POWERS OF THE CROWN

TimeFrame AD 1600-1700

NORTH AMERICA

DUTCH REPUBLIC

ENGLAND

TimeFrame AD 1600-1700

PERSIA

JAPAN

CHINA

This volume is one in a series that tells the story
of humankind. Other books in the series include:
The Age of God-Kings
Barbarian Tides
A Soaring Spirit
Empires Ascendant
Empires Besieged
The March of Islam
Fury of the Northmen
Light in the East
The Divine Campaigns
The Mongol Conquests
The Age of Calamity
Voyages of Discovery
The European Emergence
The World in Arms
Shadow of the Dictators

POWERS OF THE CROWN

TimeFrame AD 1600-1700

BY THE EDITORS OF TIME-LIFE BOOKS

TIME-LIFE BOOKS, ALEXANDRIA, VIRGINIA

Time-Life Books Inc.
is a wholly owned subsidiary of
THE TIME INC. BOOK COMPANY

President and Chief Executive Officer:
Kelso F. Sutton
President, Time Inc. Books Direct:
Christopher T. Linen

TIME-LIFE BOOKS INC.

EDITOR: George Constable
Executive Editor: Ellen Phillips
Director of Design: Louis Klein
Director of Editorial Resources:
Phyllis K. Wise
Editorial Board: Russell B. Adams, Jr.,
Dale M. Brown, Roberta Conlan,
Thomas H. Flaherty, Lee Hassig,
Jim Hicks, Donia Ann Steele,
Rosalind Stubenberg
Director of Photography and Research:
John Conrad Weiser

EUROPEAN EDITOR: Sue Joiner
Executive Editor: Gillian Moore
Design Director: Ed Skyner
Assistant Design Director: Mary Staples
Chief of Research: Vanessa Kramer
Chief Sub-Editor: Ilse Gray

PRESIDENT: John M. Fahey, Jr.
Senior Vice Presidents: Robert M.
DeSena, James L. Mercer, Paul R.
Stewart, Curtis G. Viebranz,
Joseph J. Ward
Vice Presidents: Stephen L. Bair, Bonita
T. Boezeman, Stephen L. Goldstein,
Juanita T. James, Andrew P. Kaplan,
Trevor Lunn, Susan J. Maruyama, Robert
H. Smith
Supervisor of Quality Control: James King

PUBLISHER: Joseph J. Ward

Correspondents: Elisabeth Kraemer-Singh
(Bonn); Christina Lieberman (New York);
Maria Vincenza Aloisi (Paris); Ann
Natanson (Rome). Valuable assistance
was also provided by: Karel Ornstein,
Saskia Vanderlinde, Wibo Vanderlinde,
Erik Van Zwam (Amsterdam); Yang Jin-
quan (Beijing); Otto Gobius, Robert
Kroon (Geneva); Trini Bandres (Madrid);
Elizabeth Brown (New York); Mary
Johnson (Stockholm); Dick Berry, Mieko
Ikeda (Tokyo); Traudl Lessing (Vienna).

TIME FRAME
(published in Britain as
TIME-LIFE HISTORY OF THE WORLD)

SERIES EDITOR: Tony Allan

Editorial Staff for *Powers of the Crown:*
Designer: Mary Staples
Writer: Fergus Fleming
Researchers: Caroline Alcock,
Paul Dowswell
Sub-Editor: Christine Noble
Design Assistant: Rachel Gibson
Editorial Assistant: Molly Sutherland
Picture Department: Amanda Hindley
(administrator), Zoe Spencer (picture
coordinator)

Editorial Production
Chief: Maureen Kelly
Production Assistant: Samantha Hill
Editorial Department: Theresa John,
Debra Lelliott

U.S. EDITION

Assistant Editor: Barbara Fairchild
Quarmby
Copy Coordinator: Colette Stockum
Picture Coordinator: Leanne G. Miller

Editorial Operations
Copy Chief: Diane Ullius
Production: Celia Beattie
Library: Louise D. Forstall

Computer Composition: Gordon E. Buck
(Manager), Deborah G. Tait, Monika D.
Thayer, Janet Barnes Syring, Lillian
Daniels

Special Contributors: James Chambers,
Stephen Downes, Neil Fairbairn, Ellen
Galford, Robert Irwin, David Nicolle
(text); Sheila Corr, Timothy Fraser,
Barbara Moir Hicks, Caroline Lucas,
Jackie Matthews (research); David E.
Manley (index)

CONSULTANTS

General:
GEOFFREY PARKER, Professor of Histo-
ry, University of Illinois, Urbana-
Champaign, Illinois

CHRISTOPHER BAYLY, Reader in Modern Indian History, St. Catharine's
College, Cambridge University, Cambridge, England

Japan:
I. J. McMULLEN, Lecturer in Japanese,
Oxford University

China:
DENIS TWITCHETT, Gordon Wu Professor of Chinese Studies, Princeton University, Princeton, New Jersey

Persia:
DAVID MORGAN, Reader in the History
of the Middle East, School of Oriental
and African Studies, University of London

England:
NICHOLAS TYACKE, Senior Lecturer in
History, University College, London

Dutch Republic:
JONATHAN I. ISRAEL, Professor of
Dutch History and Institutions, Universi-
ty College, London

North America:
G. V. SCAMMELL, Fellow of Pembroke
College, Cambridge University, Cam-
bridge, England

**Library of Congress Cataloging in
Publication Data**

Powers of the crown : time frame AD 1600-
1700 / by the editors of Time-Life Books.
      p.   cm. — (Time frame)
    Includes bibliographical references (p.   )
    ISBN 0-8094-6454-3
    ISBN 0-8094-6455-1 (lib. bdg.)
    1. History, Modern—17th century.
I. Time-Life Books. II. Series.
D246.P69 1990   909'.6—dc20   89-20509
                                                              CIP

Time-Life Books Inc. offers a wide range of fine
recordings, including a *Rock 'n' Roll Era* series.
For subscription information, call 1-800-621-
7026 or write Time-Life Music, P.O. Box C-
32068, Richmond, Virginia 23261-2068.

CONTENTS

TOKUGAWA JAPAN

1 For the 8,000 men camped on Matsuo Hill under the command of Kobayagawa Hideaki, the night of October 21, 1600, was an evil time to be abroad. The weather was seasonally foul; as darkness fell, a light evening drizzle had developed into a raking downpour. And their hilltop position above the village of Sekigahara in central Honshū, the main island of Japan, exposed them to the full force of a westerly gale howling through the defile from nearby Lake Biwa. Nevertheless, they could consider themselves lucky on two counts: The storm had not deteriorated into one of the *taifu,* or "great winds," that frequently devastated Japan in late summer and fall; and at least they were not on the move—unlike their allies in the valley below.

For, in the hours after midnight, Sekigahara had witnessed the drenched arrival of some 70,000 men, the combined armies of the warlord Ishida Mitsunari. Almost blinded by the rain and hampered by knee-deep mud, they had struggled ten miles through the night to reach this defensive position. Their journey represented the climax of two months of campaigning, during which Mitsunari had battled with the powerful eastern lord Tokugawa Ieyasu for control of Japan. A clash the day before had both revealed Ieyasu's strength—approximately equal to that of Mitsunari—and suggested his strategy: to sweep through the pass at Sekigahara and then to take the ancient capital of Kyōto and the key port of Ōsaka. Now, at Sekigahara, where the mountains protected his flanks, Mitsunari hoped to draw the pursuing Tokugawa forces into a decisive confrontation.

As dawn came, the storm passed over, leaving behind drizzle and thick, blanketing fog. Secure on their hill, Hideaki's men could hear, through the whiteness, the muffled curses of the last bedraggled units arriving in Sekigahara below them. Visibility was down to a couple of paces, and there was only the noise of the men in front to guide the troops. Accordingly, it was some time before anyone realized that the clash and rumble of marching men came not from Mitsunari's men alone: Into their ranks had stumbled the vanguard of the Tokugawa army.

For a while confusion reigned. The enveloping fog prevented anything but a muddled withdrawal by both sides. The Tokugawa advance guard, which had already been marching hard for four hours, took up their posts while the rest of the army arrived. It was an hour before the mist lifted, rolling away up the slopes of nearby Mount Ibuki, to give a clear view of Sekigahara. Then battle commenced.

Safe on the hilltop, Hideaki watched for four hours as fighting raged along the line with neither side gaining advantage. According to plan, he was to wait until the Tokugawa army was fully engaged, then swoop down to attack them on their left flank. By noon, the time was ripe. Some 60,000 of Ieyasu's men were pressing into the valley, and Mitsunari gave the signal for Hideaki to move.

Not a man stirred on Matsuo Hill. For weeks, the twenty-two-year-old Hideaki had

In a detail from a seventeenth-century silk scroll painting, an aging Japanese warrior prepares for battle. The man portrayed, Nabeshima Naoshige, began his career as a minor retainer of a southern warlord; he fought bravely in the civil wars that split the nation in the late sixteenth century, supporting the victorious military leader Tokugawa Ieyasu, who with his heirs imposed unity on the divided nation. Naoshige died in 1618 at the age of eighty, having lived to savor, as a provincial noble, the first fruits of the long Tokugawa peace.

9

been playing a waiting game. In each battle that he had fought on Mitsunari's side, the young general had covered himself against mishap by making overtures to the enemy. Today was no exception; Ieyasu fully expected that the troops on the hill would play for him the role expected of them by Mitsunari. Initially, however, he too was disappointed. Hideaki—still undecided as to where his opportunities might best lie—failed to respond to Ieyasu's signal also. Only after being prompted by a hail of Tokugawa arrows did he send his troops into action against Mitsunari.

Mitsunari was not entirely unprepared. He had been aware of his young ally's plotting. What the general did not expect, however, was that his leaders on the left flank would take their cue from Hideaki and would also turn against him. Attacked on all sides, his formations disintegrated. Mitsunari himself was killed, and his men fled westward in disorder through the pass to Lake Biwa. That night, Ieyasu's victorious army bivouacked on the battlefield. The road to Ōsaka was open.

The battle at Sekigahara marked a turning point in the fortunes of Japan. Not only did it give Tokugawa Ieyasu complete mastery of the nation, but it also heralded an era of extraordinary isolation and stasis. Under the direction of Ieyasu's successors, the

The story of Japan's political reunification in the late sixteenth and early seventeenth centuries is in part a tale of three cities, all of them on the central island of Honshū. The nation's imperial capital was the ancient city of Kyōto, where the emperor—a venerated figure who wielded little real power—presided over a glittering court. The true rulers of the country were a succession of military leaders, the greatest of whom, Toyotomi Hideyoshi, chose to rule from the port city of Ōsaka on the Inland Sea, from which he mounted two unsuccessful invasions of Korea. When Tokugawa Ieyasu won power after Hideyoshi's death, he moved the seat of government to the eastern city of Edo—today's Tokyo—which lay at the heart of the rich agricultural region of the Kanto plain, his power base in the earlier civil wars.

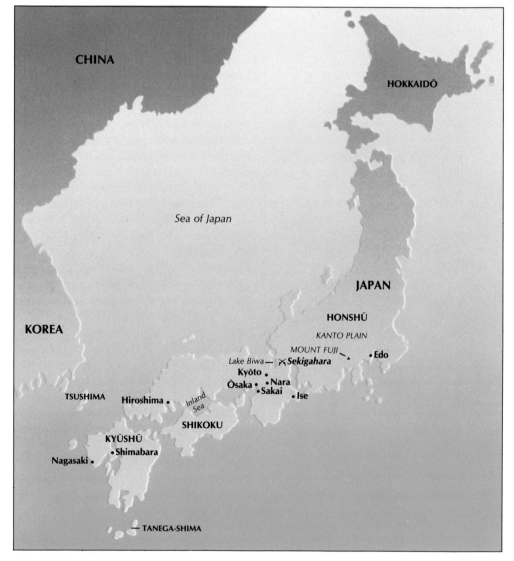

country would make the momentous decision to close itself off almost entirely from the outside world.

Japan's choice was all the more surprising in that it was made at a time when horizons elsewhere in the world were widening. The seventeenth century was a period of global change and ever-increasing prosperity, as well as of exploration and pioneering settlement typified by the European colonization of North America. Elsewhere, the age took its character from a clutch of exceptionally capable and long-lived monarchs, who increased their control over their realms with the help of firearms, printing and improved communications in general—all products of relatively recent technological advancement.

During the course of the century, Japan's neighbor China fell to a new dynasty that produced one of the greatest emperors the nation had known in two millennia of imperial rule. Persia experienced a revival as well, under Shah Abbās the Great, who fought off enemies to the east and west and built the city of Isfahan in order to reflect his glory. In Europe, no monarch ruled more resplendently than France's Sun King, Louis XIV, whose Palace of Versailles became a temple to the fashionable doctrine of royal absolutism.

Two nations, however, were exceptions to the rule: In England, two kings were dethroned, one was to be beheaded; and the Dutch Republic, newly independent of Spain, chose—to the horror of its royalist neighbors—to opt for a republican form of government. Yet such events meant little to Japan, which by that time had emerged from the trauma of its civil wars to wrap itself in a cocoon of isolationism.

For centuries, the mountainous archipelago of Japan had been ruled by a blend of ancient tradition and military pragmatism. The symbolic head of the nation was the emperor, descended, according to legend, from the sun goddess who had created the islands. Presiding over his court in Kyōto, he conducted sacred rites to ensure Japan's continued prosperity, and was himself worshiped as a semidivinity. It was by imperial decree that the state was officially governed; and it was to the emperor that all Japanese paid homage.

In terms of real rather than ceremonial power, however, the emperor's influence was less than that of his mightiest subject, the military dictator known as the shogun. Since the late twelfth century, when armed forces had seized control of the state, it had been to the shogun's commands that the emperor assented and to the shogun's administration that imperial approval was given. Resistance to shogunal demands was useless, as the imperial family had soon learned: The shogun was the nation's greatest landowner, as well as its commander in chief. And power lay in the land, the myriad tiny thatched villages whose rice crops provided not only the nation's staple but also the medium of exchange by which all wealth was counted.

In addition to yielding food, the land provided a work force. The countryside was divided into fiefs, each run by a provincial lord, or daimyo. Within his domain, the daimyo kept order by means of his samurai, armed retainers to whom he allotted small portions of land in exchange for their continued loyalty. The daimyo himself owed allegiance to the shogun, whether in gratitude for the grant of his land or through fear that it might be taken away from him. These local lords acknowledged the sovereignty of the emperor; but it was to the banner of the shogun that they rallied in times of war.

Just as there was no single ruler of Japan, so there was no one religion to which all Japanese subscribed. The indigenous faith of the islands, Shinto, acknowledged

Portrayed in court dress by an anonymous artist, Tokugawa Ieyasu is shown in this posthumous portrait as he appeared shortly before his death in 1616 at the age of seventy-three. By that time, all his rivals were dead and he was firmly established as shogun, or military governor of the nation. Ieyasu, who personally fought in more than fifty battles, pursued his objectives with cunning, patience, and enormous tenacity; his soldiers called him "the old badger." He built the fortunes of his family, which was to rule Japan for the next 250 years, not just on military supremacy but also on his skill in administering his domains, increasing revenues, and dispossessing his enemies—talents that his successors in the Tokugawa dynasty also inherited.

innumerable divine spirits, both animate and inanimate. It was to Shinto deities that the emperor offered reverence; through them, believers thought, all human activities were sustained and allotted both good and ill fortune. From China, in the sixth century AD, the Japanese had acquired Buddhism, by whose tenets the individual could, after undergoing numerous reincarnations, ultimately achieve release from the trials of mortal existence. Coexisting with these faiths was the philosophy of Confucianism, also imported from China, with its emphasis on dutiful subordination, filial loyalty, and public service.

Despite this mélange of conflicting fealties, the nation had achieved a certain degree of stability for a while. By the mid-fifteenth century, however, the complex strands of Japanese harmony were beginning to break apart. Part of the trouble was that Kyōto was an unsuitable and unrealistic seat of power. Situated on the main island of Honshū, it lay 225 miles to the west of the Kanto plain, the richest tract of agricultural land in the nation. Too far away for easy control, this fertile plain was, however, near enough to provide a base from which to threaten the capital. More disadvantageously still, the city was about thirty-five miles from the Inland Sea, which—hemmed in by Honshū, the western island of Kyūshū, and the southern island of Shikoku—was the true heart of the archipelago. Maritime cities like Ōsaka and Sakai in the east or Nagasaki in the west could not easily be dominated from the

A detail from a screen that formed part of the trousseau of a daughter of Tokugawa Ieyasu shows the general's troops sweeping to victory in the battle of Sekigahara in 1600. Outmaneuvered and betrayed by allies who switched their loyalties during the conflict, the army of Ieyasu's rivals flees from the blazing remains of their fortified camp; the banners they have left behind indicate that many of them were Christians. To the right and on the left, Ieyasu's troops surge forward under cover of a low cloud that suggests the mist that delayed the start of combat by more than an hour. The fighting was actually more obstinate, protracted, and confused than this picture, commissioned by the victor, would suggest; but afterward no Japanese lord dared to meet the Tokugawa armies in open warfare again.

inland capital. And the whole western coast, which formed Japan's gateway to the outside world, lay beyond Kyōto's vigilance.

The strategic weakness of the capital did not in itself matter, so long as the shogun was the undisputed master of Japan. Over the years, however, the daimyo had gradually accreted power to themselves and their families. Local forces became stronger while the shogun's strength diminished, since the only way the shogun could reward his followers was by granting them estates of their own, thereby diminishing his own land base while increasing that of his subjects. In addition, the religious establishment was becoming restive. Many Buddhist monks saw no incongruity in being warriors as well as clerics, converting their temples into fortresses and acquiring large tracts of land.

The crisis came in 1467, when the shogun found himself unable to make his ruling accepted in a case of disputed inheritance, and the contending parties came to blows in the streets of Kyōto itself. Prolonged fighting within the walls of the capital reduced the once-populous city to a charred wasteland across which armies could maneuver as if in the open countryside. The imperial house was reduced to penury. Central power vanished, and civil war spread throughout the land. Here, great lords were overthrown by lesser; there, confederations of samurai asserted their power; elsewhere, Buddhist warrior-monks, supported by breakaway bands of peasants, established their dominance. Different daimyo supported rival claimants to the shogunate; during the course of the sixteenth century, only one shogun escaped being deposed, and he was murdered.

The interminable wars were not entirely destructive; indeed, the nation's economy flourished. The fighting usually did no more harm to towns and villages than was unavoidable, for no lord wished to devastate lands he might come to own. Successful commanders could establish, for a while at least, unified control across entire provinces, making possible large-scale improvements in irrigation and drainage. Agricultural production grew steadily, and the daimyo were not the only ones to benefit. In the nationwide convulsion, peasants could easily avoid high taxes and repression by fleeing to neighboring estates; the more enlightened rulers, therefore, sought to govern by efficient and beneficial methods. Several families set up private codes to regulate their own behavior, emphasizing such virtues as impartial adjudication and honest administration.

Urban dwellers prospered as well. The incessant campaigns had to be supplied, and towns could grow wealthy by providing munitions. Some cities even took advantage of the precarious balance of power to achieve a moderate degree of independence. In most of the wars, for example, the flourishing port of Sakai remained neutral, and hostile lords who visited the city had to surrender their weapons and keep the peace within the walls.

The lack of supervision also benefited seafarers, who could do virtually as they pleased. Japanese pirates and marauding slave traders were dreaded all along the Chinese coast. More peaceable commerce was conducted as far afield as Indonesia. Japan generally gained from such exchanges: In the 1530s, when skilled Chinese and Korean engineers and metallurgists were imported to work in Japan's mines, silver and gold production began to soar.

Not long afterward came the double-edged benefits of Western civilization. In 1542, when Portuguese sailors first reached the southern island of Tanega-shima,

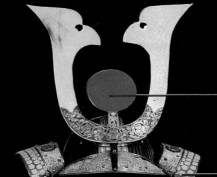

This suit of ceremonial armor was the favorite outfit of Tokugawa Yoshinao, lord of Owari (modern Nagoya) and Ieyasu's third son. Like all the best work of its day, it combines lightness and strength to a remarkable degree. Made mainly of silver or scarlet-lacquered iron, it follows exclusively Japanese traditions in its use of laced plates and strips rather than the solid steelwork preferred by Europeans. By this time, however, suits designed for battle use rather than for display often incorporated some European features to give increased protection against firearms.

KABUTO
Made of joined iron plates, this crested helmet served to identify its wearer on the battlefield.

FUKIGAESHI
These helmet flaps were a help in protecting against sword cuts.

HO-ATE
The nose and upper lip of this face mask could be removed to permit the wearer to talk and drink. Below hangs a flexible neck protector.

SHIKORO
Lacquered iron plates hanging from the helmet guarded the neck and shoulders.

SODE
Oversleeves of loosely laced lacquered plates shielded the upper arms and body from sideways sword thrusts or arrows.

DO
This breastplate was made up of small, tightly braided plates of lacquered iron. It provided good protection against spears, swords, and arrows, but not against musket balls.

KOTE
Chain mail sewn on a silken base was reinforced with iron strips to protect the forearms and hands.

GESAN
The plates constituting the skirt were larger and more loosely laced than the *do's* to give flexibility for riding, at the same time protecting the lower body.

HAIDATE
This underskirt of silk sewn with chain mail was studded with iron plates to protect the front of the upper legs.

TSUNE-ATE
Hinged iron strips mounted on cloth, these shin guards afforded protection for only the front of the leg. The calves were left free to allow a mounted samurai to grip his horse.

they astonished the inhabitants with their "exotic" ways—especially their firearms. Gunpowder, a Chinese discovery, had been known in Japan for some time; but the European matchlock harquebus, an efficient, portable, armor-piercing weapon, was something new. Within a year, the smiths of Tanega-shima were turning out imitations of the guns that would do everything except shoot. On a later visit, a Portuguese gunner disclosed (in exchange, it was said, for a Japanese master smith's daughter) the secret of making Western-style gun barrels. Thereafter, the "Tanega-shima pieces," as they became known, spread through the country. Rare at first, they were increasingly valued, particularly by the Buddhist warrior-monks. Ultimately, they would threaten Japan's social order: A humble infantryman armed with such a weapon was a match for even the most skillful samurai.

The Europeans brought other innovations: tobacco; spectacles; new styles of clothing and of cooking; as well as improved armor, with wrought-iron plates instead of the traditional Japanese lacquered silk and bamboo, that offered some protection against harquebus bullets. They also brought Roman Catholic Christianity, whose Jesuit missionaries were potentially even more threatening to the established order than firearms: A Japanese Catholic had loyalties that transcended those to his country and his emperor. Initially, however, the missionaries made few converts. They were nonetheless greatly impressed by the cleanliness and intelligence of the Japanese, while also lamenting their cruelty and the cunning of their merchants, who commonly had two sets of scales—an accurate one for weighing what they received and another to mislead purchasers. They further noted with sadness the fact that such a beautiful land should be overwhelmed by incessant war.

The spiral of violence seemed set to continue indefinitely when, in the late sixteenth century, a leader came to prominence who was to set Japan on the path to centuries of peace. In 1568, after eight years of battles, sieges, and betrayals, a thirty-five-year-old daimyo named Oda Nobunaga had grown strong enough to march into Kyōto and nominate his own candidate for shogun. In this enterprise, he was aided by two outstanding lieutenants: Kinoshita (later known as Toyotomi) Hideyoshi, a small, withered figure of uncertain parentage and deep guile who had risen from being a humble foot soldier—or, according to some, a bandit—to serving as a loyal samurai; and Tokugawa Ieyasu, a young warrior who was originally opposed to Nobunaga but who had changed allegiances and advanced to become one of Nobunaga's most favored generals.

In itself, Nobunaga's achievement was not unprecedented. Unlike other successful commanders, however, he was not ambitious simply for himself and his family. Instead, he was inspired by the aim of restoring peace and unity throughout the land. He saw only one way to achieve this goal. His motto, stamped on his official documents, was Rule the Empire by Armed Force. Father Luis Frois, a Jesuit who knew him in Kyōto, left a vivid description of Nobunaga. He "is extremely warlike," wrote the priest, and he "despises all other Japanese kings and princes and speaks to them over his shoulder in a loud voice as if they were lowly servants." Further, he "intensely dislikes any delays or long speeches."

An early casualty of Nobunaga's intolerance was the puppet shogun whom he had helped to install. Their relationship was difficult from the beginning. On assuming office, the shogun showed his gratitude by inviting the general to an evening's entertainment—thirteen successive pieces of classical drama. Nobunaga's patience snapped after the fifth. By 1573, relations had deteriorated to the point that Nobunaga deposed his nominee and, without venturing to take any official title, thereafter gave orders in his own name.

Nobunaga reserved a particular detestation for the Buddhist warrior-monks, burning their temples, melting down their statues to cast guns, and mercilessly slaughtering their supporters. It was from the unmounted Buddhist warriors, however, that he learned the importance of infantry. In 1575, Nobunaga's foot soldiers, clad in waterproof straw jackets and toting matchlocks, decimated the armored cavalry of the Kanto. By 1582, the great monastery of Ōsaka had been destroyed, its monks burned alive within it, and the rich port of Sakai had lost all pretensions to independence and had submitted to Nobunaga's authority.

Nobunaga now controlled all the central region of Honshū. The Buddhist monks had been crushed, and it remained only to subdue the remaining daimyo. To this end, Ieyasu's armies advanced eastward into the Kanto, while the western front was put in the hands of Hideyoshi, now a trusted general (though his master still called him Monkey). It was while his subordinates were thus occupied that Nobunaga met his death. He was attacked and murdered in Kyōto by one of his own daimyo.

Possibly the treacherous act was carried out at the instigation of Hideyoshi, who lost little time in taking advantage of the situation. Within eight days, he had returned to Kyōto, where he killed Nobunaga's assassins and seized control of the capital. Taken completely unawares by the coup d'état, Ieyasu put up a token show of resistance but ultimately had little choice other than to submit to Hideyoshi's rule.

The new ruler's first priority was to make himself respected by those lords who continued to think of him as a successful peasant nicknamed Monkey. There was no shogun in office, nor did Hideyoshi aspire to such a position, not being of the traditional lineage. Instead, he legitimized his status by taking the aristocratic title of *kanpaku*, or "imperial regent," one of the great ceremonial offices of the emperor's court. Armed with this resounding title, he built up his strength until by 1591, through a combination of force and persuasion, he had obtained oaths of loyalty from every daimyo in the country.

The new regent decided to rule from the port of Ōsaka rather than from Kyōto. There he built a castle worthy of his position: The moats were more than 300 feet across; the walls, lined with dozens of towers, were built of massive masonry, and their gates were reinforced by blocks of stone measuring twenty by thirty feet; and in the center the great keep, with whitewashed walls and sweeping golden roofs, rose eight stories high. Within, Hideyoshi lived in bejeweled luxury, surrounded by elaborate gilt decorations and whole walls covered with gold. He also kept a palace in Kyōto, where he entertained the emperor with feasts of unexampled magnificence.

Amid all this grandeur, Hideyoshi made an attempt to show that he also appreciated the more austere traditions of Japanese culture. Notable among these was the tea ceremony, which initially had been imported from China but which had developed in Japan into an aesthetic ritual calling for a refined simplicity of manners and a heightened appreciation of texture and form. Japan's greatest master of the art, Sen Rikyū, did his best to educate the regent's taste in these matters. Hideyoshi's response, however, was to commission a portable teahouse in which every accessible surface, including the ceiling, was plated with gold.

Such were the trappings of Hideyoshi's power. The reality that underlay them was

During the civil wars of the sixteenth century, Japanese society had become unusually fluid. The fortunes of war favored some upwardly mobile samurai who became known as "sudden lords"; and even a few peasants had a chance to attain the coveted status of warriors. In the seventeenth century, however, the Tokugawa shoguns enhanced their regime's stability by imposing a rigid class system, based on Confucian principles of loyalty and obedience.

Under Tokugawa legislation, four principal groups were recognized. A warrior elite had the highest status, followed by peasants, artisans, and merchants—in that order. Class distinctions were regarded as hereditary and unchangeable. Nevertheless, a degree of social mobility survived. Favored artisans could be rewarded with privileges far above their station; and by the end of the century, many merchants enjoyed wealth and positions of trust that were the envy of their social superiors.

THE FOUR ORDERS OF SOCIETY

Details from contemporary paintings illustrate the four estates of Tokugawa society. A warrior *(top left)*, commander's baton in hand, rides a richly caparisoned warhorse. At center left, a peasant hoes a rice paddy. The skilled workers shown preparing beams for a temple *(bottom left)* were members of the artisan class. Lowest of all in status was the merchant *(below)*, shown toting his wares to market.

a complete reform of the system of land tenure, intended to make Japan a stable country in which civil war and rebellion would be as difficult as possible. With this aim in mind, Hideyoshi ordered a survey of land ownership throughout Japan, and he used the results to impose a rational and uniform system of taxation. He rewarded those daimyo who had chosen to become his vassals with grants of land that were conditional on his pleasure. His most dangerous rival, Ieyasu, received the governorship of the Kanto, where, from the eastern castle of Edo, he served Hideyoshi loyally. He lacked the opportunity to do otherwise: The lands between the Kanto and the capital that he had formerly held under Nobunaga were given to trusted supporters of Hideyoshi.

Resistance to the new order was widespread. In the long civil wars, many peasants had grown accustomed to a tax-free and unregimented existence. But protest was literally disarmed in 1588, when Hideyoshi ordered the confiscation of all weapons from the peasantry and from those warrior-monks who had survived Nobunaga's massacres. After the Sword Hunt, as it became known, only samurai were allowed to bear arms. Hideyoshi consoled his subjects with the promise that the confiscated items would be melted down to construct a great statue of the Buddha, to the spiritual benefit of the unwilling donors.

In the cities, the regent's control was no less firm. The urban guilds that had established local monopolies were abolished, and trade became free; even foreigners were encouraged. Chinese, Portuguese, and Spanish merchants arrived in some numbers, attracted by the new abundance of precious metals. Conversely, Japanese vessels sailed to distant waters: By 1600, a few pirates had established themselves as far away as the Mediterranean port of Tunis.

Continuing contact with Europeans, however, had consequences that Hideyoshi did not entirely welcome. Under Nobunaga's rule, Christianity had become almost fashionable in court circles, and by the 1580s, the converts, who were found primarily on the western island of Kyūshū and especially around the port of Nagasaki, numbered 100,000 or more. Hideyoshi regarded them with suspicion as a possible source of disloyalty and, in 1587, issued an edict expelling all Christian missionaries from Japan. Merchants were still welcome, however, and the two classes of foreigners were easily confused. Protected by judicious bribery as well as by distance, the Jesuit missions in Kyūshū managed to continue their work while Hideyoshi turned his attention to other matters.

He had risen far; now he aspired even higher. Concerned no doubt to keep the nation's battle-hardened samurai occupied with foreign wars, he conceived the ambition of using the armies of his newly reunited country to invade and conquer Korea. In 1592, a force of Japanese soldiers numbering some 160,000 landed in the south of that country and poured up the peninsula. By the winter of 1593, however, they were floundering. The weather was execrable, and communications with Japan were precarious. The Korean peasants resisted the invaders with a bitter guerrilla campaign. Worst of all, the Chinese came to the Koreans' aid. By summer, the Japanese had been driven back to the south. Negotiations followed and failed; undaunted, Hideyoshi declared war on China.

By now, Hideyoshi was no longer the shrewd, careful commander who had risen to power as Oda Nobunaga's understudy. Possibly infected with syphilis—a disease that Iberian seafarers had brought to Japan as they had to every other accessible nation—he now saw enemies everywhere. The tea master Sen Rikyū, accused of treason because his statue had been placed above a gate through which Hideyoshi rode, was driven to suicide. A number of Japanese Christians and Portuguese missionaries were executed. The regent's own nephew and all his family were killed, accused of plotting to capture Ōsaka castle. Driven by ever-present fears of treachery, Hideyoshi flung his energies into his plan to conquer China, and his affections into a boundless love for his infant son Hideyori, who he was determined must succeed him despite any plots by his untrustworthy daimyo.

Paranoid Hideyoshi may have been, but he managed to hold on to his power. Another 100,000 warriors were sent to Korea. They fought heroically—a temple in Kyōto became the repository for the ears and noses of 37,000 Chinese killed in a single battle—and by the autumn of 1598, victory seemed to be within Hideyoshi's grasp. But by then, Hideyoshi knew he was dying. In his last lucid moments, he appointed Ieyasu as the guardian of his cherished son, with a Council of Elders to govern until Hideyori should be old enough to rule.

With the death of Hideyoshi in 1598, the Council of Elders lost no time in abandoning Korea and making peace with China. They knew that all Japanese forces would be needed at home for the power struggle that must ensue. In this conflict, Ieyasu had several advantages. The Kanto plain had made him the wealthiest lord in Japan; and, having avoided sending troops to Korea, he had a labor force as well as rice fields.

Kazuko, daughter of the second Tokugawa shogun, Hidetada, rides in a curtained carriage out of Nijo castle, the Tokugawa stronghold in Kyōto, on her way to marry Emperor Go-Mizuno in 1620. The scene is shown in a detail from one of a pair of painted screens, decorated with gold leaf, illustrating sights in and around the imperial capital. The marriage was designed to strengthen the ties between the imperial house and the Tokugawa family, thereby tightening the shoguns' hold on power.

With such strength at his command, he soon began to receive pledges of support from other daimyo. But Ishida Mitsunari, one of Hideyoshi's most faithful vassals, worked tirelessly to organize a coalition against him. In the early months of 1600, two years after his master's death, Mitsunari felt strong enough to launch an all-out attack on his rival. The fortunes of war seesawed until Mitsunari met defeat and death at Sekigahara. Ten days later, the victorious Ieyasu entered Ōsaka as the military master of the country.

He quickly set about consolidating his position. Eighty-seven daimyo houses were extinguished, their lands absorbed into Ieyasu's holdings and then redistributed to reward his followers. By 1603, Ieyasu had persuaded the emperor to make him shogun, and at his castle at Edo—the future Tokyo—he accepted the submission of all the remaining daimyo.

Nor was he content with mere oaths of loyalty. He required his vassals to provide men and materials for the construction of a new seat of government at Edo. During the next two years, hills were leveled, marshes were drained, canals were dug, and walls were raised to enclose a massive castle, a brooding symbol of power whose white-plastered buildings were adorned with dark tiles picked out in gold.

With Japan's daimyo safely subdued, the only remaining threat to Ieyasu's security was Hideyori, still ensconced in his father's great castle of Ōsaka. Yet Ieyasu kept for years the promise he had sworn to the dying Hideyoshi; perhaps he did not feel strong enough to attack the prince he had promised to defend, perhaps he hoped it would not be necessary. For their part, Hideyori's guardians also kept the peace, since Hideyori was young and Ieyasu by now was old.

The crisis was postponed until 1614. Now seventy-four years old, Ieyasu had little more than a year left to live, and he may have known it. Hideyori had been careful to give no offense, but Ieyasu found it all the same. One of the bells in a newly rebuilt Ōsaka temple bore a Chinese inscription that Ieyasu falsely claimed was insulting to the house of Tokugawa. Scholars, obedient to his command, examined the bell and confirmed that the Chinese symbols were indeed treasonable. Ieyasu's wrath could only be appeased by outright surrender. When the twenty-one-year-old Hideyori refused, Ieyasu took to arms and, in December, brought 150,000 warriors against Ōsaka castle.

But the attackers lacked artillery and Hideyoshi had built well. In addition, there were many old enemies of Ieyasu to fight for the young prince. By the end of the winter, Ieyasu's armies had lost many men and had nothing to show for it. When Ieyasu offered favorable peace terms, it seemed that Hideyori had won a victory. He was to be allowed to keep the castle and all his lands, and none of the garrison were to be punished. In return, Ieyasu asked only for a few hostages and that, as a face-saving gesture, part of the outer moat of Ōsaka castle should be filled in.

Peace came, besiegers and garrison mostly went home, and a troop of laborers—stout, reliable men from the Kanto—arrived for the symbolic moat filling. The task was more onerous than expected. To reach the moat, the workers had to demolish the outer battlements. More and more laborers arrived; more of the outer moat was filled in; by some mistake, parts of the inner moat were filled also; and then the inner parapets were brought down. Desperate to keep the peace, Hideyori tried to reason with Ieyasu's officers. They evaded his questions and referred his protests to superior authorities, while the demolition went on day and night. Eventually, they admitted there might have been some error, but they pointed out that walls and moats were of little use in peacetime. The workers left with apologies; soon thereafter Ieyasu arrived with his army. Hideyori defended the ruins from May into June, before finally committing suicide.

In the aftermath, Ieyasu ruthlessly crushed all remnants of opposition: The whole of Hideyori's family was destroyed, save for two small children; the progeny of Ōsaka's commanders were executed; and the castle's surviving defenders were mercilessly hunted down, their heads displayed in rotting thousands along the road to Kyōtō. And lest anyone be in doubt as to Ieyasu's intentions, the daimyo were summoned before him to hear how the country was now to be run.

To the cowed lords he dictated stringent terms. All opposition parties or factions were to be immediately denounced; traitors were to be expelled from their estates; new castle construction was forbidden and any repairs were to be reported; movements between estates were restricted; samurai were to live frugally and were not to adopt costumes or ornaments inappropriate to their rank; all daimyo marriages were to be sanctioned by the shogun; and very strict limits were established for the personal escorts of the nobles.

These guidelines, encapsulated in a document running to thirteen clauses, confirmed Ieyasu's position as undisputed master of Japan. He did not have long to savor his triumph, for he died the following year. But his work survived him; the legacy of social peace he bequeathed to his successors was to keep the Tokugawa dynasty in power for more than 250 years.

By the time of his death, Ieyasu had made the Tokugawa by far the richest family in Japan. His estates, yielding 32 million bushels of rice, accounted for 25 percent of the nation's wealth. Ieyasu's eldest son and successor, Hidetada, enriched the clan still further by confiscating the estates of hostile daimyo, bringing his revenues to 55 million bushels. There were rumblings of discontent from the nobles, but these were quickly stifled when Hidetada's son, Iemitsu, came to power in 1623. The new ruler summoned the great lords to his palace in Edo. They arrived, were escorted in, and left alone. They waited, growing colder and hungrier, until after nightfall. Then, with a sudden blaze of torches, Iemitsu appeared and spoke: "I am the shogun by right of succession, and you will henceforward be treated as hereditary vassals. If any man does not like this, let him go back to his estates, and make up his mind; between him and me, battle shall decide." All of the lords decided for peace. Nonetheless, Iemitsu was subsequently to make further charges of treason the pretext for confiscating yet more land—worth an additional 19 million bushels of rice a year—a maneuver that gave the Tokugawa direct control of more than 50 percent of the wealth of Japan.

Under Hidetada and Iemitsu, Japanese life took on a new shape. Ieyasu had governed in the style of a successful general; his successors created a bureaucracy out of what had been an armed camp. Efficient administration and tight control became the maxims of the new rulers. Every aspect of government was carefully regulated. Activities thought to be subversive were investigated by a ministry of information, whose findings were swiftly, and usually mercilessly, acted upon by commissioners of police and justice.

As Tokugawa control spread, Japanese society started to ossify into rigid strata. Whatever social mobility had existed in the civil wars now vanished, to be replaced by an inflexible class system. At the top stood the warriors, who made up about five percent of the population. Beneath came, in descending order, farmers, artisans, and traders. At the bottom of the heap was a floating population of outcasts who carried

FROM RITUAL TO RIVALRY

The seventeenth century saw a revolution in Japanese theater. At its start, the national tradition was enshrined in the Nō plays, a style that had developed at least 200 years earlier and had its roots in religious ritual. The highly stylized Nō performances had something of the character of sacred dances. Two or three masked actors would act out a sacred historical episode, often involving the appearance of a ghost or a demon, while a chorus commented on the action. Naturalism was not the goal; for example, members of the imperial house—even great warriors—were played by boys, to denote purity.

Although this classic drama continued to be staged in the ensuing centuries, no new Nō plays were composed after the sixteenth century. Instead, a new style called kabuki—literally, "the art of singing and dancing"—won popularity. Kabuki had its origins in the troupe of an actress named O-Kuni who organized dances and dramatic performances in Kyōto from about 1596. The plays she and her successors favored were full of devices that were anathema to the refined purveyors of Nō: buffoonery and melodrama, acrobatic feats and realistic dialogue. Their complex plots, sometimes drawing on recent events, sought unashamedly to entertain. Critics complained of the vulgarity of the new drama, but kabuki found an enthusiastic audience in the burgeoning cities, and throughout the Tokugawa period, its leading actors were popular heroes, regarded as the incarnations of disreputable glamour.

This Nō mask, made in Edo in the eighteenth century, would have been worn by a male actor playing the part of a beautiful young girl; there were no actresses in Japan's classic drama. Deprived of the possibility of portraying mood by facial expression, the players had to use gesture and movement to convey emotion.

Nō actors wore demon masks such as this poly-chromed wood example to portray any of the many evil spirits known to contemporary religious life. The tiny eyeholes of the masks posed problems for performers, who could see little of the stage.

Backed by an orchestra, three kabuki actresses dance for an audience whose attention is divided between the events on stage and their own concerns. This painting is a detail from a hand scroll extolling the merits of a popular actress, called Uneme, who ran a theater in the Shijo quarter of Kyōto in the early seventeenth century, before female performers were banned from kabuki, as from Nō, on grounds of public morality.

This fox mask was made for a *kiyogen* play: a brief comic interlude that served to relax an audience's emotions after the performance of a serious Nō drama. In this particular example, an old fox disguises himself as a human in an attempt to persuade the trapper who is pursuing him to give up the hunting life.

Portrayed in a painted wooden statuette, the powerful Buddhist priest Ishin Suden sits enthroned with a staff at his side. Under Ieyasu and his successor, Hidetada, Suden—the abbot of a monastery of the Zen sect in Kyō-to—was one of the nation's most influential figures, helping to draft the laws prohibiting Christianity and governing the behavior of the elite warrior class. Zen, which stressed individuality, was popular with Japan's military rulers, who sought advice from its exponents.

out such menial tasks as butchery and tanning. In principle, no man could rise above the class into which he was born, although many peasants chose deliberately to downgrade themselves, preferring the comfortable life of an artisan to the hardships of the paddy fields. Gradations in status were spelled out in an elaborate code of etiquette governing such matters as dress, precedence, and modes of address.

To strengthen their hold on men's minds, the shoguns stressed the ancient Confucian virtues of piety and obedience—traditions that had come to permeate all Japanese thought, whether Buddhist or Shinto, and that, though grossly violated in the civil wars, had always received lip service. With its emphasis on loyalty and its attendant obligations, particularly between ruler and subject, Confucianism provided a suitable ethical code for Tokugawa rule.

With the country at peace, the only threat to Tokugawa supremacy came from the outside world. Too many foreigners had reached Japan for its rulers' taste, and what the Japanese had learned from them they did not like. Protestant Dutch and English merchants had alerted the shoguns to the conquests the Spanish and Portuguese had made all over the world, and as close as the Philippines; the Roman Catholics, for their part, had reported on the faithlessness and rapacity of Protestant merchants. Furthermore, no foreigner could be trusted to obey the shogun, and the Christianity they brought also risked corrupting Japanese obedience. Ieyasu had encouraged foreign trade, and he had done little to persecute Christians even in the ranks of his enemies. His successors decided otherwise.

The great persecution of Japanese Christians started in 1618. Over the next sixteen years, all churches were destroyed, and all priests that could be found were executed or expelled. With them perished a multitude of converts. At first, the aim was simply to extirpate the faith: Hundreds of people were crucified, burned at the stake, broiled on wooden gridirons or thrown into the sulfurous fumaroles that abound throughout volcanic Japan. Later, however, persecutors vied with one another to make Christians deny their faith. One popular method was to wrap the victim in a sack, bind him up tightly to impede circulation, and suspend him upside-down over a pit; only the left hand remained free to make the sign of recantation. One priest described the consequences: "Soon blood began to ooze from the mouth, the nose, and the ears. For most, death came only at the end of two, three, and even six days. Care was taken to bleed victims in the temple of the head, to prevent too rapid a congestion and to prolong the pain." Another priest wrote of Christian women being forced to crawl naked through the steets, before being publicly violated and thrown into snake-filled pits. To escape such fates, many people—even Jesuit priests—abandoned their faith. Other Christians managed to remain covertly committed to their beliefs, despite the fact that if a convert was discovered, the five families living closest to both sides of his dwelling were executed as well—unless they had denounced the offender to the authorities.

Extreme though it was, the suppression of Christianity constituted only a small part of the campaign to remove all foreign influences from Japan. Iemitsu, after being taught geography by a French trader and realizing "the size of the world, the multitude of its countries, and the smallness of Japan," was, according to the merchant's account, "greatly surprised and heartily wished his land had never been visited by any Christian." Considered in this light, the decision that Iemitsu made in 1633 was not extraordinary. Showing the same thorough application to detail that characterized his internal administration, the shogun resolved to restrict Japan's contact with the outside world, and over the course of the next six years, a series of laws was promulgated that put this plan into effect.

The Japanese were forbidden to travel abroad, and all seagoing vessels were destroyed. Citizens caught returning to the country from overseas were executed forthwith. No foreigners were allowed to enter the country either, except at the port of Nagasaki in Kyūshū, where an artificial island was constructed in the harbor to accommodate foreign merchants. The Spanish and Portuguese were barred because of their connection with the Jesuits, and the English left of their own accord. Some Dutch merchants were permitted to remain, having impressed the Japanese with their trading vigor and being (on the testimony of the Spaniards) not truly Christians at all, and a colony of Chinese stayed to manage the mainland silk trade, over which the shogun held a monopoly. The only other foreign trade permitted was with Korea and with the Ryuku Islands to the south.

Few Japanese protested as Iemitsu slowly closed the lid on their already boxed-in society. Only in Kyūshū, where Christians were most numerous and foreign trade most flourishing, did the population take a stand. In January 1638, some 20,000 peasants, armed with matchlocks and led by a few Christian samurai, captured a castle at Shimabara on Shimabara Bay along the west coast of Kyūshū, and assembled there with their families. Toughened by adversity, they managed to hold out for four months against the shogun's armies and against bombardment from a Dutch warship that came to the government's aid. Defeat, however, was inevitable; shorn of supplies, the rebels were surrounded by more than 100,000 of Iemitsu's men. Gradually, the guns on the ramparts fell silent as their ammunition was exhausted. The climax came at noon on April 11, when the forces of the shogun broke through the outer walls. By the following dawn, they had reached the inner keep. The starving defenders, fighting with anything they could get their hands on—stones, wooden beams, and even their rice pots—were massacred almost to a person. Only 105 prisoners were taken from the ruins at Shimabara. Thereafter, apart from the Dutch, there were no known Christians in Japan.

The revolt at Shimabara was almost the last flicker of opposition to the Tokugawa shogunate. The daimyo, for their part, were too busy traveling to and from Edo to plan revolt: In 1635, Iemitsu had ordained that leading nobles must spend four months of every other year in the shogunal capital, leaving their families there as hostages in the interval. Even the imperial court was not exempt from the decree.

But when Iemitsu died in 1651, to be succeeded by his ten-year-old son Ietsuna, discontent flared up. The root of the trouble was not the pretension of the nobility but the plight of numerous samurai, veterans of the earlier wars who had lost employment when their masters were dispossessed by the shogun.

These out-of-work warriors, who were qualified only for military service, were known as *ronin,* or "wave-men." Rather than drop caste by turning to the land as farmers, many of these wanderers set up weapons shops or martial academies, and these establishments became meeting places where discontented fellow samurai could safely gather to air their grievances. One ronin, a halberd instructor of enormous strength named Marubashi Chuya, had a particular grudge: His father had been killed at the siege of Ōsaka, and Chuya yearned for revenge on the Tokugawa family. Another malcontent, Yui Shosetsu, was inspired by Hideyoshi's vertiginous rise to power to nurture hopes of becoming far more than a humble armorer. When the two men went into partnership to establish an ironworks, they set out in earnest to realize their dreams. Their plan was ambitious: to blow up the main gunpowder store in Edo, burn down the city, storm the castle, and eliminate the government.

The plotters gathered support among their brethren. A date was set for the coup in June 1651. Chuya, however, fell ill and, in his delirium, began to shout out details of the plan. The government moved swiftly; within weeks, the conspirators had been arrested, tortured, and executed, along with their wives, children, and parents. But the conspiracy of the ronin alarmed the regents who governed on Ietsuna's behalf. They subsequently took steps to supervise the multitudes of wandering samurai and, where possible, to teach them useful administrative skills.

For the whole nature of the samurai class was changing. They were still warriors, although by a decision of the shogunate their style of fighting was deliberately antiquated; Japan's rulers had seen what peasants with muskets could do, and they did not care for the prospect. Instead, the samurai were encouraged to use weapons that demanded long practice, notably swords and bows and arrows. Dog-shooting contests, in which mounted archers galloped around an enclosure after their agile targets, became a popular spectacle in Edo, and samurai were permitted to practice their swordsmanship on condemned prisoners, or on any peasants who showed disrespect. Such measures helped to bolster samurai self-esteem, but without wars to fight, they became mere salaried servants rather than honored feudal knights. By the mid-seventeenth century, samurai were no longer rewarded with grants of land, which might have accorded them real local power. Instead, they were allotted rations of rice, and were forced to live in their lords' castles or in cities, where they could be easily watched.

With the great lords tamed and the samurai a dependent salariat, the peasants continued to work the land as they had always done. But now the disruptions of war were replaced by the heavy taxation and strict regimentation of the Tokugawa peace. A village had little freedom except to determine how the tax assessed on the community should be divided among the families; this decision was made by the headman, whom the local lord, assisted by the village elders, appointed. On these also fell the burden of settling any disputes within the village, and of ensuring that all obeyed the shogun's regulations. Failure in these duties carried diverse and hideous penalties. Nevertheless, agricultural output grew by leaps and bounds, and the peasants had more children; by the end of the seventeenth century, there were approximately 26 million Japanese.

An expanding rural population in turn helped feed growing cities. Japan now had three metropolises: Edo, the new capital, made glorious by the shogun's court; Kyōto, the aristocratically elegant seat of the emperor; and Ōsaka, the thriving hub of coastal trade. In their streets sprang up sprawling masses of insubstantial wooden buildings, each structure two or three stories high. Earthquakes, typhoons, and fires—so frequent that flames became known as "flowers of Edo"—did little to impede urban growth. The flimsy dwellings, so easily destroyed, were just as easily rebuilt, and there was always profit to be made from disaster: Many entrepreneurs grew wealthy from the construction trade.

Such opportunism was just one aspect of the burgeoning commercial spirit that infused the newly peaceful nation. Everywhere, goods were on the move. Small boats—truly seaworthy vessels were still not allowed—carried their cargoes along rivers and canals and hugged the islands' coasts, and the excellent roads that spanned the country, originally constructed to give the shogun's armies easy access to every province, were now packed with merchants' wagons.

Rice remained the most prestigious item of trade, but tea, silk, cotton, and tobacco were also widely bartered. Timber from the mountain forests was constantly in demand; fisheries were abundant and profitable; and although the flow of gold and silver that had given such dazzling wealth to Hideyoshi's court diminished as the more accessible lodes were exhausted, copper mining flourished, providing the main export item in the small amount of foreign commerce. Artisans produced a range of goods that were abundant, intricate, and carefully made.

Barred from foreign trade, enterprising families found opportunities within Japan.

A painting by an unknown Japanese artist familiar with Western oil-painting techniques shows a massacre of Christians in 1622, one of a series that culminated in the total suppression of the religion in Japan. Fearing that the first loyalties of Christians would lie outside the nation and viewing the message of the faith as incompatible with their warrior ethic, Japan's rulers decided to eliminate it by torturing and killing those who would not renounce their beliefs. In the mass execution depicted, which took place in Nagasaki, thirty Japanese Christians were beheaded *(foreground)*, while at least twenty-two others, including nine Spanish missionaries, died at the stake in the fiery pit shown at center; "among them," according to an English merchant who witnessed the event, "little children of five or six years, burned alive in the arms of their mothers."

The fortunes of the powerful Mitsui family, for instance, rose through the efforts of a provincial patriarch who became a brewer of rice wine in the 1620s. Turning his attention to moneylending and rice dealing, he managed to amass enough money to allow his son, a half-century later, to establish a dry-goods store in Edo, selling cotton and drapery at fixed prices for cash. Within a decade, the Mitsui house had branches in the towns of Kyōto and Ōsaka, and was making a handsome profit from commodity brokering. By the 1690s, the firm was acting as financial agent for the shogun, the emperor, and several leading daimyo. In addition, the company managed a large network of wholesale associations, for which its stores provided outlets; operated a speedy courier service between Edo and Ōsaka; and was heavily involved in the real-estate market.

For the Mitsui and such other merchant houses as the Sumitomo, the seventeenth century signaled the start of more than 300 years of commercial paramountcy. To the military rulers of the time, however, they were objects of scorn. Segregated in special quarters of the towns, as befitted their low status, they were subject to strict regulations and were forbidden any participation in the running of the nation.

Freed from onerous responsibility and unshackled by social obligations, Japan's merchant class found time to escape the rigors of office and abacus in a round of worldly delights. The cities offered endless gratification for those who had the money: expensive clothes and rich food, conversation in tea and wine shops, the pleasures of paintings, novels, theaters, bathhouses, and brothels. In the areas around the merchant quarters, patrons of restaurants and bathhouses enjoyed the attentions of geishas, professional courtesans who provided an alternative to the boredom of an arranged marriage or the routine sensuality of the brothel. Theatergoers hired private boxes, where, secluded behind gold screens and split-bamboo curtains, they whiled away the evenings with picnic hampers and bottles of rice wine. And merrymakers thronged the waterways of such towns as Edo and Ōsa-

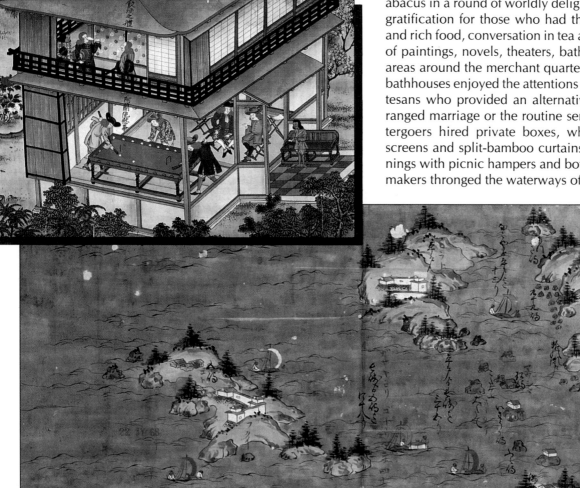

ka, where the wealthy maintained their own luxuriously appointed pleasure boats, staffed with cooks, musicians, and dancing girls. The poor took their own supplies and caroused along the canals in more modest, hired vessels.

Ukiyo, or the "floating world," the Japanese called this urban playground, using a phrase that in Buddhist teaching signified all that was transitory and insubstantial in life. Expenditure on these fleeting delights was so lavish that it called forth frequent rebukes from the military government. Nevertheless, many samurai discarded their swords and forgot their principles of frugality and self-control to taste its fruits. One such temporary renegade described a visit to the theater:

> *Many went . . . with their faces wrapped in towels, wearing only a short sword so they would look like common people. These disguised samurai broke over the bamboo fence of the theater, whereas the real common people paid their fees. If the management tried to stop the intruders, they uttered a menacing roar and strode on to take the best seats.*

The arts were quick to reflect the new urban lifestyle. A new type of prose literature appeared, heroic romances that satisfied the townsfolk's taste for adventure. Among its greatest exponents was the novelist Ihara Saikaku, whose down-to-earth heroes provided a stark contrast to the courtly paramours of traditional tales. He frankly extolled the life of pleasure. "Why offer money to Buddha?" he once wrote. "Is not a land of women paradise? Give your money to women."

In the theater, the popular kabuki style gradually began to replace the ceremonial Nō performances that had bored Nobunaga to distraction. And in the visual arts, carvers and painters employed colored woodcut prints to satisfy a large and growing market for representations of the floating world: merchants desirous of having mementos of their favorite geishas, theaters needing handbills, book publishers requiring illustrations. From simple line cuts, the works became increasingly sophisticated; a series of fine-grained blocks, each printing a single color, was kept accurately in register to build up the required image. In their style, the prints incorporated elements of European art learned in the period of open contact or later through the continuing influence of the Dutch at Nagasaki: Perspective, dramatic chiaroscuro, and modern pigments such as Prussian blue all combined to enhance the design. Demand grew and print runs lengthened. By the end of the century, a few small coins could purchase colorful masterpieces depicting popular entertainers, bustling urban scenes, or majestic landscapes.

Native connoisseurs regarded this new fashion as vulgar, preferring older styles of Japanese art ultimately derived from China. But even for purists, the nation's poetic renaissance had something to offer. The making of intricate, allusive verse had long been a courtly skill in Japan. This tradition had crystallized in the form of the haiku, a three-line verse drawing concise imagery from nature to suggest an emotion. In the seventeenth century, the greatest master of haiku appeared, an ex-ronin who used the pseudonym of Matsuo Bashō.

A wandering recluse known simply as Bashō, the poet studied the doctrines of Zen, a contemplative Buddhist sect whose adepts sought to savor both the uniqueness of every object and moment and the complex web of destinies linking them. Far removed in spirit from the gaudy venality of the floating world, Bashō's terse, allusive poems were tinged with a contemplative melancholy:

A page from a late-seventeenth-century map shows the walled artificial island of Deshima *(below, center)* built near the port of Nagasaki to receive Dutch merchants, the only Europeans permitted to trade with Japan. Within the enclosure, they enjoyed a comfortable existence, drinking, smoking, and playing billiards in well-appointed quarters *(inset)*. But they were allowed minimal contact with the Japanese; the dark-skinned servant standing outside the door would have come with the traders from the Dutch settlement in Indonesia.

An important item in the tea ceremony, this cast-iron kettle of an early, restrained style is etched with bamboo, and plum and pine trees, symbolizing strength.

THE REFINED PLEASURES OF THE TEA CEREMONY

When the Japanese adopted from China the custom of drinking tea, they imported not only a refreshment but a ritual. Beginning in the eighth century AD, the Chinese had made the preparation and sharing of a bowl of the beverage a symbol of inner harmony. Under the influence of Zen Buddhism, with its emphasis on austerity and the renunciation of worldly attachments, this practice was refined into a style of ceremony known as *wabi,* or "simplicity."

In the sparsely decorated surroundings of a humble garden hut, the host would welcome his guests, boil water in a kettle,

put the tea powder into a bowl, whisk in hot water, and then he would offer the drink in a spirit of modesty. This style reached its peak under the sixteenth-century tea master Sen Rikyū.

But in the seventeenth century, tea masters revived the ostentatious daimyo ceremony, named for Japan's warrior nobility, which permitted larger surroundings, richly decorated utensils, and separate seating for lords. In later years, this style was formalized and codified by tea schools, under whose influence the ritual became popular with Japan's burgeoning middle class.

The elegant simplicity of this bamboo tea scoop belies its creation at the hands of Kobori Enshu, a seventeenth-century tea master who developed the luxurious daimyo ceremony. By tradition, the scoop was always carved by the master himself.

The *natsume* style of tea caddy, shaped like a jujube fruit and made out of dark lacquer, was a favorite of Sen Rikyū. This seventeenth-century example, decorated with golden feathers, is in a later and more ornate style.

A ceramic tea bowl, bearing an enamel pattern of fish scales and waves, epitomizes the courtly grandeur of the later daimyo style. The height of the ceremony was reached when the master ladled hot water from the kettle on to the powdered tea in the bowl from which the guests were to drink.

The most formal type of ceremony calls for two servings of tea; the first "thick," or unwhipped, and the second "thin," whisked up to a foam. The tea whisk is made from a single piece of bamboo, carefully split into tines at one end and bound with silk thread at the base of the tines. This example was bought by a Dutch merchant at Deshima.

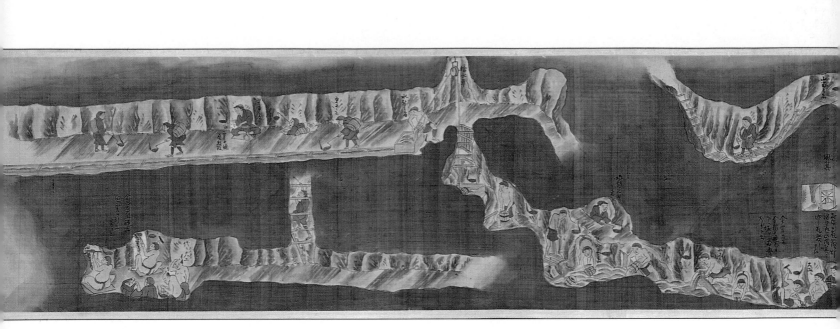

*On a withered branch
a crow has settled;
autumn nightfall.*

Bashō himself died in 1694, but his works had a lasting influence. In years to come he would be honored as Japan's greatest poet, and as the hectic existence of the towns began to pall, many followed Bashō in seeking meditative repose in nature. Shortly before his death, Bashō composed his last haiku:

*On a journey, ill
and my dreams o'er withered fields
are wandering still.*

Tokugawa culture developed in seclusion. Iemitsu had forbidden the handful of Dutch traders restricted to the island of Deshima to import books, and Japanese interpreters were allowed to discuss with them only the commonplaces of trade. In time, however, such intellectual isolation proved unsustainable. The eighth Tokugawa shogun, Yoshimune, had scientific leanings, and he was aware that in earlier centuries much learning had come from abroad. In 1744, he reversed his predecessor's ruling. Japanese scholars were sent to learn Dutch, and Western books were permitted so long as they made no mention of Christianity.

Through this narrow crack in the wall of self-imposed isolation, Western influences slowly began to trickle into Japan. Daimyo collected such novelties as clocks and field glasses, and they drank out of glass goblets. Artists departed from tradition and tried out Western oil-painting techniques. Individuals of a more scientific bent studied Western medicine, carried out experiments with asbestos and electricity, peered at the heavens through telescopes, and avidly discussed European advances in agriculture and botany. Even the shogun's palace was embellished with imported meteorological equipment. But his subjects balked when Yoshimune ambitiously

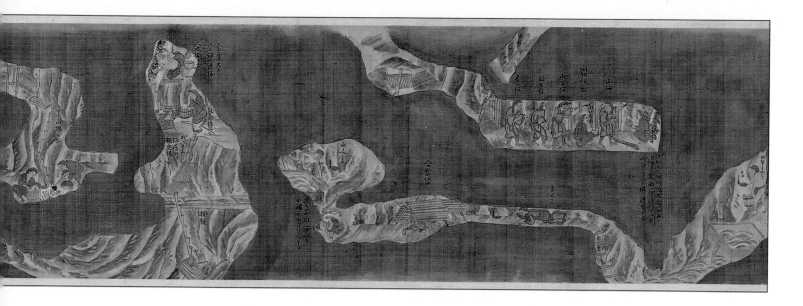

Shown in an eighteenth-century copy of an earlier scroll, Japanese miners toil underground to win the precious metals of the mines on Sado Island, off northern Honshū. While some miners work on the rockface, others repair scaffolding supporting the tunnel and remove underground water by means of buckets and a pulley. To the right, officials inspect a newly excavated shaft; on the left, porters carry loads of the mined rock back to the pit entrance. The scroll also shows a circular device *(center)* that served as a rotary ventilator to freshen air made smoky by the oil lamps that many of the miners carry. The ores of Sado were a valuable asset for the shoguns; the gold, silver, and copper that they produced were the nation's main export.

proposed replacing the traditional Chinese calendar with the Gregorian version.

Such interests were limited to a very small minority of the population. Still, the seeds of doubt were being sown, and by the turn of the nineteenth century, educated Japanese were growing uneasily conscious of the threat posed by more technologically advanced nations overseas. In 1807, Russian raiders attacked the northern islands of Sakhalin and Yezo (later renamed Hokkaidō). The following year, a British warship sailed into the harbor at Nagasaki and threatened to bombard the port unless the governor provided it with supplies.

In the decades that followed, such incursions were repeated with alarming frequency. The shoguns found themselves struggling with forces they could not control, and the passing of sumptuary laws intended to promote frugality—the banning of barbers, the arrest of prostitutes, the prohibition of gambling—did little to invigorate an economy that was rapidly deteriorating. Crop failures and famines sent prices skyrocketing, creating growing unrest among the peasantry. Attempts by the shogunate to curb rampant inflation by debasing the coinage merely incurred the enmity of the samurai. And increasingly, local daimyo broke away from the tottering central government and took charge of their own affairs.

The long Tokugawa peace was already failing when, in 1853, Commodore Matthew Perry of the U.S. Navy ended Japanese isolation by sailing with four gunboats into Edo harbor and, despite Japanese protests, demanding that his country be given trading rights. The shogun had neither the military nor the economic strength to resist the challenge. Assailed by foreigners from without and attacked by contemptuous daimyo within, the shogunate limped on for another fifteen years. Then, in January 1868, the bubble burst. A group of rebel lords from the western provinces announced that thenceforth the country would be ruled by the emperor. The discredited Tokugawa government disintegrated almost without a struggle. For two centuries, Japan had lagged behind the Western powers. Now, in the name of their emperor, Japan's samurai prepared to rectify the situation.

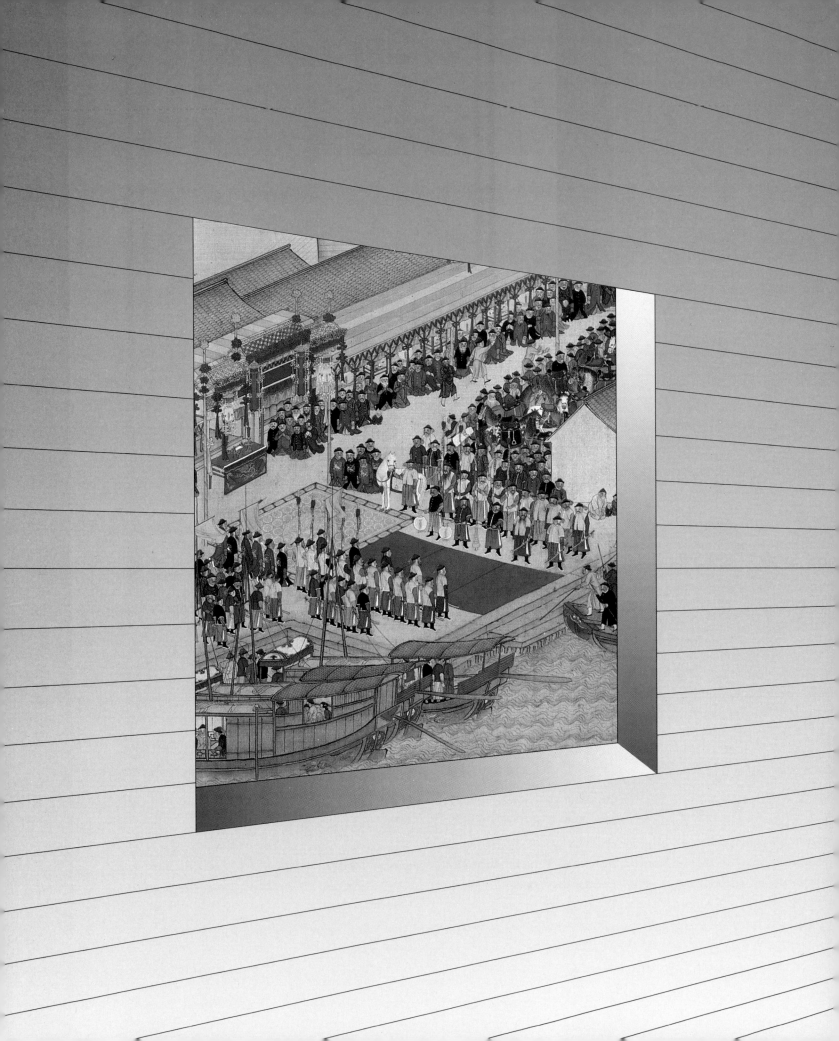

CHINA'S MANCHU OVERLORDS

2 The Kangxi emperor of China was in a satirical mood. When Monsignor Mezzabarba, legate from Pope Clement XI, appeared before his throne near the end of his long reign, which stretched from 1662 to 1722, the emperor held up three pieces of cloth that lay on a table before him. "If anyone should maintain that this red stuff is white, and that the white is yellow, what would you think of it?" he asked. Mezzabarba understood that his host was mocking the way successive popes had contradicted themselves in edicts regarding religious worship in China. The monsignor then attempted to explain the infallible nature of papal authority, but Kangxi would have none of it. "Is it possible," the emperor abruptly demanded, "that the pope can judge of the nature of the rites of China, which he has never seen, or had any personal knowledge of, any more than I can judge of the affairs of the Europeans, who are unknown to me?" With this confident challenge, Kangxi dismissed his suitor. He was beginning to lose patience with Europeans who tried to lecture him. "How can they presume to talk about 'the great principles of China'," he wrote. "After all, they know only a fraction of what I know."

Kangxi had every reason to be self-assured. He presided over the largest and wealthiest empire on earth, a fact that even the most culturally confident European visitors were forced to acknowledge. From the forests of Manchuria to the jungles of Southeast Asia, bounded on the west by Tibet and the plains of central Asia and on the east by the South China and the East China seas, this vast country was at peace both with the European powers and with its immediate neighbors. Nowhere else on earth did so many people enjoy such a prosperous life. One hundred and fifty million or more subjects of the Celestial Empire, as the Chinese called their country, were experiencing an economic and cultural renaissance that would have seemed inconceivable just fifty years earlier.

Yet the emperor who helped create this peace—the man venerated as the Son of Heaven—was not even Chinese. He was a Manchu whose grandparents had lived in the wild lands to the north of the Great Wall. This "barbarian" people had poured into China in the mid-seventeenth century, replacing the corrupt and moribund Ming dynasty with their own Qing administration. How the Manchu managed to establish their authority, cope with the ever-increasing attentions of the Western powers, and revitalize the ancient civilization of China is one of the most remarkable stories of the seventeenth century.

China was an old, enfeebled state when the Manchu swept from the north toward Beijing in 1644. The Ming dynasty, which had assumed power nearly three centuries earlier in the wake of 100 years of Mongol occupation, had grown increasingly inward looking over several generations of timid, inefficient rule. Ming officials relied

Dignitaries of the city of Suzhou in eastern China crowd the banks of the Grand Canal to welcome the Kangxi emperor in 1698. This detail from a contemporary scroll painted on silk shows an honor guard dressed in imperial yellow uniforms lining up before an elaborate altar; a groom waits with the emperor's white horse. Kangxi was the greatest ruler of the Qing dynasty, which replaced the decadent Ming regime in 1644.

upon agriculture for national revenue, generally mistrusting merchants who might subvert the state with foreign ideas. By the sixteenth century, the isolationist policies of China's rulers had brought to an end the wide-ranging expeditions in mighty, oceangoing ships that had marked the early, confident years of Ming rule. As the once-proud Chinese fleet dwindled to a collection of coastal junks, maritime trade was gradually given over to foreigners, while Turks and Mongols continued to dominate commerce across the landmass of central Asia.

Despite the dead hand of official policy, the industrious Chinese people invested the Ming economy with a surprising vitality. Fresh land was continually brought into agricultural production, and faster-growing strains of rice allowed farmers to harvest two crops in a season. In some favored regions, agriculture was shifting from subsistence farming to cash crops such as tea, cotton, citrus fruit, and mulberry trees for the silk industry. Fish ponds supplied the hungry cities, and some pioneering farmers experimented successfully with newly introduced crops from the Americas, including peanuts, corn, and sweet potatoes.

Industry, too, made steady advances, though with little encouragement from the

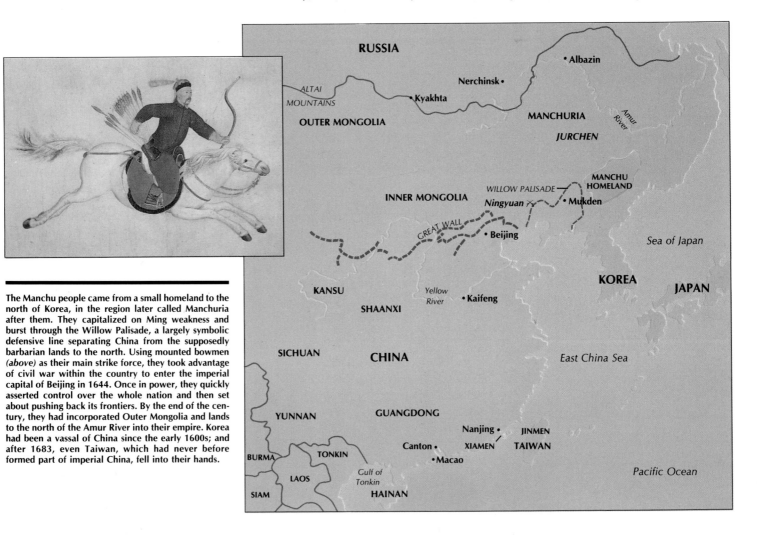

The Manchu people came from a small homeland to the north of Korea, in the region later called Manchuria after them. They capitalized on Ming weakness and burst through the Willow Palisade, a largely symbolic defensive line separating China from the supposedly barbarian lands to the north. Using mounted bowmen (above) as their main strike force, they took advantage of civil war within the country to enter the imperial capital of Beijing in 1644. Once in power, they quickly asserted control over the whole nation and then set about pushing back its frontiers. By the end of the century, they had incorporated Outer Mongolia and lands to the north of the Amur River into their empire. Korea had been a vassal of China since the early 1600s; and after 1683, even Taiwan, which had never before formed part of imperial China, fell into their hands.

central government. Chinese silks, cottons, and especially ceramics were highly prized in Europe. It was not until the early eighteenth century that Europeans learned the secret of manufacturing porcelain, and even then authentic Chinese ceramics remained the envy of collectors throughout the world.

In one essential industry, the Ming authorities reluctantly enlisted Western aid. Although the Chinese were excellent metallurgists—more knowledgeable in some respects than the best smiths of Europe—they admitted Western superiority in the manufacture of firearms. Undoubtedly the most advanced cannon and handguns were either imported from Europe or made under the supervision of Western experts. The Ming had, in fact, been purchasing European matchlock muskets and light artillery from the Portuguese in Macao since the sixteenth century, as well as encouraging the manufacture of Chinese copies. As the threat of rebellion and frontier warfare grew even more menacing during the seventeenth century, the Ming government relaxed its deep-seated suspicion of Western barbarians and sought aid in the manufacture of weapons from an apparently unlikely source—Jesuit missionaries.

The Jesuits had been accepted at the imperial court in Beijing since the beginning of the seventeenth century. Although they had come to China to win converts to Christianity, Chinese intellectuals were less interested in their faith than in the news they brought of Europe's recent scientific and technological discoveries. These highly educated clerics were natural diplomats, who quickly realized that Catholicism was unlikely to win the hearts of the people unless the emperor himself blessed their work with his approval. Consequently, they adapted to Chinese society, learning the language and assuming Chinese dress. On June 21, 1629, a Jesuit astronomer astonished his hosts by successfully predicting a solar eclipse. This apparent prophetic magic led to the employment of Jesuits at the Board of Astronomy, where they were to remain for nearly two centuries. When embattled Ming officials needed more firepower to fight off the growing menace of the Manchu, they naturally invited the holy fathers to supervise the casting of heavy artillery.

But guns alone could not preserve the failing dynasty. As cash crops turned farming into a lucrative business, land had become concentrated in the hands of wealthy landlords. Powerful local landowners could defy government tax collectors, while an increasing tax burden fell upon the smaller peasant farmers. The result was a wave of peasant uprisings in almost every province of China. Some of these blazed into full-scale regional rebellions; others sputtered into banditry, the plague of life in provincial China in the early seventeenth century.

Quick to exploit the opportunity for easy plunder, China's neighbors harassed the country from all sides. Japanese pirates ravaged the coast. Massive Japanese armies invaded the Ming vassal kingdom of Korea, involving the Ming in years of costly warfare. To the northwest, the Mongol nations began a disturbing revival of hostilities, while beyond them an additional threat was developing: Cossack adventurers were spearheading an expansion that would extend the boundaries of Russia eastward to the Pacific by the middle of the century. Meanwhile, along China's northeastern frontier, the newly established Manchu state steadily and efficiently developed its military and political organization.

Despite superior technology and vast manpower, the Ming government was slow to defend itself against these challenges. Decades of extravagance and neglect of the economy had left the Chinese state unable to pay for an adequate army. Private militias supplemented the undermanned national force, halfheartedly defending the realm in campaigns that often threatened to degenerate into banditry and rebellion.

Natural disasters added to China's woes. Bad harvests in the 1620s led to devastating famines in the impoverished northwest. Plagues accounted for millions of deaths between 1639 and 1644, further weakening the Ming armies.

At the heart of this smitten empire was the dissolute and self-absorbed court at Beijing, whose emperors had virtually abdicated political responsibility; after 1582, they even refused to conduct court business or attend meetings with government ministers. Power consequently fell into the hands of eunuchs. A feature of Chinese court life for more than two millennia, these household servants had often seen their influence on affairs of state wax as imperial fortunes waned. Now, with their private armies, secret police, and factional rivalries, the eunuchs terrorized the Chinese administration and the common people alike.

Court life reached a nadir during the reign of the Tianqi emperor (1620-1627), an illiterate who withdrew entirely from politics in order to devote his life to carpentry. In his absence, the state was effectively ruled by the emperor's former nursemaid Mistress Ke and by a cruel and self-seeking eunuch named Wei Zhongxian. Wei's great influence and untrammeled delight in torture and murder silenced most of his critics. One brave court officer, however, presented the uncaring emperor with a list of Wei's "twenty-four great crimes." "Can your majesty employ as your right-hand man a creature whose flesh the whole empire desires to eat?" the anguished official demanded. He received an unambiguous reply two years later when he was savagely tortured on Wei's commands and left to die in prison.

On the death of Tianqi, his seventeen-year-old brother assumed the imperial throne, taking the reign title of Chongzhen. This young man attempted to restore a measure of integrity to Ming politics. The eunuch Wei found an easy escape in suicide. His companion in misrule, Mistress Ke, suffered death by slicing, a prolonged form of torture in which the victim was slashed with sharp knives and each wound was quickly cauterized with a hot iron to prevent too painless a death through loss of blood. But by now it was far too late for purges and reforms. Before long, internal rebellion was to tear the state asunder, while an enemy at the gate had grown too powerful to be denied.

During the steady collapse of the Ming regime, the Manchu nation rapidly increased in power, as if feeding off its effete southern neighbor. This energetic people lived in the mountains north of Korea in the region subsequently known as Manchuria. They were one of three Tungusic tribal groups collectively called Jurchen, distantly related in language to the Mongols and Turks to their west. In the twelfth century, the Jurchen had burst into history by conquering much of northern China, where they established their Jin, or "Golden," dynasty before falling prey to Genghis Khan's Mongols. The Jurchen later withdrew to their homeland in the north, but their brief ascendancy over China remained a proud and inspiring memory for them.

Under the centuries of Mongol and then Ming suzerainty, the people of Manchuria remained generally at peace with their overlords. Chinese officials used the age-old policy of "divide and rule" to dominate the tribes, and Chinese settlers were confined within the Willow Palisade, a largely symbolic frontier defense around southwestern Manchuria. Nevertheless, some Chinese did move beyond the Willow Palisade, offering their expertise to tribal rulers and playing a major role in the establishment of a local arms industry.

The Manchu—the branch of the Jurchen people who lived closest to the Chinese frontier—set about unifying Manchuria in the late sixteenth century under the rule of a vigorous leader called Nurhachi. They seized Chinese territory within the Willow Palisade, setting up a new capital in 1625 at Shenyang, which they later renamed Mukden. From here Nurhachi, having already thrown off nominal Ming suzerainty, declared the creation of a new Jin state, recalling the "Golden" empire of five centuries earlier. He built up an efficient government organized along partly Chinese and partly nomadic lines and ensured strong economic foundations by monopolizing the pearl, fur, and ginseng trades. Nurhachi simplified the complex Mongolian script

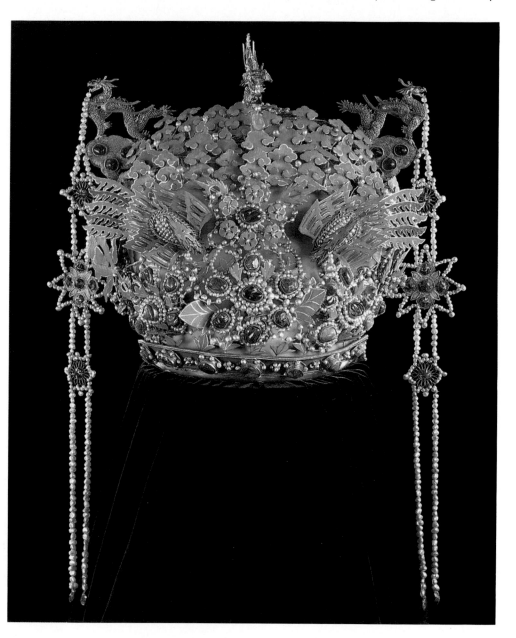

Decorated with gems, pearls, and kingfisher feathers on a base of gold, a crown made for one of the two queens of the Wanli emperor, who ruled China from 1573 to 1620, suggests the extravagance of the later years of Ming rule. At a time when the empire was committed to major military campaigns in Korea against Japanese invaders, the treasury was further burdened by massive expenditure on the repair of royal palaces and the upkeep of a court entourage that by now included 70,000 eunuchs and 9,000 female attendants, as well as on lavish spectacles celebrating such occasions as the investiture of imperial princes.

previously used by the Jurchen. Most important of all, he replaced the existing tribal military organization with the famous banner system, which provided him and his successors with one of the most formidable armies in Asia.

At first, the banner organization was quite simple: Nurhachi's troops were divided into four companies, each with their own colors—yellow, white, blue, or red. In less than fifteen years, the number of companies expanded to 200, forming eight larger "banners," their flags now fringed with red or white. Eventually each of the banners in Nurhachi's army included 7,500 men in five regiments, each comprising five companies. As the Manchu state expanded, Chinese and Mongol divisions would be added to the ranks. Leadership of the banners was, and remained, largely hereditary, although officer ranks in later years had to be confirmed by the Manchu government. The bulk of troops were tribesmen, but captives, slaves, and serfs all came to be enlisted in the ranks of one or another of the banners for administrative purposes.

These early banner armies did not receive payment; the troops were

The Jesuit Presence

China seemed promising territory to Christian missionaries in 1600. Challenged by no single dominant faith like Islam in the Middle East, proselytizers dreamed of Christianizing the entire country through the conversion of its ruler. With that hope in mind, the Italian Jesuit, Matteo Ricci, traveled to China in 1582 and set about studying Chinese culture. His example was followed by other members of his order, men of great learning who made themselves welcome at the Chinese court, where they won many souls to the faith.

Toward the end of the century, however, Dominican friars arrived in China. They found Jesuit toleration of Chinese traditions, such as the discharge of firecrackers during Mass, deeply shocking. They appealed to the pope, who condemned the practices, thereby alienating the Kangxi emperor, who later expelled most of the missionaries, Jesuits and Dominicans alike.

Made of ivory, this pocket sundial was the work of Adam Schall von Bell, a German Jesuit who became head of the Imperial Board of Astronomy under the first Manchu emperor. The device also incorporates a compass.

This portrait of a Jesuit missionary in China is thought to represent Matteo Ricci, an Italian who spent his last thirty years in the country trying to link Chinese and European culture. The book in his hand bears the title *Holy Teaching of the Heavenly Ruler*—the Chinese term for Catholicism.

expected to support themselves from the revenues of their own lands or else with plunder, as the old Mongol hordes had done. In their fighting style, however, these armies preferred Chinese to Mongol tactics, relying heavily upon foot soldiers. Their vanguard consisted of armored infantry, the first rank of which was armed with pikes, the second with swords, and the third with bows. A smaller cavalry force remained in the rear, ready to support the infantry and deliver a decisive blow should the opportunity present itself.

Such tactics left the Manchu very vulnerable to firearms, of which Ming Chinese garrisons had an increasing number. In 1626, the Manchu suffered a notable reverse against Ming artillery in the battle at Ningyuan; Nurhachi died of wounds received in the encounter. But within a few years, the Manchu had firearms of their own—Russian guns presented as tribute by Mongol tribes. The still-primitive matchlock musket was less accurate and had a far slower shooting rate than the bow, but competent archers took years to train, whereas guns required no great skill of the user.

Even before establishing the Manchu capital at Mukden, Nurhachi had forced the

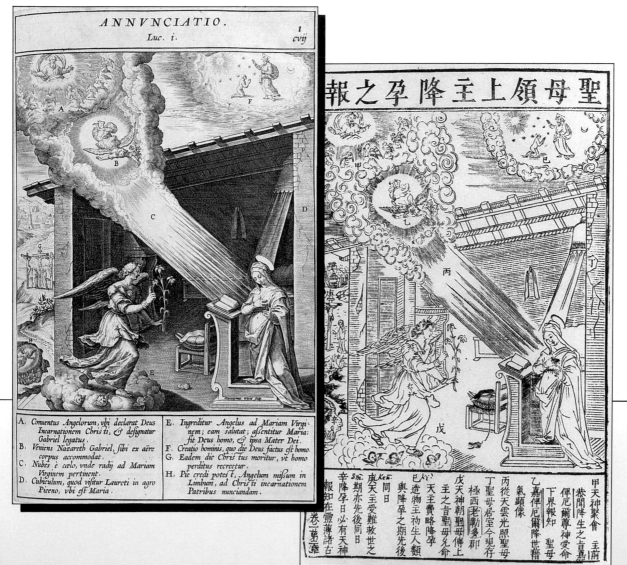

Two pictures of the Annunciation—the announcement to the Virgin Mary of her divine mission—show how the Jesuits adapted European material for a Chinese audience. The original engraving *(far left)* by Hieronymus Wierx was published in Antwerp in 1595. The copy *(near left)*, made by a local artist for a Chinese edition of *The Life of the Lord in Pictures* by the Jesuit missionary Giulio Aleni, uses an identical composition, but the style has been changed to suit Chinese artistic tastes.

eastern Mongols into submission. His son and successor, Abahai, brought more Mongol tribes into the expanding Manchu realm and also extended his authority northward into the Amur River valley, which today forms the frontier between China and the Soviet Union. Meanwhile, the decline of Ming power in China turned Manchu attention south once more. China, even in its decadence, was so much larger than the Manchu homeland that its conquest could be contemplated only if the invaders could count on substantial Chinese support. In this respect the name "Jin" that Nurhachi had given to his state was counterproductive, because it carried bitter memories of defeat and foreign domination for the Chinese. So Abahai coined a new name for his dynasty—Qing, or "Pure"—which had wholly different associations.

Despite occasional setbacks, Abahai continued to wear away the northern defenses of Ming China. In 1629, a Manchu army reached the gates of Beijing before withdrawing north of the Great Wall. Success bred success, and an increasing number of Chinese administrators, soldiers, and artisans came to serve the new Qing state, which, organized along acceptably Confucian lines stressing the importance of education and public service, offered them rich rewards and even high office. In fact, the Manchu state was becoming more Chinese all the time; Abahai even set up six government ministries, mimicking the Ming administrative system. In this way, the foundations were laid for the Manchu-Chinese cooperation that was to govern China for more than two and a half centuries.

It was not, in the end, the Manchu state that delivered the fatal blow to the tottering Ming regime. By the early 1640s, powerful uprisings were tearing the country apart. In central China, a one-eyed rebel called Li Zicheng attracted a huge army of disillusioned peasants, victims of famine and poverty. Ruthless and ambitious, Li believed that the "mandate of heaven," which alone entitled an emperor to rule, was destined to descend upon him, and he suffered nothing to stand in his way. When the city of Kaifeng resisted a siege, he cut the banks of the Yellow River, drowning hundreds of thousands of innocent civilians—along with many of his own followers—in the resulting flood.

The road to Beijing lay open to Li's army by the spring of 1644. The imperial city itself was defended by an inadequate army of eunuchs, which melted away in the face of the rebel horde. Informed that the insurgents were within the walls of his capital, the emperor muddled his senses with wine. Dressing his sons in rags to escape recognition, he told them to flee from the palace. Then he summoned the court ladies. "All is over. It is time for you to die," he announced. He killed his senior concubine with a blow from his sword. Trying to similarly dispatch his fifteen-year-old daughter, Princess Imperial,

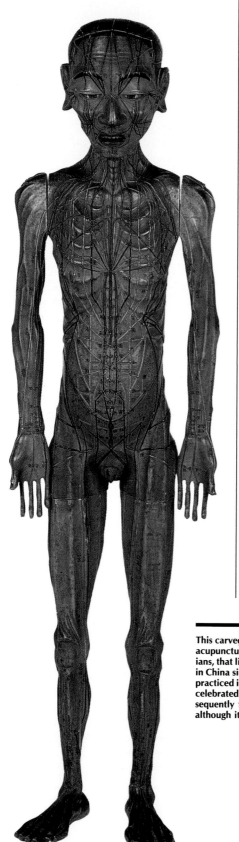

he succeeded only in chopping off her arm. Then, dressed in his ceremonial robes and attended by a loyal eunuch, the emperor wandered into the palace grounds. The bodies of emperor and eunuch were later found hanging from a rafter in a pavilion known as the Imperial Hat and Girdle Department. Pinned to the emperor's robe was a despairing farewell note. "I die unable to face my ancestors," it concluded. "May the bandits dismember my corpse and slaughter my officials, but let them not despoil the imperial tombs nor harm a single one of our people."

This last imperial command was signally ignored by Li's rebels. The people of Beijing had thronged the streets on their arrival. "Long live the new emperor," proclaimed posters along the route. But the welcome turned to terror as the undisciplined army embarked upon an orgy of looting and murder. "Hands were amputated, legs severed, stomachs ripped open, ears sliced off, hair cut away. . . . No one dared oppose them," wrote an anonymous survivor.

It was now that the Manchu finally descended upon the city of Beijing. Their soldiers met no resistance, for Wu Sangui, the Chinese general who had previously barred their way, chose to join forces with these disciplined foreigners rather than allow Li's murderous army to preside over the capital. In the face of this irresistible alliance, the rebels took flight, and the Manchu conquerors proclaimed their Qing dynasty as the rightful heir to the Ming. Abahai had died the year before. His five-year-old son became the first Qing emperor, in the Chinese manner taking the name of Shunzhi, or "Obedience and Good Order Established," for his reign; the boy's uncle, Dorgon, was the principal regent.

The most pressing task for China's new rulers was to assert control over the vast land that had fallen so effortlessly into their hands. "If there are those who disobediently resist us," proclaimed the regent Dorgon in his very first edict, "then the stones themselves will be set ablaze and all will be massacred." This was no idle threat: When Yangzhou, a walled city near the Yangtze River, attempted resistance, thousands of men, women, and children, in the words of one survivor, "went to their graves like beds."

The Ming resistance in fact presented little threat to the Manchu armies. Over the course of the next ten years, a succession of Ming claimants to the imperial throne attempted to rally loyalists to their cause, but their courts retreated steadily into the southwest, where the last serious pretender to the throne was executed in 1662.

An altogether more formidable challenge to the new dynasty came from a half-Japanese nobleman named Zheng Chenggong, known to Westerners at the time by the name of Coxinga. Steadfastly refusing to recognize Manchu authority in spite of the offer of generous peace terms, Coxinga amassed an army of more than 100,000 men and dominated the coast of central and southern China with his large, swift fleet. (So enraged was the Shunzhi emperor by Coxinga's continued successes that he is said to have hacked a throne to pieces with his sword in frustration.)

Like many heroes who have passed into folklore, Coxinga was betrayed by a human weakness. In 1659, his army seemed on the point of capturing Nanjing, the largest city of the empire.

This carved seventeenth-century figure shows the main acupuncture points and the imaginary lines, or meridians, that link them. Acupuncture, which had been used in China since at least the third century BC, was widely practiced in the late Ming period, when two of the most celebrated books on the subject were written. It subsequently fell out of favor, and in 1822 was banned, although it continued to be practiced surreptitiously.

Flushed with the prospect of victory, Coxinga and his soldiers lavishly celebrated his birthday throughout the night. The morning after "so inappropriate a ceremony"—as a censorious Dominican friar described the event—"his troops were careless with sleep and wine." Set upon by the enemy at this unhappy moment, the rebel army fell back to the sea in confusion.

Even after this demoralizing defeat, Coxinga continued his defiant rebellion from the offshore islands of Xiamen and Jinmen. Attempts to starve him into submission by evacuating a long coastal strip of mainland China caused great suffering for thousands of dispossessed Chinese civilians: "Along the coast we have nothing but ruined cities and villages," lamented one Chinese official. Two years after their defeat at Nanjing, Coxinga's army overwhelmed a small Dutch garrison on the island of Taiwan and established a permanent base there.

Coxinga himself died the following year, and leadership of his forces passed to his son. As tensions gradually eased, mainland inhabitants trickled back to their coastal homes, but the rebels remained a lingering threat to the Qing dynasty for another twenty years. It took a Manchu invasion of Taiwan in 1683 to finally put an end to resistance and to incorporate the island for the first time into the Chinese state.

In asserting their rule over China, the Manchu were assisted by the cultural and social gulf that separated the gentry from the peasants, making it difficult for the two to join together in resistance. Imbued as they were with Confucian reverence for authority, a majority of the existing elite found it easier to transfer its allegiance to the new rulers, particularly as the Manchu made great efforts to respect China's ancient codes of justice. Ming officials were welcomed back into the administration and were even allowed to retain their distinctive costumes. One new regulation did, however, cause widespread resentment. From the beginning, the Manchu insisted that all officials shave their foreheads and pull back their hair into Manchu pigtails. This humiliating symbol of their subservience to a foreign culture never ceased to rankle the Chinese nationalists. And in fact, the removal of such pigtails became a symbol of revolt against Manchu rule.

In the Manchu efforts to ease the transition from Ming to Qing, the Shunzhi emperor played an important role. This scholarly young man mastered classical Chinese, encouraged Confucian scholarship, and attempted to stamp out corruption wherever he found it. As a boy he was fortunate to fall under the influence of Adam Schall von Bell, a German Jesuit appointed head of the Imperial Board of Astronomy with the title "Master Who Searches Out Celestial Secrets." Schall was both spiritual and political adviser to the emperor, who called him *mafa*, or "grandpa." "Father Schall exercises an influence with the emperor possessed by neither viceroy nor prince," wrote a colleague. But he was unable to persuade his protégé to accept Christianity. Shunzhi became increasingly attracted to Buddhism, and by the time of his death from smallpox at the age of twenty-two, he was a devout follower of Zen.

Shunzhi was succeeded by his third son, a boy of seven at his father's death. This child was designated heir to the imperial throne partly because he had survived an attack of smallpox and so had acquired immunity to the disease that had killed his father. Shunzhi himself had scarcely met the boy—like all imperial children he had been brought up by nurses and eunuchs—but the choice was an inspired one. The child possessed prodigious curiosity, energy, and intellect, absorbing Confucian classics and dynastic history as avidly as he practiced riding and archery. Assuming

The Kangxi emperor sits cross-legged to read in this portrait on silk by an unknown artist, possibly a Jesuit missionary. Kangxi was one of the most successful of all Chinese rulers. Throughout his sixty-year reign, he not only brought stability and prosperity to his realm but also worked long hours, took firm personal control of government, and avoided the corruption that had marred the latter part of the Ming period. Despite his heavy workload, he retained a lifelong devotion to learning and did not stop reading books even when he was ill from overwork.

the reign title of Kangxi, he was destined to rule for more than sixty years and become one of the greatest figures of the seventeenth century.

Because the new emperor was too young to assume power in person, another regency ensued. Under the harsh domination of Oboi, a leading Manchu nobleman, the conciliatory pro-Chinese policies of Shunzhi were abruptly overturned. Chinese officials were forbidden to criticize the government. Those suspected of anti-Manchu sentiments were arrested and tortured. Oboi's influence would have lasted longer had these high-handed policies not offended Kangxi, who formally assumed power in 1667 at the tender age of thirteen. Two years later, finding himself unable to control his former regent, Kangxi arranged for his death. The circumstances are obscure, but according to one picturesque account, Oboi was seized and killed by a group of boys playing hide-and-seek in the palace courtyard. They were, in fact, youths trained in the martial arts, acting under orders from their emperor.

This audacious coup marked the effective beginning of Kangxi's long, autocratic reign, during which China reached a pinnacle of power, prosperity, and cultural achievement. An able military leader, a careful administrator, and an enthusiastic scholar, Kangxi set out his own sixteen moral principles, which became known as the *Sacred Edicts*. These precepts ranged from calls for filial piety and brotherly love to exhortations for citizens to cooperate in the protection of property. The emperor strove to follow them in his own life, as far as was possible for the ruler of a great empire. He cultivated China's intellectual class and controlled trade with the outside world to China's advantage. Under Kangxi, Manchu rule not only was legitimized in China but was consolidated across the entire country, while his conquest of Mongolia began the process of Manchu expansion across what is the modern-day Chinese People's Republic and beyond.

Kangxi adopted a demanding daily routine. He rose before dawn to study the Confucian classics. Imperial audiences began as early as five o'clock, although officials who lived some distance from the palace were permitted to attend a little later. Kangxi then discussed government issues with directors of the main boards and departments, next receiving the high government officials known as grand secretaries to discuss other problems. "It is the constant attention to detail that is of the greatest importance," he once wrote. Toward the end of the morning, officers of the imperial household, provincial officials, and finally foreign ambassadors were received. In the afternoon, the emperor read reports from lesser officials not permitted a personal audience. Any remaining time was devoted to his own studies, family matters, writing poems, or practicing calligraphy. Tutored by Jesuit missionaries, the emperor extended his interests beyond traditional Chinese scholarship to encompass European science, mathematics, cartography, medicine, and chiming clocks, which had a particular fascination for him. He studied Euclid's geometry and learned to play simple tunes on the harpsichord. "There is not a science of Europe that ever came to his knowledge, but he showed an inclination to be instructed in it," wrote one admiring Jesuit. It was said that Kangxi rarely got to bed before midnight.

Throughout the early years of his reign, Kangxi had to fight to secure his huge empire under Qing rule. His first major campaign was a bitter civil war that lasted nearly ten years. In the south and west of the country, three powerful Chinese generals—one of whom was the same Wu Sangui who had assisted the Manchu in taking Beijing—presided over provinces that they had transformed into virtually independent states. Their original task had been to help the Manchu crush Ming resistance, but by 1674, that job was virtually completed. Not surprisingly, however, the Three Feudatories, as they were known, resented the emperor's attempts to bring the provinces back under firm imperial control. When Kangxi moved against one of the generals, who was entrenched in Guangdong in the deep south, all three rose in revolt, their numbers reinforced by an army from Taiwan under the son of Coxinga. This powerful rebellion very nearly succeeded in driving the Manchu out of the country, but with the aid of loyal Chinese generals, Kangxi eventually prevailed in 1681. Two years later he invaded Taiwan, defeated Coxinga's grandson, and thereby stamped out the last spark of civil war.

Another military problem faced Kangxi as soon as he had crushed the Three Feudatories and occupied Taiwan. This was a growing Russian presence along the Amur River in northern Manchuria. The Manchu emperor obviously could not ignore a rival so close to the birthplace of the Manchu dynasty. For their part, the Cossacks were attracted to this relatively fertile area after their epic conquest of the harsh Siberian wastes. Beyond the Amur lay the Pacific Ocean and the lure of the Asian riches that were already bringing wealth to various European naval powers.

At the heart of the Manchu-Russian confrontation was the fortress of Albazin, built by Cossacks on the northernmost bend of the Amur in 1655. The very existence of the fortress was a provocation, but in addition, Cossack atrocities led the local tribes to demand help from their Manchu overlords. Fighting flared on and off until, after 1680, Kangxi set about the systematic consolidation of Manchu control throughout the Amur region. He established postal communications along roads and rivers from the south and set up bases, granaries, river fleets, and military colonies. Kangxi's armies proved themselves well able to deal with European troops, destroying Russian positions and Cossack colonies until, by 1686, only Albazin itself remained in enemy hands. Now at last negotiations began. A fleet of ninety ships sailed up the Amur to strengthen the Manchu bargaining position. In 1689, the two sides signed the Treaty of Nerchinsk—the first formal agreement between China and a European power. Both sides made concessions. China held the Amur valley and Russian expansion came to an end, but the newcomers maintained a base from which to trade with Beijing, a city that had in the past been loath to grant such privileges.

The army that achieved these successes was still based on the banner system, although this had changed somewhat since the Manchu conquest of China. Bannermen, who received government pensions and land grants, now included Mongols and Chinese, but these outsiders were paid less than the Manchu. And banner companies were of three types. Most bannermen came from the "external companies" based in a cordon around Beijing. Next came the garrison companies stationed in various Chinese or Manchurian cities, near the borders or along strategic roads. Somewhat separate from the main garrisons was the green-banner army. This substantial but scattered force of largely Chinese constabulary was primarily concerned with the suppression of banditry.

Manchu mounted bowmen still formed the military elite, but the role of the infantry continued to grow. Most foot soldiers fought with a shield and short sword or with a long axlike halberd. Archers and musketmen provided fire support, and a crack force of so-called shield-bearers served as an aggressive assault force.

Despite initial reservations, the Manchu became increasingly reliant upon firearms. Jesuit missionaries were persuaded to cast cannon in China, while additional artillery was purchased from Portuguese and other European traders. Russian prisoners of war were enlisted to fire the new weapons and were eventually incorporated into the banner system. In 1683, the emperor ordered that every banner in his army should include a musketry battalion, these apparently being formed of Chinese soldiers who had shown themselves to be poor horsemen.

The adoption of firearms did not mean the immediate abandonment of armor. In fact, China's traditional body defenses made of overlapping scales were probably as well able to resist seventeenth-century firearms as the plate armors of Europe. The protective scales were not always of metal. Lightweight but very resilient paper armor

In one of a sequence of paintings illustrating "The Four Pleasures of Bo Juyi," the artist Chen Hongshou shows his subject, a celebrated ninth-century poet, in meditation. In choosing his theme, Chen may have been drawing a parallel with his own day, for both poet and painter lived in times of upheaval—Bo in the latter years of the Tang era, Chen during the collapse of the Ming. The change of dynasty severely disrupted intellectual life; many Ming scholars killed themselves rather than serve the new masters. Chen himself abandoned his government post to become a Buddhist monk, but he remained torn between the inward-looking ideal of Buddhism and Confucian notions of public duty. His uncertainties were reflected in a series of pseudonyms he chose for himself, among them Huiseng (Repentant Monk) and Laochi (Old and Too Late).

remained in use, those with ten to fifteen sewn layers still being proof against everything but musket balls.

In order to sustain their formidable fighting skills, the main combat banners regularly took part in enormous hunting expeditions. The soldiers on such exercises formed circles many miles in diameter, which gradually closed in around deer, bears, tigers, and any other hapless game unable to escape. Hunts improved coordination among fighting units and sharpened the bannerman's skill with a bow. In 1683, Kangxi led 100,000 cavalry and 60,000 infantry on one such excursion north of the Great Wall. He exulted in escaping the confines of Beijing. "It is when one is beyond the Great Wall that the air and soil refresh the spirit," he wrote. An expert bowman who could shoot either right- or left-handed, he boasted of having killed 135 tigers, 96 wolves, and 132 wild boars "as well as hundreds of ordinary stags and deer." But he took equal joy in the simple outdoor life, cooking stag's liver over an open fire or chatting informally with local herdsmen. Even in the wilds Kangxi found a means to exercise his nearly obsessive love of learning. "Many of the officials could not even recognize the basic twenty-eight constellations," he complained after one trip.

For all his enthusiasm for scholarship and the hunt, Kangxi never neglected his duties to the empire. In the 1690s, a tribe of Mongols under a leader called Galdan began stirring up trouble on the northwestern frontier and at one point advanced to within 200 miles of Beijing. Kangxi personally led his armies in pursuit of the invader, and he took enormous pride in the defeat of this elusive enemy—the last man to threaten Beijing for more than a century. When Galdan committed suicide in 1697, Kangxi was exultant. "My great task is done," he wrote to a eunuch. "In two years I made three journeys across deserts combed by wind and bathed with rain, eating every other day in the barren and uninhabitable deserts. . . . The constant journeying and hardship have led to this achievement."

Victory in this war made it possible for the Manchu to establish a protectorate over what is now Outer Mongolia. Nevertheless, Mongol-Manchu competition would arise again at the beginning of the eighteenth century, when both sides struggled to dominate Tibet. Victory eventually went to the Manchu, and by the mid-eighteenth century, even the westernmost Mongols of Dzungaria and the Tianshan Mountains had lost their independence.

The civil administration of the Manchu empire was as complex, and as traditional, as its military organization. From the outset the Manchu paid particular attention to ensuring that the new dynasty was acceptable to their Chinese subjects. Accordingly, they chose the course of least resistance, taking over the existing Ming administration virtually intact. Having no long tradition of imperial rule themselves, the Manchu readily accepted Ming political institutions. The advantage of this smooth transition was that many of the Chinese people transferred their allegiance from a Ming to a Qing emperor without question; the mandate of heaven had merely passed from one ruling family to another.

Though willing to adopt the Ming system of government, the Manchu—who represented only about two percent of the population—were justifiably afraid of losing their national identity. To prevent total assimilation and guarantee their continued control over the state, they enshrined in law their separation from the Chinese. The Manchu elite was governed through a special department and had its own grades of social rank. The Manchu were barred from commerce or labor and were forbidden to marry ethnic Chinese. Chinese immigration into Manchuria, beyond an extended Willow Palisade, was still banned. The Manchu and Chinese languages were jointly used for official purposes.

In taking over much of the Ming administrative system wholesale, the Manchu also made some improvements of their own. They split up some provinces south of the Great Wall into smaller units, making a new total of eighteen such regions within China. Although the system of local government remained virtually unchanged, the tax burden on the poor was lightened and there was a widespread decline in the practice of serfdom. In 1681, the Kangxi emperor banned the selling of serfs along with land in at least one province; his successor, Yongzheng, abolished all hereditary servile groups in 1727, thus effectively liberating the serfs.

Under the new dynasty, the basic social unit remained the family, which itself formed part of a wider clan under an acknowledged clan head. Though weak in the north, the clan structure was a powerful social influence in southern China, where the state rarely interfered with an effective system of internal clan justice. The role of women was unchanged. Wives continued to be treated as subservient to their husbands. Girls of good family still had their feet bound in childhood to shape them into the "golden lily," no more than three inches from heel to toe. This practice

An engraving of Chinese beggars *(above)* shows one man who has lighted a small fire on his head to arouse sympathy and another beating himself with a stone, while a third wears a wooden collar; a group of street entertainers *(right)* includes a man suspended on a pole and another showing off trained rats. The pictures illustrate an account by the Dutch traveler Jan Nieuhof of a journey to China in the 1650s. Nieuhof was much struck by the beggars, whom he called "not only bold, but troublesome." He described how some mutilated themselves "to stir up a commiseration in such as pass by," and reported an encounter with one man, naked but for a loincloth and armed with spears, who threatened to kill himself unless given money.

confined a woman's movements, while supposedly enhancing her erotic appeal.

Although such ancient traditions continued to exert a powerful influence, Chinese life was changing, sometimes quite dramatically. The population was once again growing and agriculture was expanding, to the benefit of the peasantry who comprised about 80 percent of the population. The proportion of large landowners declined as the importance of moderately prosperous peasants—their interests protected by the state—increased.

Urban industries such as textile manufacturing and ceramics overcame the disruption of the 1630s and 1640s to reach and surpass their old levels. By the end of the century, an expansion of the cloth, ceramics, salt production, and mining industries was accompanied by increased capital input. The great wealth generated by these economic changes encouraged a leveling tendency in China's hitherto very stratified society. It became increasingly difficult to judge a person's social class merely by his dress.

The Kangxi reign also saw a considerable expansion in China's overseas trade. The main exports were channeled through Canton in the south, from which tea, silk, fine cotton textiles, porcelain, and lacquerware were shipped to Europe. Yet the Manchu government's attitude toward commerce with foreigners remained equivocal. Merchants from such neighboring countries as Korea, Indochina, Thailand, and Burma

were regarded merely as the bringers of tribute. Russian merchants were obliged to do business under the guise of conducting political missions, even after the Treaty of Nerchinsk theoretically opened the border for trade. Traders from western Europe were generally dismissed as barbarians—and reckless and uncultivated many of them undeniably were.

Amid the burgeoning economy, the ancient tradition of Chinese scholarship continued to flourish. A sophisticated upper class still cultivated formal gardens, collected antiques, wrote poetry, practiced painting or calligraphy, and patronized the theater, as it had for centuries past. These gentlemen-scholars formed a pool of talent from which the government could recruit its administrative bureaucracy.

At the same time there emerged a trend toward what was called practical scholarship, which emphasized the gathering of evidence from as wide a range of sources as possible, followed by the making and testing of new theories. These remarkably modern intellectual principles were generally applied to the study of language and literature rather than science or technology, but one exception was the work of the widely traveled scholar Gu Yanwu, who turned his attention to the practical problems of geography, frontier defense, agriculture, and trade. This gradual shift away from traditional forms of scholarship took place at the same time that European learning was beginning to alter China's view of the world outside the Celestial Empire.

The Jesuits flourished under the new dynasty, contributing greatly to the intellectual life of the Manchu court. They enjoyed their finest hour during the middle decades of Kangxi's long reign, playing the part of courtiers and enjoying high rank in the emperor's entourage. The Jesuits performed the necessary Manchu rituals without embarrassment, in the full knowledge that their favorable position depended upon the continued good will of the emperor. These rites included the ceremonial kowtow, in which a kneeling supplicant touched his forehead to the ground until the emperor invited him to come forward.

Despite such seeming indignities, the Jesuits were enthusiastic apologists for their adopted land. "China offers an enchanting picture of what the whole world might become, if the laws of that empire were to become the laws of all nations," wrote one missionary. They helped familiarize the West with Chinese ceramics, textiles, and lacquerwork, all of which were to influence European baroque and rococo art. They also helped draw Chinese civilization to the attention of the great thinkers and writers of Europe, including Spinoza, Goethe, Voltaire, Diderot, and Adam Smith.

Although it was prepared to borrow much from Europe in return, China—unlike many traditional civilizations confronted with the power of Western technology—did not find its own heritage obviously outmoded. In fact, Chinese scholars generally regarded European achievements as representing a "new science," complementing but not superseding their own. They sought to learn from both traditions in a broad-ranging effort to achieve a universally valid system of scientific thought.

In the latter part of the Kangxi reign, however, the Jesuit influence was lessened by divisions within the Christian camp. Missionaries from other orders were increasingly critical of what they saw as Jesuit sycophancy toward the emperor. Their complaints were sympathetically received in Rome, and the papacy's subsequent critical messages to the Chinese court led to the cooling in relations with the emperor. The pope's claim to spiritual superiority, even over the Son of Heaven, further undermined the Christian cause.

And Kangxi was not used to disagreement. He ruled his country with absolute authority, paternal benevolence, and unflagging energy. A man of action, he was intolerant of officials who thought physical involvement in the course of duty beneath their dignity. When a fire broke out in the Chinese quarter of Beijing, he was furious to observe Manchu officials standing by "with their hands

Among China's most important exports during the seventeenth and eighteenth centuries was porcelain made for the European market. As the two examples here show, these wares were often quite unlike traditional Chinese ceramics, being shaped and decorated specifically to appeal to Western tastes. The plate at left copies a French print of a *fête champêtre*, or "outdoor entertainment," but surrounds the scene with typical Chinese landscapes; the pot at right bears images of both Chinese and Western ships. Many millions of such pieces were shipped from the port of Canton and, along with other examples of Chinese decorative art, had a profound influence on the European rococo style.

folded in their sleeves." "We'd be better off with less talk of moral principles and more practice of them," he once wrote.

To observe the problems of his domains firsthand, Kangxi made several tours throughout China, inspecting public works, pardoning criminals, listening to grievances, and sometimes reading the examination papers of aspiring state officials. According to one astonished Jesuit, he permitted "even the meanest workman or peasant to approach his person," speaking to them "with so much affability and sweetness, as charms them to the heart." Perhaps as a result of these internal encounters, Kangxi learned to identify dialects from thirteen of the eighteen provinces. Life on tour was not all business. On at least one occasion, the emperor demonstrated his Manchu skill at mounted archery, a common touch that would have been inconceivable to his Ming predecessors.

Kangxi was less successful in governing his willful family than in ruling the empire. Of his twenty sons who survived into adulthood, it was Yinreng, the second, upon whom the emperor lavished all his attention and hope. This young man, however, repaid his father's devotion with extravagance and disobedience. Worse still, he became involved in the traffic of boys as homosexual companions. Kangxi was outraged. "He is dissolute, tyrannical, brutal, debauched—it's hard to even speak about it," he wrote. He dismissed Yinreng as his heir, later reinstating him only to dismiss him again. In growing paranoia, Kangxi executed several associates of the former heir apparent; at one point, three of his own sons were under arrest. "I cannot overcome my anger and sorrow," he wrote at the height of the crisis. As a result of this domestic turmoil, the embittered emperor refused to designate a successor.

In 1717, fearing that he would soon die, Kangxi expressed his weariness and

disillusionment in a document known as the Valedictory Edict, which he had read aloud to his sons and to leading officials. "I have prepared these notes to make my own record," he wrote, "for fear that the country may not know the depth of my sorrow." Fifty years of rule had taken their toll on the emperor: "Now that I have reached old age I cannot rest easy for a moment. Therefore I regard the whole country as a worn-out sandal, and all riches as mud and sand. If I can die without there being an outbreak of trouble, my desires will be fulfilled."

Five years later, the emperor indeed fell ill and died. The succession passed to his fourth son, who was at his bedside in his last days. Suspicion that Kangxi was killed by his heir remains speculation.

The era of prosperity established during the reign of Kangxi did not end with his death. The empire continued to expand, reaching its maximum extent in about the year 1760. By then, it included all of modern China and Mongolia, plus parts of Soviet central Asia, India, and Pakistan. The late eighteenth century, however, saw the beginnings of a decline that, within fifty years, had become an irreversible slide toward dissolution. The European powers, by then entering their colonial heyday, would quickly take advantage of China's internal weakness to win commercial advantage. In so doing, they set the stage for the end of imperial rule itself; on his abdication in 1912, the last of the Qing dynasty was also to become the last emperor.

THE GREAT SHAH OF PERSIA

In the summer of 1628, unusual visitors arrived at Ashraf, the shah of Persia's pleasure palace situated in thick forests two miles south of the Caspian Sea. The strangers were the first royal envoys to be sent to Persia from England; and before being granted audience, they had to cool their heels for four days, probably as a result of the shah's habit of consulting astrologers over favorable days for receiving important guests.

One of the Britons, Sir Thomas Herbert, later wrote an account of their reception. He noted that "the palace is large and looks into very pleasant gardens, albeit the building itself be not very regular, but rather confusedly divides itself into four *mohols,* or banqueting houses, which be gorgeously painted." When the party was finally admitted, they proceeded down a long audience chamber. They passed between rows of functionaries sitting cross-legged against the walls and sidestepped pages who ran about with flagons of wine. At last they stood before the man they had come to meet—Shah Abbās, who was "beloved at home, famous abroad, and a terror to his enemies."

Abbās—whom Herbert referred to oddly as "Potshaw," apparently an English rendering of the Persian *padishah,* or "chief ruler"—was probably the most powerful and effective Persian king from the fall of the Sassanid dynasty in AD 642 to the present day. He was the greatest monarch of the Safavid dynasty, which between 1499 and 1736 restored to the nation something of the luster of its earlier glories. Faced by enemies to the east and west, he managed to restrain both: His armies held their own against the fearsome Ottomans of Turkey and defeated the Uzbek tribesmen of the central Asian steppes. At home, Abbās encouraged a revival of commerce and the arts, and he left as his memorial the splendid city of Isfahan.

It was in pursuit of aid in his various campaigns that the shah, who at the time of Herbert's visit had only eight months left to live, had agreed to receive the English emissaries. The envoys congratulated him on his recent victories against the Ottomans, and the shah received their congratulations genially. By now some of his front teeth were missing, but he was still vigorous, and he conducted negotiations with a mixture of bullying and teasing. After some solemn talk about the future prospects for Anglo-Persian trade, Abbās pulled down Sir Dodmore Cotton, the head of the delegation, to sit beside him, deriving considerable amusement as he did so from the English ambassador's inability to sit cross-legged in the Oriental fashion. Abbās called for a bowl of wine and drank to the health of Cotton's sovereign, King Charles I of England. At the mention of the royal name, Sir Dodmore removed his hat as a mark of respect. Much struck by the gesture, the shah promptly removed his own turban in clownish imitation of this foreign ritual. Abbās had always been fond of jokes, wine, and creature comforts.

His behavior was a far cry from that of the founder of his dynasty, his great-

Backed by barren mountains, a ceramic-tiled dome crowns the sanctuary of Isfahan's Royal Mosque, built on the orders of Shah Abbās I, the greatest ruler of Persia's Safavid dynasty. When Abbās seized the throne in 1587, Isfahan, which had seen better days in the Middle Ages, was in decay. In 1598, however, the shah decided to make it his capital and, urged on by a mixture of piety and dynastic pride, commissioned and supervised the construction of many new buildings. The splendor of the monuments he created gave substance to his subjects' boast that "Isfahan is half the world."

grandfather Ismail. In 1494, at the age of seven, Ismail had inherited the guardianship of a holy shrine in Ardabīl in northwest Persia, and with it the leadership of the Safavid order of Muslim mystics, whose holy place it was. He thereby also inherited the unquestioning loyalty of many of the Turkoman tribesmen who roamed across the pastures of eastern Turkey, northern Syria, and western Persia. These doughty warriors were known as *qizilbash*—or "redheads"—from the red hats they wore as a sign of their partisanship for the Safavid house.

The qizilbash regarded Ismail with more than the normal respect accorded by believers to their spiritual leader. These tribal people were the most significant surviving supporters of the once-mighty Shiite branch of Islam, which had fallen on hard times; and as Shiites, they believed that Ismail belonged to a hereditary succession of imams—spiritual leaders drawing their authority directly from Prophet Muhammad through the line of his son-in-law, Ali. This belief put the qizilbash at odds with the established Muslim regimes in Turkey, Egypt, Transoxiana, and India, all of which subscribed to the Sunni branch of Islam, which followed a different pattern of succession from the prophet.

In the minority for most of their history, the Shiites had developed their own religious rituals and law. They also tended to espouse doctrines that were mystical, cabalistic, revolutionary, and messianic. Many Shiites, for example, maintained that the twelfth

The Safavid empire was created in the first two decades of the sixteenth century by Shah Ismail, leader of an Islamic mystical order based at Ardabīl in northwestern Persia. At the head of an unruly army of tribesmen, he conquered a realm that included all the land of modern Iran as well as territories, now part of the Soviet Union, between the Black and Caspian seas. The Safavid domain was subsequently challenged by the Ottoman Turks to the west and by Uzbek tribesmen to the east. And in the early, difficult years of Shah Abbās's reign, it seemed that his territories might fall apart under the strain of waging war on two fronts. The shah, however, made peace with the Ottomans in order to deal with the Uzbek threat; then, having defeated the Uzbeks, he was able to reopen the war in the west and retake the provinces previously surrendered to the Ottomans.

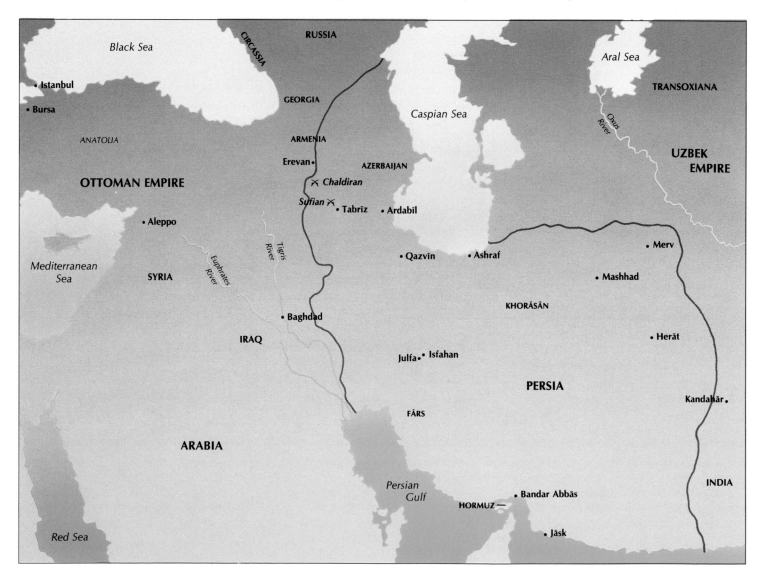

and last imam claiming direct descent from Muhammad—who had disappeared in mysterious circumstances in the year 874—had not died but had gone into a mystical form of concealment known as occultation. This was the man the Turkomans took Ismail to be; and they believed that his return to earth signaled the coming of the Last Days, in which the resurrected imam would lead the true believers to victory and establish the rule of perfect justice.

The chieftains who guided the boy Ismail drew on such expectations to assemble armies of the dedicated faithful, who rode into battle believing that they were invulnerable thanks to the protection of their mystical leader. Their early victories were gained at the expense of the rulers of much of Persia, the White Sheep Turkomans (so called to distinguish them from a rival, Black Sheep, clan). In 1501, Ismail entered the White Sheep capital of Tabrīz, where he was proclaimed king. Subsequently Ismail and his followers campaigned against the Sunni Muslim regimes that dominated the Middle East: the Ottomans of Turkey, the Mamluks of Egypt and Syria, and the Uzbek rulers of Transoxiana. Though not always successful—his forces were humiliatingly defeated by the Ottomans at the Battle of Chaldiran in 1514—Ismail had by the time of his death in 1524 succeeded in creating a Safavid empire that incorporated all of modern Iran and Iraq and some of Afghanistan, as well as parts of the southern Caucasus now in the Soviet Union.

Moreover, the empire was Shiite in faith. Although Persia had been predominantly Sunni at the end of the fifteenth century, a mixture of fierce proselytizing and even fiercer persecutions dragooned most of the population into adherence to the qizilbash creed—a legacy that was to endure through the centuries to come.

The great majority of the Safavid shahs' subjects were Persian, but the armies that defended them continued to consist mainly of Turkomans, immigrants from Turkey and Syria who at first had little in common with the civilians they protected. Grouped in tribal confederacies, the qizilbash spoke Turkish rather than Persian and followed a nomadic lifestyle.

There were religious differences, as well. Although the qizilbash were firm—even approaching fanatical—Shiites, their interpretation of the faith sometimes verged on heterodoxy, incorporating ill-digested borrowings from shamanistic Turkic folklore. They were sometimes referred to as "grass worshipers" from their pantheistic tendency to see God in natural features and natural omens. Their *dedes*, or "spiritual gurus," were so venerated that devotees would reverently sweep up and preserve the dust from their horses' hoofprints. The dedes had the pick of the young women of the tribes, whom they "blessed" by ritually deflowering them. The tribesmen also practiced ritual cannibalism on the bodies of slain enemies. A qizilbash tribesman wore an earring in his left ear as a sign of his devotion to chastity; nonetheless, hostile chroniclers made accusations that the nomads participated in orgies involving homosexuality and incest.

Though wild, the qizilbash army was nonetheless an invaluable resource for the Safavid rulers. The shahs needed cavalry to defend the extended frontiers of their empire against enemy attack, and there was no doubting that the qizilbash were splendid mounted warriors. They rode into battle equipped with a small armory of weapons that included bows and arrows, swords, daggers, battle axes, and, by the late sixteenth century, harquebuses, which they fired from the saddle. Often their zeal and élan won the day against more numerous enemies.

The shahs garrisoned the tribesmen in the dangerous frontier provinces and re-

Shown here in a portrait by an Indian miniaturist, Shah Abbās was of less than average stature, and in later life, he remained physically unimpressive. But he was robust—hunting was his favorite activity—and observers noted his keen eye and quick intelligence. He followed the fashion of the time in allowing his mustache to droop: It was considered presumptuous to point the tips toward heaven. Abbās's court dress was thought simple by the showy standards of his day; he discouraged ostentation as a matter of principle and always made a point of making himself accessible to his subjects.

warded their leaders by giving them provincial governorships. Although Persian civilians dominated the Safavid bureaucracy, qizilbash chieftains held a near monopoly of military and court offices. At times when the shah was weak, the Turkomans took the opportunity to meddle in politics. Some of them even aspired to become kingmakers. Such ambitions were encouraged by the Safavid practice of putting young princes of the ruling dynasty in the tutelage of Turkoman chiefs who acted as their guardians.

On Ismail's death in 1524, his ten-year-old son, Tahmāsp, became shah, and for a decade or so the empire fell prey to the ambitions of contending qizilbash chiefs. But Tahmāsp grew into a capable war leader and politician, and he was able to bring his unruly subjects under control. On his death in 1576, however, the Turkomans reasserted themselves. The tribesmen formed factions around two of Tahmāsp's sons, Haydar and Ismail. First, Haydar was murdered; then, after a short and bloody reign, the drug-addicted, alcoholic Ismail died, perhaps also assassinated. A third brother, the languid and half-blind Muhammad Khudabanda, was placed on the throne in 1577, but real power continued to lie with the rival qizilbash factions that contended for control of the country. Not only was Muhammad Khudabanda an ineffective ruler; to many of his subjects, his near blindness amounted almost to a formal disqualification for the throne, for Islamic tradition held that a ruler must be in full possession of all his senses.

Accordingly, when the qizilbash chieftain acting as guardian to Muhammad Khudabanda's son, the sixteen-year-old Abbās Mirza, raised the banner of revolt in 1587, the insurrection quickly gathered strength. Born in February 1571, Abbās had survived a perilous childhood in the troubled years after the death of Tahmāsp. His mother was murdered by tribesmen resentful of her influence over state affairs. His first guardian, the governor of Herāt (in present-day Afghanistan), was killed when Abbās was five. Another Turkoman chieftain was then dispatched to Herāt by the young prince's uncle, Shah Ismail II, with orders to execute the boy, whom he considered a dangerous rival. The envoy chose to disobey the order, however, and in the chaotic circumstances of the time, contrived to take over both the governorship of Herāt and the guardianship of the prince. He subsequently lost Abbās to a rival chieftain as part of the spoils of war; the victor, Murshid Quli Khan, was the instigator of the rebellion of 1587.

By that time, it was plain for all to see that Muhammad Khudabanda was not competent to rule. Ottoman armies had invaded western Persia; the rest of the country was prey to tribal strife. As Murshid Quli Khan and his royal protégé moved westward across the country, their advance soon turned into a triumphal progress. The prince reached Qazvīn, the town in northwestern Persia that Tahmāsp had chosen as the Safavid capital, in midyear. On October 1, 1587, he was proclaimed ruler of Persia as Shah Abbās I.

If Murshid entertained the notion that Abbās would be a pliant puppet ruler, he was fatally mistaken. Just nine months after his accession to the throne, the young king arranged for the murder of his overweening subject. He had already, following a common Middle Eastern tradition, had his brothers blinded to remove any threat to the throne from that quarter. The young shah also conducted a purge of the tribesmen responsible for his mother's death. There were revolts in the provinces, but they were ruthlessly suppressed.

A miniature illustrating a seventeenth-century manuscript of Persia's historical epic, the *Shahnama*, shows warriors of the legendary past fighting in costumes common in Shah Abbās's day. Over their armor, the soldiers wear surcoats of cotton to keep the metal cool; vambraces, or armguards, are attached over the coat sleeves to protect the forearms. Although the warriors shown carry only swords and bows, their real-life counterparts would have also borne firearms, whose use Abbās encouraged. The horsemen wear pointed helmets of a style long familiar in the Middle East; the example at right, more likely intended for ceremonial use than for battle, boasts a lengthy curtain of mail.

Despite these sanguinary measures, Abbās continued to feel insecure. In August 1593, he was advised by his astrologers that the stars boded ill for the ruler of Persia, since Mars and Saturn were in quadrature in the ascendant. Resourcefully, Abbās stepped down from the throne and had a condemned heretic, an adherent of a small, outlawed sect, proclaimed shah in his place. The heretic ruled under close surveillance for three days. On the fourth day, when the zodiacal aspects were more favorable, the substitute shah was executed and Abbās resumed his reign.

Persia's external enemies provided additional cause for alarm, and the problems they posed were less easily solved. The continuing threat from Ottomans and Uzbeks, dating back to the reign of the first Ismail, had grown in the time of troubles following the death of Shah Tahmāsp. The Ottomans represented the more serious danger: Abbās inherited a war against them that had begun ten years before his accession. The territories at issue were Iraq, Armenia, Azerbaijan, and the Caucasus, and much of the fighting took place in the two latter areas. For the most part, the Ottoman army had the upper hand. Its strengths were its large and tightly disciplined infantry forces, its many artillery pieces, and its sophisticated logistical backup. Time and again the

Ottoman battle tactic of placing artillery and musketeers behind carts linked to one another by chains thwarted the charges of the Safavid cavalry. In 1587, the Ottomans captured Baghdad.

Given the limitations of his army, there was little that Abbās could do to regain lost ground. Buying time, he agreed to conclude a humiliating peace in 1590. By the terms of the Treaty of Istanbul, he acknowledged Ottoman control of Iraq, Georgia, and most of Azerbaijan. To placate the Sunni Ottomans, he also swore to prohibit his subjects from cursing Umar, Abū Bakr, and Uthmān, the first three caliphs to lead the Muslim community after the death of Prophet Muhammad; in Shiite eyes they were usurpers, and the devout were fond of execrating them.

Abbās needed peace with the Ottomans so as to confront the Uzbeks, who were pressing hard on Persia's eastern province of Khorāsān. Uzbek forces had sacked the cities of Herāt and Merv and had desecrated the Shiite holy place of Mashhad. Unlike the Ottomans, however, the Uzbeks had a relatively unsophisticated military machine, consisting of levies of nomadic tribesmen. Under Abbās's leadership, his qizilbash cavalry proved more than a match for them. Mashhad, Herāt, and Merv were all recaptured in 1595 and 1596, and Safavid cavalry went on to cross the Oxus River, taking the war into Uzbek Transoxiana. The Uzbek leader Abdullah Khan II died in 1598; later that year, a large Uzbek army was defeated in a battle fought near Herāt. In the decades that followed, skirmishing continued and Uzbek raids continued to menace the towns and agriculture of Khorāsān, but the sorties no longer threatened the security of the realm. Abbās felt secure enough to redirect his attention to the Ottomans.

Conscious of the earlier failure of his army, Shah Abbās sought to remedy its weaknesses. In pursuit of this aim, he looked northward to the Christian territory of Georgia, nominally in Ottoman hands since the Treaty of Istanbul. Georgia, along with the neighboring Christian states of Circassia and Armenia, had long been the favored hunting ground of white slave traders, who culled the flower of its youth to sell at the great Islamic courts. The women were highly esteemed for their beauty and were favorites in the harems of the shahs. At least since the reign of Shah Tahmāsp, the men had been organized into a military corps; the best of them were handpicked to enter palace service.

These were the people to whom Abbās turned for help. Despite their nominal subjection to the Ottomans, the semi-independent Christian rulers of Georgia resumed the practice of sending slaves as tribute to Persia in the 1590s. Their lowly origin notwithstanding, the Georgians came in the course of Abbās's reign to constitute a third ethnic element in the ruling elite, competing for office with Turkomans and Persians.

The Georgians' most significant role was in the army. Abbās may not have been the first ruler to make use of Georgian troops, but he was the first to deploy them on a large scale. Hitherto the shahs had supplemented the intimidating yet undisciplined tribal forces of qizilbash cavalry with a much smaller standing army that was also recruited from the qizilbash but organized on a nontribal basis. Now Abbās began to form regiments composed of the military slaves from Georgia and other regions of the Caucasus. Among them was an elite force of cavalrymen, 10,000 strong, who owed their loyalty not to any tribe but to the shah alone. Abbās also formed a bodyguard of 3,000 soldier slaves.

He innovated further by creating a regiment of musketeers and a corps of artil-

Taking her ease in a flower-bedecked garden, a lady clasping a flagon of wine considers whether to accept the shawl offered to her by an admirer; the painted and glazed tiles that carry the scene probably once adorned a pavilion in Abbās's palace in Isfahan. Strict Muslims in seventeenth-century Persia denounced the mingling of the sexes and the consumption of alcohol, as well as the portrayal of human figures in art, which, they felt, was proscribed by the Koran. Their fulminations notwithstanding, languorous and willowy men and women picnicking, daydreaming, and drinking in verdant orchards were part of the stock in trade of the painters and poets who catered to the hedonism of the Safavid court.

lerymen. Abbās recruited Persians into these infantry regiments and in so doing became the first of the Safavid shahs to give the native people of his realm a role in the defense of their own country. The guns themselves came at first either as spoils of war from the Ottomans and Uzbeks, or from the Portuguese, who maintained a naval and mercantile base on the island of Hormuz in the Persian Gulf. Later, Abbās set up his own gun foundries.

Abbās's military reforms, which drew upon the Ottoman example in the use both of slave-soldiers and of massed firepower, had important implications for the internal politics of Persia. With a standing army of around 37,000 men, the shah was no longer totally dependent on the Turkomans to repel foreign invasions or to suppress internal disorder. The power of the qizilbash at court and in the provinces declined accordingly. Although qizilbash chiefs continued to hold most of the provincial governorships, Abbās now felt strong enough to send them to provinces that were far from the lands of their own tribes, the sources of their strength. Leading offices of state were increasingly given to palace servants and Georgian officers, and some Georgians were even given provincial governorships.

One such appointee, the Georgian Allahverdi Khan, owed his tenure of high office to his participation in the murder of Murshid Quli Khan in 1589. He was rewarded in the first instance with the governorship of a small town, but by 1595, he had become commander of the slave regiments and governor of the important province of Fārs. Later he was appointed commander in chief of all the Safavid armed forces, and in that role, he was the principal architect of Abbās's army reforms. Abbās valued Allahverdi Khan's military ability and favored him for his readiness, repeatedly demonstrated, to act against enemies of the shah.

For all the advantages, both military and political, that the standing army brought, it had one major disadvantage: It had to be paid regularly. To meet the extra expenditure, Abbās presumably increased taxation, although no detailed records survive. He certainly increased the extent of crown lands. Under his predecessors, most of the revenue from land in Persia was collected by the tribal chiefs, who had tenure of estates that could be as large as a whole province. They then sent a portion of the money collected to the central government. Abbās, however, did away with these middlemen in many areas, claiming the land directly in his own name.

After ten years on the throne, Abbās felt sufficiently certain of his position to embark on a great work that was forever after to be associated with his reign. He decided to create a new capital city to replace Qazvīn, which was uncomfortably close to the Ottoman war zone and, besides, was in a region dominated by the qizilbash warlords and their tribesmen.

Seeking a new location closer to the heart of his empire, Abbās settled on the small town of Isfahan, on the high central plateau of Persia. The site had been occupied since before the time of Muhammad, and in the eleventh and twelfth centuries, the town had briefly been the nation's capital, although it had subsequently declined in importance. Now Abbās planned to extend and transform it into a garden city that would advertise his rule and his empire's prosperity.

Advice on the layout of the city was sought from the Lebanese poet and engineer, Bahā al-Din al-Amili. (Al-Amili is alleged to have designed a bathhouse whose pool was kept hot by the flame of a single candle burning under its water tank.) And the royal astrologers were consulted about the time at which the building should begin.

Construction finally started in October 1598; it was to continue throughout Abbās's reign and beyond it.

The city that the shah and the poet created was splendid indeed. Its principal axis was provided by the Chahar Bagh, a 165-foot-wide avenue built along a central canal, which was spanned by little bridges and flanked by fountains and pools. The street was shaded by plane trees and poplars and lined with palaces, mosques, shops, and gardens. At the end of the day, princes and populace alike would ride or stroll down the avenue to enjoy the tranquil pleasures of the evening. Shah Abbās himself liked to mingle with the crowds, cracking jokes with the street entertainers and examining the goods for sale in the booths.

East of the Chahar Bagh was a warren of pavilions, courtyards, harem quarters, reception chambers, administrative offices, service rooms, stables, imperial work-shops, and storehouses that together made up the royal palace. This edifice was no monumental pile in the European manner; rather it was a small village of separate buildings scattered among shady gardens, on the lines of the Ottomans' Topkapi Palace in Istanbul.

Beyond the palace was the maidan, or town square. Covering twenty acres, this was the main communal space in the city. When no special event was being staged there, it was covered with market stalls; at night there was a lantern-lit fun fair. At other times, it might be used at the shah's behest for parades, public executions of criminals, or sports such as wolf baiting, for which a live wolf would be loosed into the square while it was crowded with young men eager to show off their courage. Although one or two people might get bitten, no serious harm ever came to any of the participants other than the wolf.

No sport played on the maidan pleased the shah as much as polo, the preeminent game of the Safavid court and its military elite, prized both as recreation and as training for mounted warfare. A French visitor, noting that it was the favorite exercise of the ruler and his retainers, observed that "their horses are so well trained to it that they run after the ball like cats." The royal orchestra accompanied the game, sound-ing a fanfare every time Abbās hit the ball.

The dominant feature of the northern end of the maidan was the archway leading into the great covered bazaar, a maze of shops and workshops extending over more than one and a half square miles. In it, tradesmen were grouped into separate quarters, for carpet weavers, textile workers, metalsmiths, and so forth. The royal mint and the royal caravansary (providing lodging and protection for dealers in luxury goods) were located near the bazaar's entrance. Elsewhere small enterprises pros-pered, for although the shah was the nation's wealthiest individual, enjoying a near monopoly on the expanding silk trade as well as the growing fruits of customs duties, others also flourished in the prosperity that his reign generated.

Among the greatest beneficiaries were the Armenian merchants and artisans en-couraged by the shah to settle in the Christian suburb of Julfa, just south of Isfahan proper, which enjoyed tax privileges and a degree of self-government. With Abbās's compliance, the Armenians came to dominate the overland trade in luxury com-modities, especially raw silk. Julfa-based entrepreneurs dispatched caravans across the Syrian desert or the Anatolian plateau to Aleppo, Bursa, or Istanbul, where fellow Armenians, subjects of the Ottoman sultan, handled the sale of the merchandise. Apart from finished commodities, popular trading goods included natural substances such as opium, civet (the richly perfumed secretions of the Asian civet native to

India), and bezoar (a stone formed in the stomach of the wild goat), which was valued at the time as an antidote to poisons.

The shah's policy of toleration encouraged Christian missions from western Europe to use Julfa as a base. Augustinians, Carmelites, and Capuchins all established houses there. In the light of the shah's friendly attitude toward Europeans and their faith, a number of missionaries managed to convince themselves that the ruler himself was on the verge of converting to Christianity. The error was fostered by Abbās's mischievous sense of humor: On one occasion, he joined a band of Portuguese Augustinian friars in their tent, singing psalms with them and serenading them on the lute. But the truth was that Abbās had no inclination to abandon Islam; he valued Europeans primarily for the military assistance that they could give him against the mutual enemy, the Ottomans.

Merchants and traders were not alone in benefiting from the internal peace of Abbās's reign. The arts also revived. Miniature painting, in particular, flourished under royal patronage. Some of the greatest Persian painters held posts in the Safavid royal library, for a librarian in seventeenth-century Persia was not just supposed to look after books and assist readers' access to them: He was also expected to add to their number by creating original manuscripts.

One such was Abbās's first royal librarian, Sadiqi Beg, who described himself without false modesty as "the rare man of his time." Contemporaries regarded him as ill-tempered, self-seeking, and above all arrogant, at the same time conceding that he had much to be arrogant about. He was born into one of the leading qizilbash tribes and at first pursued the military career expected of him, distinguishing himself by feats of foolhardy bravery. Then, when he was in his early thirties, he took the unprecedented step of giving up warfare for painting. He studied under the poet and calligrapher Mir Sani and subsequently worked as court artist for Shah Ismail II. In the turbulent times that followed the death of Ismail, Sadiqi Beg took up the life of a wandering dervish, or ascetic, before returning to a military career. Finally, on Abbās's accession to the throne, he became royal librarian and returned to painting and writing, composing poetry in Persian and prose in the Chagatai dialect of Turkish. Among the works for which he was best remembered was *The Assembly of Worthies,* a biographical dictionary in which he took pains to establish his superiority over most of his contemporaries.

For many years, Sadiqi Beg's preeminence among Persian artists was universally, if reluctantly, acknowledged; but then a newcomer named Ali Riza appeared in Isfahan and, in the words of a contemporary critic, "snatched the ball of precedence from his forerunners." For a time, the two painters worked together, but relations were probably tense as the shah came to prefer the hair-fine brushwork of the younger man. Abbās held Riza's work in such reverence that, it is said, he would hold a candle for him while the painter worked. In the long run, however, Riza fell into bad company. He became an aficionado of wrestling and spent much time in the company of the lowlifes that practiced and admired the sport. He took to dissipation and boasting and fell out of favor. By that time Sadiqi Beg was dead; outshone by his younger rival, he had been dismissed from his appointment at the library, apparently for stealing a precious illustrated book.

The demand for such luxury items as miniature paintings was stimulated by the hectic diplomatic activity of Abbās's court. Indeed, the exchange of diplomatic gifts with

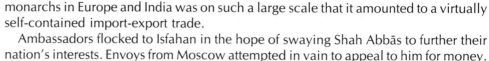

monarchs in Europe and India was on such a large scale that it amounted to a virtually self-contained import-export trade.

Ambassadors flocked to Isfahan in the hope of swaying Shah Abbās to further their nation's interests. Envoys from Moscow attempted in vain to appeal to him for money. Missions from the Mogul court at Delhi came with extravagant presents. Papal emissaries talked enthusiastically but a little vaguely about creating a grand alliance against the Ottoman Turks. A legation from Spain sought to protect the Portuguese base on the island of Hormuz in the Persian Gulf. (From 1580 to 1640, Spain and Portugal were jointly ruled by one king.)

Among the diplomats clustered at Abbās's court were a couple of English citizens who were to have a significant influence on the latter part of his reign. Though not officially accredited by Queen Elizabeth, Anthony and Robert Sherley had been dispatched by her favorite, the earl of Essex, to explore informally the possibility of an alliance with Abbās against the Turks. The two brothers arrived in Qazvīn in November 1598, not long after the shah had won victory over the Uzbeks. The returning qizilbash cavalry streamed into the town wearing necklaces of Uzbek ears and carrying the earless heads aloft on lances. The Englishmen thoughtfully surveyed the scene, then hastened to congratulate the shah on his success.

They were well received. Anthony Sherley was dispatched by the shah back to Europe with letters for the Holy Roman emperor, the king of Spain, the pope, and other monarchs, including Queen Elizabeth. Sherley carried off his mission flamboyantly, but no grand alliance was forthcoming.

The shah's relationship with Robert Sherley, who stayed behind as a virtual hostage during his brother's travels, was ultimately to prove more fruitful. Abbās rapidly found useful employment for him as a military adviser, in which capacity the Englishman's knowledge of artillery and tactics proved invaluable. Abbās carried out his successful reorganization of the Persian army with the assistance of Sherley, who served as an officer and won for himself the title of "Master General against the Turks."

In 1611, Robert Sherley was sent back to England to determine whether he could interest Elizabeth's successor, King James I, in opening up direct trade with Persia via the Gulf, thereby freeing the shah from the necessity of exporting his silk overland through Turkey. Although the Levant Company, which controlled English trade with the eastern Mediterranean, preferred not to imperil its traffic with the Turks by making a deal with Persia, officials of the British East India Company, which was based in India, expressed an interest in the idea. The company later established a base at Jāsk on the Persian Gulf, and the British gradually took over from the Portuguese as Persia's principal European trading partner. In

A miniature dating from 1626 shows a wandering dervish announcing his presence by blowing on a horn. Holy men vowed to a life of poverty, the dervishes survived by begging for food, which they carried with them in baskets like the one shown here. Such men helped the first Safavid shah, Ismail, to seize power, and their support was an important prop for the dynasty in the sixteenth century. Abbās, however, distrusted his dervish following, and during his reign, the itinerants were occasionally persecuted.

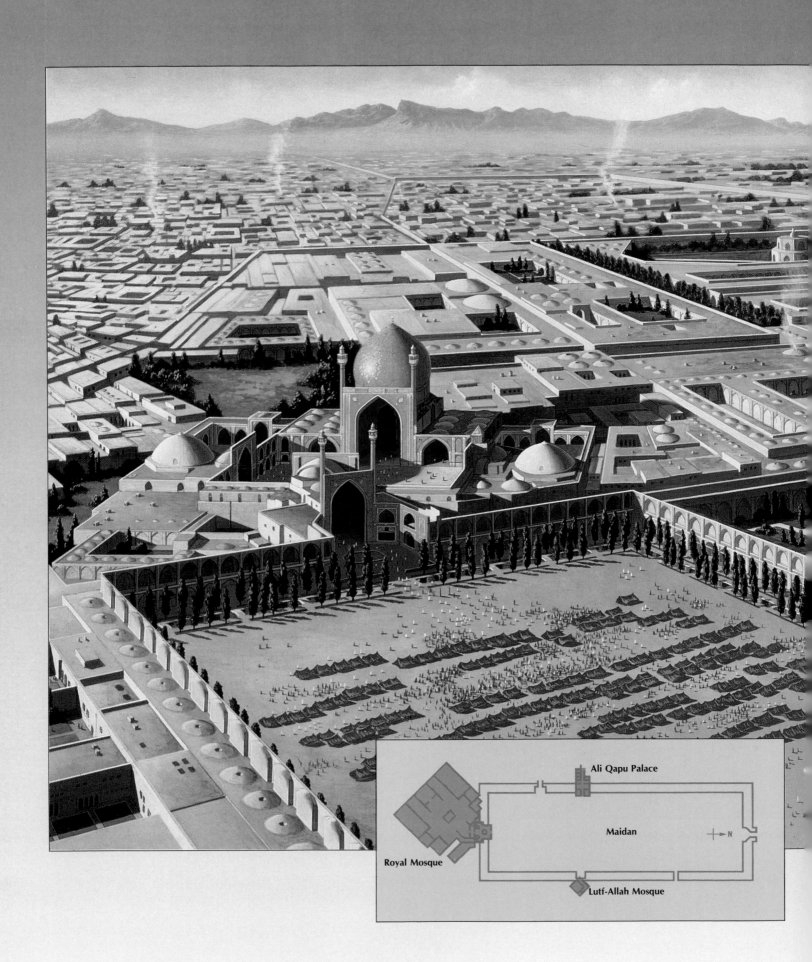

Ali Qapu Palace

Maidan

N

Royal Mosque

Lutf-Allah Mosque

David Bergen

Backed by a residential district stretching southwest toward the Zagros Mountains, the maidan, or open space (shown schematically in the inset) was the centerpiece of Abbās's planned city of Isfahan. Measuring almost 1,700 feet by 520 feet, it was surrounded by low arcades of shops and workplaces, as well as by trees and water channels. Soaring above its southern end, the Royal Mosque, with its great dome and four minarets, was the center of public worship. The lofty balcony of the Ali Qapu Palace—to the right foreground of the main picture—gave the shah and his intimates a commanding view of all that happened below. The threshold of the royal residence was regarded as sacred ground, and any criminal who managed to reach it and kiss its gate was safe from arrest. Behind the palace lay spacious royal gardens.

A great deal of Isfahan's public life was transacted in the maidan. On most days it housed a public market, and all the square, except for the immediate vicinity of the palace, was covered with stalls. But the great open space also served by turns as a parade ground, an execution yard, and a sports arena for polo matches, horse races, archery tournaments, and wrestling. Sunrise and sunset were marked by concerts from the imperial orchestra.

At night 50,000 lamps illuminated the square, which was transformed into a fun fair thronged with hucksters, water sellers, prostitutes, preachers, jugglers, acrobats, and animal tamers. Abbās himself, contemptuous of European sovereigns who in his view "always sat indoors," liked to walk about in the evenings, sampling the goods on display and admiring the performances.

Profits From Silk

The splendors of Shah Abbās's court could not have been paid for without the revenues from the cultivation and export of silk and the artifacts made from it, principally carpets and textiles. The weaving of rugs had traditionally been a cottage industry, but Abbās set up royal workshops for their production, adding the revenues from them to the monopoly he already had of silk production. The carpets were distinguished by the intricacy of their designs and by the density of the knotting made possible by the use of fine silk thread; a rough judge of quality was to press a thumb against the edge to gauge how many threads were covered by the thumb's breadth.

The chief silk-producing regions were in the southern Caucasus and near the coast of the Caspian Sea. Both areas were contested between the Safavid shahs and the sultans of Ottoman Turkey, but production went on despite the wars. So for the most part did the overland carpet trade; the goods were carried by camel caravan to the Ottoman domains for shipment to Europe, where they became known as Turkey carpets. Shah Abbās, however, encouraged English and Dutch merchants to purchase and export silk directly by sea from the port of Bandar Abbās on the Persian Gulf.

1622, a joint Anglo-Persian force attacked and captured the Portuguese base at Hormuz. The island entrepôt eventually fell into ruins—its streets were torn up by bounty hunters searching for nonexistent buried treasures—and its place as a commercial center was usurped by a new port on the mainland that the shah named after himself, Bandar Abbās.

The testing time for the shah's reforms came in the early years of the seventeenth century, when Abbās resumed hostilities against the Ottomans with the aim of reversing the humiliating Treaty of Istanbul. The time was propitious, for the Ottoman Empire had been weakened in the intervening years by growing internal dissent. Beginning in the 1590s, much of Anatolia had passed into the hands of rebellious tribal peoples and unemployed soldiers whom the government in Istanbul stigmatized as bandits. As the Ottomans struggled to reassert control over the empire, refugees streamed into Persia by the tens of thousands to put themselves at the service of Shah Abbās. Many of the rebels harbored Shiite sympathies, because throughout the Ottoman lands there were pockets of religious dissidents who favored the faith of the Safavid shahs.

In the autumn of 1603, the shah set off on what he claimed was a hunting trip, although it was noted that his retinue seemed unusually large for the purpose. Suddenly he swooped on the city of Tabrīz, retaking the Safavids' original capital from the Ottomans. After a prolonged winter siege, the strategically important fortresses at Erevan in Armenia were also captured. In 1605, the Turks made an attempt to regain Tabrīz, but they were heavily defeated in the battle at Sufian. The Sufian debacle led to additional revolts in Anatolia, and for a while, the Persian armies were able to advance into eastern Turkey before being forced to withdraw. In 1612, the two nations eventually agreed on peace, on the basis of the frontiers established in the mid-sixteenth century. Although both parties to the treaty tried to improve on the agreed terms by mounting raids and skirmishes, a temporary status quo had in fact been reached, and this was recognized by the formal reaffirmation of the 1612 agreement six years later.

Yet Abbās's conflict with the Turks was still not at an end. In 1622, the Ottoman governor of Baghdad rebelled against his sultan. In conjunction with another rebellion in Anatolia, this event persuaded Abbās to reopen the anti-Ottoman offensive. In 1623, he invaded Iraq, recapturing Baghdad in November. The sultan then sent a large army to besiege the city. The shah did not dare to attack the Ottoman forces, but he did blockade them. Doubly besieged, the starving inhabitants of the city were reduced to eating palm leaves. It seemed so certain that the beleaguered city must fall that when Abbās's astrologer predicted its defenders would successfully hold out, Abbās for once refused to believe him. Yet the astrologer's forecast proved to be correct. The Turks were forced by the shortage of supplies to abandon the siege. Abbās's forces allowed them to march back to Turkey, leaving their cannon and their sick behind them. The recapture of Baghdad was Shah Abbās's last great triumph, although the war continued to smolder for the remaining years of his reign and well beyond.

In the meantime, Abbās had other troubles closer to home to occupy his attention. In the course of his reign, he had fathered five sons. At first, he followed the practice of his predecessors in sending the children to provincial capitals to learn the arts of government under the guardianship of qizilbash chiefs. In 1589, however, the governor of Mashhad and guardian of Abbās's second son attempted to follow the example of the kingmaker Murshid Quli Khan by raising the standard of rebellion.

Abbās put down the uprising, but from that time forward, he kept his sons in the royal palace, where they were reared

Exotic birds and beasts adorn this silken kilim—a patterned textile in which colored weft threads are woven with warp threads only where needed to form the pattern. The cloth, too delicate to use as a carpet, may have graced a Persian divan.

in the closely guarded harem under the supervision of loyal eunuchs. Ever mindful of the safety of his throne—such was his fear of conspiracy that he moved from bedroom to bedroom in the palace to confuse potential assassins—he had his sons carefully watched. In 1615, he arranged for the assassination of his eldest son after certain courtiers had accused the young man of plotting against his father. (In remorse, the shah subsequently forced the man who carried out the deed to murder his own son.) Six years later, Abbās became dangerously ill, and his oldest surviving boy made the mistake of prematurely celebrating his forthcoming accession.

When Abbās recovered his health, he had the youth blinded. Five or six years later, he condemned his last remaining son, Imam Quli Mirza, to suffer the same fate, once again on suspicion of conspiracy against him. A Carmelite missionary reported that Abbās "was wont to say that he would have killed 100 children in order to reign alone for a single day."

Soon after the blinding of Imam Quli Mirza, Abbās began to dream of his own death. Then a fever came upon him. Despite the sickness, he continued to hunt until he was too weak to leave his bed. As it became clear that the shah was dying, his courtiers turned their attention to the task of finding a successor. All of Abbās's sons had either died or been disqualified by blindness; but there were several grandsons. Abbās died on January 19, 1629; nine days later, the eldest of these, Safi Mirza, was installed on the throne.

Abbās's treatment of his sons revealed the darker side of his character. Throughout his reign, he had made terror one of the instruments of his government. His adoring chronicler, Iskandar Munshi, reported that no one dared disobey the shah:

> For instance, should he command a father to kill his son, the sentence would be carried out immediately, even as the decree of destiny; or should the father, moved by parental tenderness, make any delay, the command would be reversed; and should the son then temporize, another would slay both. By such awful severity the execution of his commands attained the supreme degree of efficiency and none dared hesitate for an instant in the fulfilment of the sentence as inevitable as fate.

Thomas Herbert, in his account of the Persians, thought that "to record the variety of tortures here too much used by man-eating hags of hell, cannibal hounds . . . and their death-twanging bowstrings, ripping up men's guts and the like—what could be the effect but an odious and unnecessary remembrance?" Yet despite the horrors, the sovereign always remained popular with the crowds and with foreign visitors, Herbert among them.

In other respects, Abbās was a model of prudent kingship. He made little or no use of the messianic trappings that had carried his great-grandfather Ismail to power. He preferred to reign as a secular monarch, employing the force of arms, the persuasive power of money, and the lavish use of spectacle as well as terror to command the obedience of his subjects. He was not a great innovator, but he was a wise reformer, many of his best moves being developments of policies first initiated by his grandfather Tahmāsp. In other areas, Abbās copied the institutions and practices of his neighbors, the Ottoman and Mogul sultans. He took full advantage of the growing European interest in Persia and of the technological and economic opportunities that could be had as a result.

Seen here giving audience to ambassadors from Mogul India, Shah Abbās II was not of the same moral or intellectual stature as his great namesake. Acceding to the throne as a boy in 1642, thirteen years after the death of Abbās I, he allowed the army to decline in numbers and quality in the course of his twenty-four-year reign. Addicted to opium and alcohol, he died, probably of syphilis, at the age of thirty-three. His successors were no more impressive; but such was the strength of Abbās I's legacy that the Safavid dynasty held power until well into the eighteeenth century.

Abbās's successors, brought up in the rarefied atmosphere of the harem, lacked experience of the real world and were often the pawns of factional intrigue. None of them possessed his flair and flamboyance, yet the strength of his legacy was such that the Safavids were to remain in power, using mostly the institutions he put into place, for almost a century after his death.

It was not until the early eighteenth century that the lack of decisive leadership finally took its toll. Sultan Husayn, the last Safavid, was a debauchee and a heavy drinker who paid little attention to affairs of state. The neighboring Baluchis and Afghans took advantage of his negligence to invade the nation and seize border provinces already alienated by Husayn's attempts to enforce rigid Shiite orthodoxy throughout his realm.

Finally one Mahmud, a former vassal of the Safavids from Afghanistan, besieged the ruler in his capital of Isfahan. The starving citizens were reduced to cannibalism before finally surrendering to the rebel warlord, who took for himself the title of shah. Husayn was murdered in the *madrasa,* or "mosque-school," constructed in his mother's name. The Shiite faith survived; but once more Persia found itself under the rule of foreigners.

Soldiers looting a farmhouse

AGONIES OF THE THIRTY YEARS' WAR

over the thirty years, around one million of them died.

Nor was the suffering confined to the military. The huge numbers of soldiers drained dry the countryside over which they fought. The civilian mayhem was on a par with that inflicted by the Mongols who had raided Europe 400 years earlier. It led the most celebrated German poet of the time, Martin Opitz, to write:

The trees stand no more
The gardens are desolate
The sickle and the plow
are now a cold, sharp sword

And its horrors inspired a French artist, Jacques Callot, to produce a famous series of engravings called *The Miseries of War,* some of which are reproduced here and on the following pages.

Although the Thirty Years' War was fought by many nations, most of the carnage took place on the soil of the Holy Roman Empire, a loose collection of about 1,000 semi-independent, small states nominally controlled from Vienna by its emperor, Ferdinand II. Ferdinand was a member of the Hapsburg family, which collectively ruled nearly half of Europe, including Spain and sections of Italy and the Netherlands. Ferdinand's share included present-day Germany, Czechoslovakia, and Austria, as well as parts of Hungary, Poland, and Yugoslavia; it stretched from the Baltic Sea in the north to the Adriatic in the south, from the Rhine River in the west to the Carpathian Mountains in the east.

The force that set off the destruction throughout this vast land was religion. In medieval times a source of unity throughout western Europe, Christianity had been transformed by the Protestant Reformation of the sixteenth century into a cause

F or what can war but endless war still breed?" When the poet John Milton posed that question in 1648, he was addressing the civil war that was then devastating his native England. Yet he could have found a more apt illustration of his aphorism across the English Channel, where, at the time that he was writing, parts of continental Europe were being devastated by a conflict more enduring, more widespread, and more savage than any they had previously known. History was to call the struggle the Thirty Years' War, but to those whose lands it laid waste and whose children it butchered, it must have indeed seemed endless. It was a conflict that fed upon itself, destroying agriculture and creating a whole class of beggared peasants whose only hope of survival lay in joining the ranks of the plunderers and pillagers who had reduced

them to ruin. This was total war, and it transformed some of the Continent's wealthiest provinces into wasteland.

The conflict started as an internal dispute within the Holy Roman Empire and swelled to involve most European nations. Its outcome was hardly inconsequential: It established the status quo in Europe for almost a century. But the Thirty Years' War was to be remembered by later generations not so much in terms of battles won and territories gained but as an orgy of violence, a glimpse of the hell that man could create on earth.

It was a war that saw terrible advances in the methods of mass destruction. Muskets and cannon became less unwieldy and more deadly. New, shallow formations exposed more soldiers to fire and to hand-to-hand fighting and death. Unprecedented numbers of soldiers fought, and

Enrolling the troops

of conflict between and within nations. Parts of the Holy Roman Empire, together with the Scandinavian countries, England, Scotland, and most of Switzerland, had converted to Protestantism, chiefly the Lutheran or Calvinist denominations; Italy, Spain, most of France, and the remainder of the Holy Roman Empire—along with the emperor himself—had remained Catholic, retaining their loyalty to the pope in Rome. The new pattern cut across old diplomatic ties; traditional allies such as Spain and England now found themselves at odds over religion. Moreover, religious affiliations did not neatly follow national boundaries. All major states now found themselves confronting an enemy within—a religious minority whose first, uncompromising loyalty was to its creed.

Within the Holy Roman Empire, the religious rift upset what had always been a precarious balance between the individual principalities and their would-be rulers in Vienna. When, in 1618, the zealous Emperor Ferdinand tried to assert his imperial authority by debarring Protestants in Bohemia from public office and by closing down two of their churches, the balance was not so much upset as destroyed. An anti-imperial revolt duly broke out in Prague, the Bohemian capital. This started a chain reaction whereby not only German states but also a number of neighboring European powers were drawn into the conflict.

They ranged themselves in the beginning primarily by religious affiliation. Protestant England, Sweden, Denmark, and the Dutch Republic joined the Bohemian side; Roman Catholic Spain, Poland,

and the pope were on the imperialist front. But the motives of the individual combatants—especially the German ones—varied at any one time between the spiritual and the secular, the aggressive and the defensive, and between self-assertion and self-preservation. The prime secular issue was the desire of the German princes and dukes and the rising nation-states neighboring the Holy Roman Empire to counteract the multinational power of the Hapsburg family.

The struggle fell into two phases. During the early years, local issues were paramount and the most heartfelt of these were religious. But after 1635, naked politics took over; the goal of the warmongers was no less than to alter the balance of power in Europe.

By that time, the war had created a momentum of its own. With all Europe divided into two camps, diplomatic initiatives were difficult: There were no neutral parties to serve as mediators. Fighting was the only way of resolving the conflict, and the fighting was inconclusive. So the war dragged on.

Since no state in this period received sufficient tax revenue to support a large standing army, their rulers had recourse to the crude and ultimately ineffective method of hiring mercenaries. The notion of fighting purely for financial gain, for a state not necessarily one's own, had entered Europe toward the end of the Middle Ages, when the old obligation of feudal vassals to fight for their lords began to wane. The use of mercenaries had grown steadily, and by the seventeenth century, they were indispensable.

The job of recruiting and running these

The battle

temporary armies was farmed out to private entrepreneur-generals, such as the ambitious and unscrupulous adventurer, Count Peter Ernst von Mansfeld. The illegitimate son of a minor Catholic prince, Mansfeld began his career in the Hapsburg army. The stigma of his birth held back his progress through the ranks, however, and at the start of the war he transferred his allegiance to the Hapsburgs' Protestant opponents. In the first eight years of the conflict, he led armies for Savoy, France, Britain, the Netherlands, and a variety of German states; a contemporary engraving showed him preparing a steam bath in which the German states were portrayed sweating money.

While some of the soldiers led by Mansfeld and his ilk had a religious or political commitment to their cause, most were no more idealistic than their leaders. Many had been forcibly conscripted; others had joined the army to escape destitution or the gallows. Few fates, however, were so terrible as to make soldiering seem a desirable alternative. The men, clothed in lice-ridden uniforms, lived constantly under threat of death from disease or battle, in that order. Mutiny and desertion were savagely punished.

Under the mercenary system, all wages were channeled through the regimental commanders. The soldiers' allegiance accordingly lay with these officers rather than with the cause for which they were fighting. If a commander swapped sides, his troops would follow him as a body. But their loyalty was poorly rewarded. The commanders themselves, and the officers who served under them, regularly skimmed off a percentage of the already-

low pay provided by the rulers who had hired them. Quite often, the supply of cash dried up altogether. "Neither they nor their horses can live on air," Mansfeld complained for his soldiers when funds were cut off by one of his employers, the duke of Savoy.

If the revenues did run out in mid-campaign, rulers would authorize army commanders to extract payment from the local citizenry, in the form either of taxes or of free board and lodging. Such impositions were made all the heavier by the community of servants, wives, children, freebooters, prostitutes, and traders that accompanied every army. And the countryfolk suffered even more acutely from the acquisitive instincts of individual soldiers. For the one attraction that a soldier's life did offer was the hope of booty. Each soldier became a small, property-acquiring industry at the expense of the local populace.

A contemporary novel, *Simplicius Simplicissimus,* by the German writer Hans Jacob von Grimmelshausen, described graphically how stealing from local farmers became a way of life for the book's eponymous antihero, a musketeer in the imperial forces. "If I was not on patrol," says Simplicissimus, "I went out looting, and neither horses nor sheep were safe from me in their stalls, which I raided for miles around. To avoid being trailed, I knew how to put boots or shoes on cattle and horses until I brought them to a much-used highway." For pigs, "I made a well-salted porridge with meal and water, and soaked a sponge therein, to which I had tied a strong rope, and let those that I wanted to keep swallow the sponge full

The maimed and wounded seeking refuge in a hospital

of porridge, keeping the rope in my hand, whereupon they followed patiently without further dispute, and paid the bill with hams and sausages."

Simplicissimus was driven to soldiering when his father's farm was similarly raided; the invaders slaughtered some of its occupants and tortured others with thumbscrews or by burning them over a fire. Such incidents were far from being products of Grimmelshausen's imagination. One well-attested brutality inflicted by marauding bands of soldiers and camp followers was to force-feed local farmers with liquid excrement, either out of wanton cruelty or as a means of getting them to divulge the whereabouts of valuables.

In some parts of Germany, particularly those on the river supply routes, the vicious depredations of soldiers were a regular occurrence. Hans Heberle, a shoemaker who kept a diary of the war years, described how on thirty separate occasions plundering soldiery drove him and his family from their village to take refuge in the nearby city of Ulm. Yet even if they escaped with their lives, Heberle and his like would often be left penniless in a countryside that had been stripped of all its crops. An Englishman named William Crowne, who journeyed through Germany in 1636 as a member of a diplomatic mission, gave an eyewitness account of their sufferings. At Neustadt on the Aisch River, he wrote of "wretched children sitting at their doors almost dying of hunger." And he recorded that in the village of Bacharach on the Rhine, "the poor people are found dead with grass stuffed in their mouths"—a final, desperate bid to escape starvation.

Unsurprisingly, villagers driven to such extremes sometimes retaliated against their oppressors. "The boors on the march cruelly used our soldiers," a Scots officer who served in the war noted, "in cutting off their noses and ears, hands and feet, pulling out their eyes, with sundry other cruelties which they used; being justly repaid by the soldiers in the burning of many dorps on the march, leaving also the boors dead where they were found."

Thus, civilians and soldiers alike were drawn into an accelerating spiral of violence that proved almost impossible to stop. The bloodletting could end only when every possible permutation of national and international hostility had been exhausted, and when sufficient destruction had been done to have drained every emotion except the desire for peace.

By 1643, that process was well under way. The population of Germany as a whole had fallen by perhaps 20 percent. In areas directly affected by the fighting, the figure was higher. Up to three-quarters of the population had disappeared—a result of disease, war, and mass migration to the cities, whose walls and protection money kept most armies out. In the much-fought-over southern duchy of Württemberg, the number of inhabitants declined from 450,000 in 1620 to 100,000 in 1639.

Nor was the depopulation confined to Germany alone. In Sweden, wholesale conscription stripped the land of adult males; once shipped off to fight in Germany, a man was unlikely to come back alive. Many died within a year of enlistment. "We may indeed say that we have

The hangman's tree

conquered lands from others and to that end ruined our own," wrote a depressed member of the Swedish government.

By the 1640s, therefore, the mood was conducive to peace; achieving it, however, turned out to be a cumbersome process, requiring an international conference that dragged on for four years and met simultaneously in two different cities. The French and their Roman Catholic allies negotiated with the emperor in Münster in northwestern Germany, while the Swedish and Protestant delegations met him thirty miles away, at Osnabrück. The delegates stuck to their task, and the result was the triumphant announcement on October 24, 1648, of the long-awaited Peace of Westphalia.

To guarantee that the peace would be lasting, the negotiators had determined to obtain the agreement of all the parties, not just some. For, as the Swedes' perceptive ambassador Count Johan Salvius put it: "The first rule of all politics is that the security of all depends on the equilibrium of the individuals." And all the individual states participating in the conference did indeed get enough out of the peace to ensure a new equilibrium.

Sweden won financial compensation and a strategic slice of northern Germany, while France secured sufficient territory on her eastern border to break what had threatened to become encirclement by the Hapsburgs. The emperor (now Ferdinand III) kept his title and most of his territory, but the German states within his empire won recognition of their supreme power in their localities. The concessions to the German states not only diminished the concern of other countries over the excessive power concentrated in Hapsburg hands; it also resolved the tensions within Germany—and there was consensus by this time that a stable Europe depended on a stable Germany.

The treaty included some specifically religious clauses, but they were not of enormous moment. Since 1555, the rulers of the German states had had the right to determine whether their subjects should adhere to the Roman Catholic or to the Lutheran church; now Calvinism became a permitted option. The peace treaty also decreed that any future religious disputes within the empire should be settled by "amicable" agreement between the Catholic and Protestant members of the Imperial Diet, or parliament. The optimism of this clause was a measure of how far down the list of priorities spiritual considerations had sunk; never again was religion to spark a European war.

Now that the threat of Hapsburg domination had subsided, it was the turn of other European nations, notably France, to kindle their territorial ambitions. Not for another two centuries would the diverse states of Germany be welded together, under Wilhelm I of Prussia, into a power sufficiently unified to threaten the Continent's stability.

And for almost a century, the warweary German people were left in peace to rebuild their lives and livelihoods. They did so with surprising speed. By 1700, parts of Germany had returned to their prewar housing and population levels. But the memories were not so easily erased. For centuries to come, the Thirty Years' War would endure in European minds as a byword for calamity.

CIVIL WAR IN ENGLAND

On February 23, 1642, the warship *Lion* set sail from England for Holland. Its most distinguished passenger was Henrietta Maria, the thirty-three-year-old, French-born wife of the English king, Charles I. Ostensibly, the queen was taking her ten-year-old daughter, Mary, to join the fifteen-year-old Dutch prince, William of Orange, to whom she had been married ten months earlier. In fact, however, Her Majesty had even more important business to accomplish. Her luggage contained the crown jewels of England and most of her own jewels as well, and she was on her way to pawn them in Europe and use the money to buy arms. The king of England was preparing to go to war against his own subjects.

The conflict that was about to erupt was to be the first and the most critical act in an extended drama that changed the balance of power in England. At a time when most other European nations were increasingly subjected to the will of absolute monarchs, the English would forcibly resist the claims of their king to rule by divine right. In the course of the century, two separate rulers of the Stuart dynasty would be driven from the throne: one to face execution; the other, exile. As a result, the nation would enter the following century set firmly on the path of constitutional monarchy and would provide a model for the rest of the world of the checks and balances that could be used to shackle royal absolutism.

The Stuarts had succeeded to the English throne in 1603, when the last ruler of the preceding Tudor dynasty, Elizabeth I, died childless. By the laws of succession, the throne passed to her cousin, James Stuart, who had by then been ruling in Scotland as King James VI for twenty years. Tall and broad-shouldered, though with thin legs and a tongue that seemed too big for his mouth, James had a reputation as an intellectual; before his arrival in England, he had published *The True Law of Free Monarchies,* a scholarly, if unoriginal, treatise on political theory arguing the case for the divine right of kings. But James was also conceited and lazy. A bisexual, he showed a penchant for worthless favorites, the last of whom, George Villiers, he addressed as "sweetheart" and "wife." In his character, good and bad qualities were mixed in a way that led his fellow monarch, Henry IV of France, to describe him as "the wisest fool in Christendom."

Nevertheless, to the English in 1603, James had much to recommend him. He subscribed to the Protestant faith of his predecessor, and he had an established reputation as a ruler. Although Scotland retained its status as a separate country with its own distinct constitution, the fact that one king would henceforth reign in Edinburgh and in London seemed to promise a period of peace between the two nations, which had often in the past been at loggerheads. And his penchant for handsome young men nothwithstanding, James was married to a daughter of the king of Denmark, who had borne him two sons and a daughter; the succession seemed to be

Dressed in ceremonial armor, King Charles I of England gazes proudly from a portrait by his court artist, the Flemish master Anthony Van Dyck. Charles's regal bearing in the painting was more impressive than his demeanor in real life—he was a short, slightly built man with a stammer—but it accurately reflected his exalted conception of kingship. This was, he believed, bestowed by divine right, making kings answerable for their actions to nobody but God. This view brought him into conflict with the elected representatives of his people in Parliament, a conflict that ended in civil strife.

ensured. As he traveled southward in April of 1603, his future subjects turned out in large crowds to welcome him.

By inheriting the English throne, James also became king of Ireland, a largely Roman Catholic country established as a separate kingdom under the rule of the English monarch by Elizabeth's father, Henry VIII. Yet for all its appurtenances, James's new throne was not as rich as he might have hoped. For their daily expenses, the monarchs of England were expected to "live of their own," which for the most part meant living off the income from the revenues of royal estates and the fines imposed by their courts. In addition, Parliament traditionally voted customs duties known as tonnage and poundage to each monarch for life at the beginning of his or her reign. These resources had once been enough to support a royal household, but their value had recently diminished. Although Queen Elizabeth had been extremely thrifty in everything but the cost of her wardrobe, she had been forced to reduce the income of her heirs by selling off large tracts of royal land in order to pay for the war she had waged against Spain.

Even if James had been as careful as Elizabeth, he would have had difficulty making ends meet. In fact, he was impetuously profligate. He spent lavishly on new buildings, on gifts to courtiers, on splendid balls, and on spectacular theatrical productions written by Ben Jonson and designed by Inigo Jones, respectively the leading play-

At the start of the Civil War in 1642, Royalist forces loyal to King Charles controlled the north of England, Wales, the west Midlands, and Cornwall, while supporters of Parliament held the richer south and east of the country *(shaded yellow)*. Since London was in Parliamentary hands, the university city of Oxford became the Royalist capital. Most of the major battles of the conflict, from Edgehill in 1642 to Naseby in 1645, were fought in the disputed territory near the boundaries of the two hostile zones.

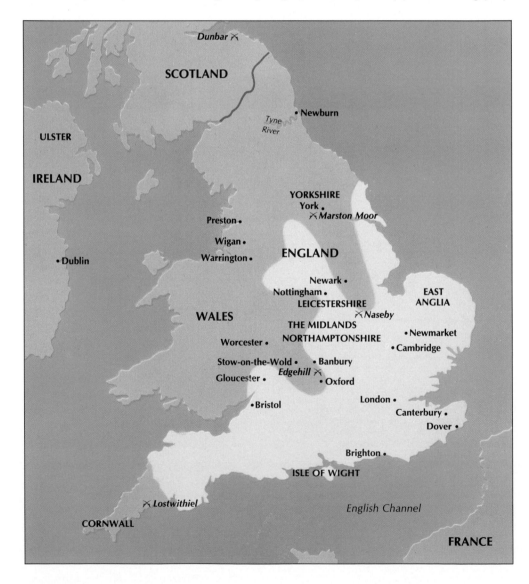

wright and architect of the day. Fortunes were squandered on jewelry and clothes for his queen, Anne of Denmark, a lady of extravagant fancies who once attended a Christmas ball dressed as a mince pie.

In an effort to meet his debts, James exploited the royal prerogative. He sold titles, imposed new import duties, and rewarded his courtiers with grants of monopolies, at the cost of the populace at large; and despite the fact that most of his reign was spent at peace, he sold off royal estates too.

The only other way in which James could raise substantial sums of money was by seeking approval for additional taxes from Parliament; and here lay the seeds of future conflict. This institution, which had parallels in every other major western European country, had evolved from the habit of medieval kings of summoning consultative assemblies of their subjects. At first, such gatherings had consisted exclusively of the great nobles and the leaders of the church; later, however, lesser landowners and representatives of the cities had also been included. Since the fourteenth century, kings had conceded to this body the right to approve the raising of taxes.

In the ensuing centuries, Parliament had split into two separate chambers: the Lords, for the bishops and hereditary nobility, and the Commons, for the representatives of the cities and shires. Certain guarantees of the right of free speech had also developed. One was that the king never entered the debating chamber in person; in his place, the House of Commons elected a Speaker to preside over its debates and speak on his behalf.

Although the House of Lords had originally been the dominant body, it gradually lost its preeminence during the sixteenth century, when the Commons had consolidated its influence—primarily by loyal support of the Crown. Under the Tudors, the House of Commons had developed powers and privileges that were real, though limited. It had the right to petition and protest to the monarch, and was an important arena for the airing of grievances. It was expected to debate measures proposed by the king, and its consent was part of the formal process by which new laws were enacted. But neither it nor the House of Lords had any authority to dictate policy or to take part in the executive government of the kingdom, except in authorizing the raising of taxes.

Nevertheless, the parliament that James inherited was very different from the docile gathering that had assembled under the early Tudors. The country gentlemen who made up the bulk of the House of Commons had benefited greatly from a wave of economic expansion, based on wool and the textiles made from it, that had enriched England in the previous century. The boom had raised the price of real estate and had increased the rents paid by tenants to landowners. The beneficiaries of the new wealth were not politically sophisticated, but they were resolute, ambitious, and eager to protect their interests.

Many of them also held religious opinions that divided them from the king. Ever since Henry VIII had broken with Rome in the 1530s and established an independent Church of England, the nation had been torn by theological controversy. Henry's church owed allegiance not to the pope but to the English monarch, but in other respects differed little from the Catholic model it supplanted. Yet the upheaval engendered by the English Reformation, and the anti-Catholic rhetoric it encouraged, inevitably fostered the Protestant doctrines being preached by Martin Luther on the Continent at the time. An attempt by Queen Mary Tudor in the 1550s to restore the Catholic faith did not survive her death.

Under Queen Elizabeth, the Church of England had finally begun to find its identity as a compromise between the conflicting parties. In dogma, the Anglican church was Protestant, but its liturgy continued to be reminiscent of Catholicism, and it was still organized under a hierarchy of bishops and archbishops. Loyalty to the Anglican church was strictly enforced. The Roman faith was proscribed, and priests were sent to the gallows. There were still Catholics in England, numbering among their ranks some of the greatest families in the land, but now they were forced to practice their faith in secret.

The bitterest enemies of the Roman Catholics were the strict Protestants known as Puritans—devout and serious-minded folk who wanted to "purify" the Church of England by removing all remaining traces of what they considered to be "popery." Many Puritans took their ideas from the French reformer, John Calvin, whose austere insistence on salvation by faith alone had already come to dominate the Scottish church. A radical minority belonged to a variety of Nonconformist, or dissenting, sects, which were to grow in strength as the seventeenth century progressed. All of these groups shared a distaste for ecclesiastical show or ostentation. Believing the important part of any act of worship to be the Word of God, pure and unadorned, they tended to favor gatherings of equals in bare rooms where the Bible could be read and explained without distraction. These groups were strongly represented in the House of Commons.

Because Scotland had moved further in the direction of ecclesiastical reform than England—the Scottish church was organized along largely Presbyterian lines, being run by the clergy and lay elders known as presbyters rather than by bishops—the Puritans hoped that James would support their cause. But he had learned by bitter experience. Exasperated by the interference of Scottish synods in the affairs of state, he was unwilling to encourage similar developments in his new kingdom. His refusal was unequivocal. Although he agreed reluctantly to impose penalties on Roman Catholics, his gesture did little to appease the Puritans and only earned him additional enemies among the Catholics, a few of whom hired a fanatical explosives expert called Guy Fawkes, who very nearly managed to blow up both king and Parliament in the Gunpowder Plot of 1605 *(right)*.

After their disappointment, the Puritans in Parliament were inevitably unsympathetic when the spendthrift king asked for more money. The Commons demanded in exchange a statute forbidding any further imposition of customs duties, and the abolition of certain feudal privileges such as wardship—the right to the custody, and property, of an infant heir of a feudal tenant—and purveyance, the royal right to requisition provisions. Negotiations on these matters collapsed in 1610 and again in 1614. By then, a pattern of confrontation was set that was to be repeated in the ensuing decades and that would finally culminate in civil war.

In 1621, members of a subsequent parliament summoned by the king even attempted to influence foreign policy. Rightly fearing that James was hoping to heal the wounds of Christian Europe by marrying "Baby Charles" to the daughter of the Catholic king of Spain, Parliament refused to grant more than a fraction of the money that James needed unless he promised to declare war on Spain and marry his heir to a Protestant.

In a fury, James dismissed Parliament and ripped the offending pages from its records. When his efforts at matchmaking foundered, however, he turned to Parliament again. This time, the members did at least grant him sufficient funds to embark on a new conflict, on behalf of the Protestant cause in the Thirty Years' War, although they laid down conditions as to how the money was to be spent. But by this point, the king had only a year to live.

Under the twenty-four-year-old Charles I, who succeeded to the throne in 1625, the relationship between king and Parliament deteriorated further and faster. Charles shared his father's indolence and his faith in the divine right of kings, but in other respects, he was a very different man. He was short in stature, and by temperament pious, devious, and indecisive. In order to hide his deep insecurity, he adopted a pose of earnest and often pompous formality, and like most insecure men, he did not always keep his word.

Besides James's kingdoms, debts, and war with Spain, Charles also inherited the dubious influence of his father's last and most cherished favorite, George Villiers, who had been created duke of Buckingham. Widely resented for his arrogance, the duke by now virtually dictated English foreign policy. After the failure of the planned Spanish marriage, the extrovert duke arranged a match between Charles and Henrietta Maria, the ardently Catholic sister of the king of France. The couple were married by proxy; when the big-eyed, buck-toothed queen, then sixteen years old, finally arrived in England with several priests in her entourage, she burst into tears at the sight of her husband. She hated Buckingham; and she despised Charles for his weakness as much as he disliked her for her frivolity. For their first three years together, until the death of Buckingham, their mutual antagonism was so great that some said the marriage was not consummated.

As part of the marriage contract, Charles had promised to relax the penal laws against Roman Catholics and had lent the king of France some English ships, which were subsequently used against the Huguenots—as French Protestants were known. Deeply suspicious of the new king's intentions, Parliament failed to vote adequate taxes for an expedition to Cádiz, planned by Buckingham as part of the ongoing war with Spain, which ultimately ended in fiasco. Worse still for Charles, Parliament refused to grant him tonnage and poundage. The king had no choice but to raise the

Shown in a contemporary engraving, conspirators plan the failed coup of 1605 known as the Gunpowder Plot. Roman Catholics, incensed by an edict banishing priests, the plotters sought to blow up Parliament on November 5, 1605, when the king and members of both houses would have been assembled for its ceremonial opening. Enlisting the help of a soldier and explosives expert named Guy Fawkes, they rented the cellars beneath Parliament. Fawkes installed barrels containing almost two tons of gunpowder in the vaults and covered them with firewood and iron bars. But one conspirator aroused suspicion by telling his brother-in-law not to attend the ceremony. The cellars were searched, Fawkes was arrested, and before his execution, he revealed under torture the names of his fellow plotters.

Oliver Cromwell, seen here in a miniature by Samuel Cooper, was one of England's greatest soldiers and statesmen. Until 1642, he was simply a country gentleman with Puritan religious inclinations who sat as a member of Parliament and more than once had considered emigrating to America. After the outbreak of the Civil War, however, he became the best cavalry commander in the Parliamentary army, and his disciplined and dedicated troops, nicknamed Ironsides, played a key role in the army's victory.

money himself. Charles's methods, however, went far beyond anything that his father had ever attempted.

He levied tonnage and poundage without parliamentary consent and thereby incensed the merchants. He imposed a forced loan to the Crown on property holders and imprisoned those who refused to pay, which infuriated the landed gentry. And—having fallen out with his brother-in-law and having decided to send an expedition to help the Huguenot rebels in France—he angered everyone along England's southeast coast by billeting his troops in the houses of the local population and by imposing martial law on soldiers and civilians alike.

When Charles summoned Parliament in 1628, there was hardly a representative in it whose family had not suffered from the exercise of the royal prerogative. Despite the anti-Catholic swing in his foreign policy, both the House of Lords and the House of Commons refused to supply him with any money until he had, unwillingly, assented to a document known as the Petition of Right, which outlawed forced loans, compulsory billeting, martial law, and imprisonment without cause.

Some months later, the hated duke of Buckingham was assassinated by a disgruntled Puritan naval officer who had served on Buckingham's unsuccessful foreign expeditions. Nevertheless, Parliament was still hostile when it convened again after a six-month recess. In the first place, the members were angry because the king was still collecting unauthorized tonnage and poundage. In the second place, they were deeply concerned for the future of the Church of England, which was being modified in a Roman Catholic direction by the clergy the king was appointing to bishoprics, particularly by the new bishop of London, William Laud. To the passionate reformers in Parliament, it seemed as though the differences between the Church of England and the Church of Rome were being reduced to the vanishing point.

A confrontation quickly materialized. On March 2, 1629, a member from Cornwall, Sir John Eliot, proposed a motion bitterly critical of the Crown. When the king ordered Parliament to be dissolved, the members barred the door, forcibly held the Speaker down in his chair so that their proceedings would still be legal, and passed resolutions condemning as enemies of the state all those who collected or paid tonnage and poundage or abetted popery.

On the following day, when Parliament was dissolved at last, Eliot and the other leaders of the debate were arrested and imprisoned in the Tower of London, where Eliot subsequently died. For the next eleven years, Charles ruled England without summoning another parliament. Under Laud, who became archbishop of Canterbury, altars were restored to the churches, and a series of strict regulations banning dancing, archery, and other amusements on Sundays—which had been introduced in James's time to placate the Puritans—were rescinded. Many disillusioned Puritans simply gave up all hope and emigrated to North America.

By avoiding war and living frugally, King Charles managed to keep his expenses to a minimum. Like his father, he granted monopolies, and he imposed new taxes and resurrected old fines. But at the end of those eleven years, his need for money suddenly increased dramatically.

An ill-advised attempt to impose a Laudian prayer book on Scotland resulted in a full-scale rebellion. In the spring of 1640, Charles summoned what was to be known as the Short Parliament and asked it to finance an army. Inevitably, both houses refused to grant him a penny until he redressed their many grievances. On May 5, after making little effort to negotiate, the king simply dissolved Parliament and began to muster as much as he could of the militias—the volunteer regiments that all the counties in England were required to maintain for the defense of the realm. These troops were ill-equipped and ill-prepared; they seldom trained for more than a few hours each year before retiring to the nearest tavern.

The sullen militiamen, many of them press-ganged into service, were no match for angry, well-armed Scots, who were led by professional officers who had served in continental armies. The English were put to flight. In the treaty that followed, Charles allowed the Scots to occupy part of northern England and agreed to pay the expenses of their army until a full peace was arranged.

That autumn he summoned another parliament. It was to sit for the next twenty years, winning for itself the title of the Long Parliament. One of its earliest enactments prevented it from being dissolved without its own consent.

The humiliated king could do nothing but accept its terms. The Scots were waiting, and the citizens of London were rioting in protest at the popish innovations of his bishops. Charles submitted meekly to the curtailment of his prerogative, particularly with regard to the imposition of duties and taxes. By the time the Scots had been paid off, he had seen his archbishop imprisoned in the Tower and had signed a death warrant for his closest adviser, Sir Thomas Wentworth, the earl of Strafford, who had been attainted for treason by Parliament.

Despite everything, a majority of the members of both houses were intent on reform, not revolution. But there was a growing body of Puritans, led by a landowner named John Pym, who had set their sights not merely on bishops and the Book of Common Prayer but also on the king's monopoly of executive power. Once the immediate problems of the Scottish war had been resolved, the Puritans began to argue their case for setting limits on the royal prerogative. As the ensuing heated debates rose to a climax, fate played into the Puritans' hands. News reached London of another rebellion.

This time it was in Ireland. Despite nominal allegiance to the English king, their sovereign, Ireland's impoverished inhabitants were for the most part bitterly hostile to their foreign rulers. In an attempt to make the nation more governable, James I had dispossessed thousands of Catholic farmers in the northern province of Ulster, granting their land instead to Scottish Protestant settlers. The simmering grievances left by the Plantation of Ulster, as it was called, now burst into insurrection. Four or five thousand of the newcomers were massacred, and many more fled to the hills, where they faced starvation.

There was no longer any good reason for Parliament to refuse to finance an effective army. But once the king had control of such a force, there was a real possibility that he would use it not to crush the Irish rebels but to overpower his foes in the Commons. Many members were already alarmed by rumors of royal plots, and the extremists exploited their anxiety. Pym persuaded both houses to protect themselves by requesting the right to appoint the army's senior officers. When the king adamantly refused to surrender any more of his sovereignty, Pym and his supporters introduced the Grand Remonstrance.

This document was a long list of all the wrongs that the English church and state had suffered at the hands of the king, followed by a summary of Parliament's accomplishments and a number of specific proposals. One demanded that a synod should be summoned to supervise a religious reformation; another insisted that, in the future, all the king's ministers should be approved by Parliament.

The Commons was divided in its attitude toward the remonstrance. The prospect of radical religious reform was too much for many members. After two weeks of fierce debate the remonstrance was adopted, but only by 159 votes to 148; one-third of the house had abstained.

If the king had only waited, the missing members might well have rallied to his cause and the Grand Remonstrance might have been overturned. Instead, he over-reacted violently. Urged on by the taunts of his contemptuous queen, he ordered his attorney general to impeach his leading opponents in both houses of Parliament. On January 4, 1642, he went down to the House of Commons himself at the head of a contingent of armed guards, with the intention of arresting five of its members. It was the first time that an English monarch had entered the premises. But when he sat down in the Speaker's chair and looked around the astonished house, he saw that the five members had already departed. One of the queen's ladies-in-waiting had warned them of the impending raid.

London rose in outrage at the king's breach of parliamentary privilege. The city's 6,000-strong citizens' militia, known as the Trained Bands, was mobilized to protect Parliament; and unlike other volunteer forces, the Trained Bands took their soldiering seriously and drilled regularly under experienced professionals. A contingent from the Royal Navy, long discontented over pay and conditions, marched up mutinously from the docks to join them. Fearful for his own safety, King Charles abandoned his capital on January 10. He was not to return to it as a free man.

Negotiations continued for a while, but the king would not accept the terms of Parliament, and Parliament would not trust the word of the king. On a wet and windy English summer's day in 1642, King Charles I raised his standard at Nottingham. His herald could hardly read the declaration of war because the king had altered it so many times, and during the night, when the wind increased, the standard was blown down into the mud. The English Civil War had begun with an unpropitious omen for the Royalist cause.

The English did not divide by class to fight the war. They chose sides in accordance

A sequence of illustrations from a seventeenth-century military manual shows the correct way to fire a musket. Such works helped familiarize English officers with the new drill and tactics then being used on the Continent in the drawn-out conflict that became known as the Thirty Years' War. The strategic innovations were designed above all to get maximum benefit from firearms, which were available in ever-growing numbers but still generally lacked finesse. The musket seen here was a heavy, hazardous weapon fired not by a spark from a flint but by a match—made from cord boiled in vinegar—which was kept permanently burning.

Rest your Musket. | Drawe out your match | Blowe your match. | Cock your match. | Try your match. | Gard your panne. | Present | Giue fire.

with their consciences, their personal loyalties, and the demands of self-preservation. Nevertheless, a majority of the greater landowners fought for "King and Country," while there was a tendency for those who had grown wealthy in the booming cloth industry to support "God and Parliament." In general, the Royalists were strongest in the north and west, while the Parliamentarians were dominant in the richer south and east. But in every town and in every county—and even within some families—there were supporters of two parties. There were also many people who hoped to stay neutral and let the war pass them by. At the outset, according to Edward Hyde, the earl of Clarendon, who wrote a famous history of the conflict, "the number of those who desired to sit still was greater than the number of those who desired to engage in either party." As the war dragged on, however, more and more citizens were forced to choose one side or the other in order to protect themselves from plunderers, press gangs, or persecution.

Even within Parliament the divisions were not clear-cut. Although a majority of the members of the House of Lords were Royalists, there were around 30, more than one-quarter of the total, who sided with Parliament and provided it with its first generals; and approximately one-third of the House of Commons, more than 170 members, remained loyal to the king. Most of them had been his opponents since the Long Parliament first sat, but when it came to war, they could not bring themselves to fight him. Sir Edmund Verney, who became the king's standard-bearer and saw his own family divided by the conflict, spoke despondently for many of them:

> I have eaten his bread and served him near thirty years, and will not do
> so base a thing as to forsake him; and choose rather to lose my life (which
> I am sure I shall do) to preserve and defend those things which are against
> my conscience to preserve and defend.

The first volunteers to join the Parliamentary army were the apprentices of London, who wore their hair cropped short; as a result, the dour, determined Parliamentary soldiers were given the nickname Roundheads. The carefree and reckless Royalists, on the other hand, were called Cavaliers, after the brutal Spanish caballeros, or noble horsemen, who had oppressed Protestants in the Netherlands during the Dutch struggle for independence. Despite the nickname's connotations, the king himself authorized its use, saying that it signified "no more than a gentleman serving his king on horseback."

In the beginning, both sides recruited and paid for their armies in the same way. Wealthy supporters sold silver plate and other treasures—Queen Henrietta Maria's

PARLIAMENT VICTORIOUS

The Battle of Naseby, fought on June 14, 1645, was the decisive encounter of the English Civil War. The disposition of troops at the start of the engagement was later depicted in the engraving shown here, which was published two years after the battle. It shows the Northamptonshire village of Naseby in the foreground, with the Parliamentary baggage train on its left and spectators on a hill to its right. Below them, the cavalry of Oliver Cromwell, on the right flank of Parliament's New Model Army, faces the Royalist cavalry of Sir Marmaduke Langdale. On the other wing, the horsemen of Cromwell's son-in-law, Henry Ireton, confront the high-spirited troopers of Charles I's nephew, Prince Rupert. Although the artist depicted the king in front of his infantry, Charles in fact commanded his army from the group at the rear, near the top of the hill.

The battle opened with a charge by Rupert's horsemen. Despite a devastating musket volley from Parliamentarian dragoons who had dismounted and hidden in a hedge, his men kept going and chased the bulk of Ireton's cavalry back as far as the baggage train. Behind them, the two advancing lines of infantry engaged. But it was Cromwell's men who won the day. As their front ranks drove off Langdale's horsemen, the hindmost wheeled to attack the flank and rear of the Royalist infantry, who were surrounded when the dragoons from the hedge rode across to attack their other flank. Returning to the field after only an hour, Rupert's forces were already too late to save the day.

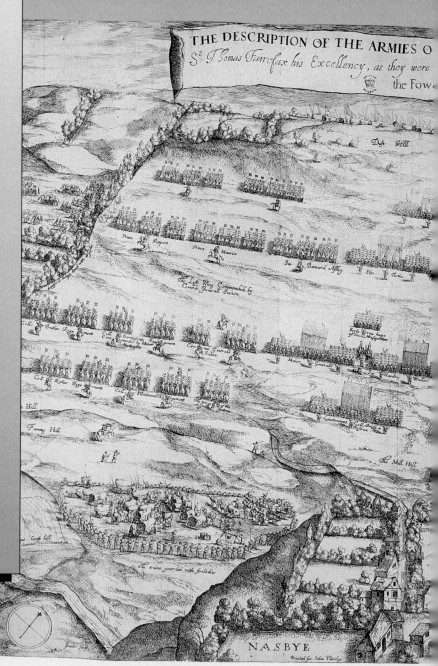

The standard of King Charles I, who commanded the Royalist army at Naseby, combines symbols of England, Ireland, France, and Scotland. Though personally brave, Charles was a bad general; he gave battle when his men were outnumbered, and failed to commit his cavalry reserves when there was a chance of saving his infantry.

ND FOOT OF HIS MAJESTIES, AND
ll bodyes, at the Battayle at NASBYE
of June 1645

The standard of Sir Thomas Fairfax, commander in chief of the Parliamentarian army, flew over his headquarters as a means of location. A scholar as well as a soldier, Fairfax fought for Parliament from the outset. Never a radical, he was shocked by the execution of the king and played a leading role in the restoration of his son, Charles II, to the throne.

jewels among them—in order to provide the sort of wages that would induce men to enlist, and some large landowners even raised entire regiments from among their own tenants. But as time passed and the resources of the wealthy ran out, the financial advantage tended toward the Parliamentarian cause. Parliament was able to borrow from the bankers in the city of London. Parliament introduced systems of assessment and imposed taxes on land and property that were actually more efficient than any that had previously been imposed by the Crown. And since Parliament controlled not only the navy but also almost all of the ports in the nation, it was able to impose import duties.

With very few ports at his disposal, and with his former navy blockading them, the king found it hard enough to get supplies from the Continent, let alone impose duties that would pay his soldiers' overdue wages. But, at the outset at least, the king did have the advantage in the quality of his recruits. The Welsh hills and the moors of Cornwall provided him with hardy and tenacious infantry; and the great landowners and their followers provided the perfect raw material for first-class cavalry. Long experience in the hunting field had made them expert horsemen. Trained and led by

A contemporary depiction of the execution of Charles I shows a woman fainting as the executioner holds up the head of his royal victim. The beheading was carried out on January 30, 1649, outside the Banqueting House of Charles's own palace of Whitehall. Although this painting shows the king kneeling at a high block, he in fact had to lie with his head on a low one, so that he could have easily been tied down if he had chosen to struggle. The crowd that assembled to watch the proceedings was held back by soldiers. But once the ax had fallen, some people scrambled onto the scaffold to dip handkerchiefs in the royal blood to keep as sacred relics.

the king's twenty-two-year-old German nephew, Prince Rupert of the Rhine, they became the first effective shock troops of the war.

At the end of August 1642, the Parliamentary army marched north from London to Nottingham under the command of the earl of Essex. By then, however, the king had gone west to collect his Welsh recruits, and by the time Essex caught up with him, he was already marching toward London. On October 23, Charles halted his army and turned to face his pursuers on the crest of Edgehill near Banbury in The Midlands. As the armies prepared for the first great battle, Sir Jacob Astley, the sixty-three-year-old commander of the king's infantry, uttered a prayer that became celebrated:

> *Oh, Lord! Thou knowest how busy I must be this day:*
> *If I forget thee, do not thou forget me.*

Both armies numbered around 13,000 men, and each was drawn up in a similar formation. Units of steel-helmeted cavalry stood ready on either wing. The centers were made up of alternating squares of musketeers in large felt hats and helmeted pikemen bearing pikes that ranged in length from twelve to eighteen feet. Both armies also had a few cannon, but the big guns were to be of more use in siege warfare than on the battlefield. After each shot, it took five minutes to cool their barrels and reload them—and cavalry could cover a great deal of ground in five minutes.

The Roundheads wore orange sashes and the Cavaliers red ones, but apart from that, the regimental uniforms on either side were very much the same. The red coats of the king's Life Guards, for example, were echoed in the Roundhead regiments of Lord Robartes and Denzil Holles. On several occasions during the war, the similarity in uniforms, particularly among officers, enabled commanders to pass unnoticed through enemy lines; more often, it led to fatal mistakes.

The battle opened with a brief and ineffective exchange of fire from the artillery. Then Prince Rupert led the cavalry on the Royalist right in a massed charge against the Roundhead left. After long argument, he had persuaded the Royalist commanders to abandon the traditional maneuver in which cavalry rode up to the enemy in a column, halted rank by rank to fire their side arms, and then rode away again. Instead, Rupert used the tactic introduced by King Gustavus Adolphus of Sweden during the Thirty Years' War, which was then raging in Germany. Rupert's horsemen charged in line abreast and drove home the attack with their swords as they slammed into the enemy at a full gallop.

The effect was dramatic. The horsemen on the Roundhead left broke and fled, and so too did the infantry next to them. Soon afterward, a charge from the Royalist's other flank had a similar effect on the Roundhead right. Although Rupert had taught his men to fight, he had not succeeded in instilling discipline. Instead of rejoining the battle, they set off after the fugitives and attacked the Roundhead baggage train.

When they rallied and returned at last, they were only just in time to avert disaster. Unsupported by any other cavalry, the Royalists had been forced back by a frontal assault from the Roundhead infantry and flank attacks from their mounted reserves. Their guns had been captured, and the enemy had come so close to the king himself that his standard-bearer, sad Sir Edmund Verney, had been killed. What could have been a crushing victory had ended in a bloody stalemate.

The earl of Essex withdrew westward. The road to London lay open. But the Royalist commanders knew that the capital would be well defended. Ignoring Prince

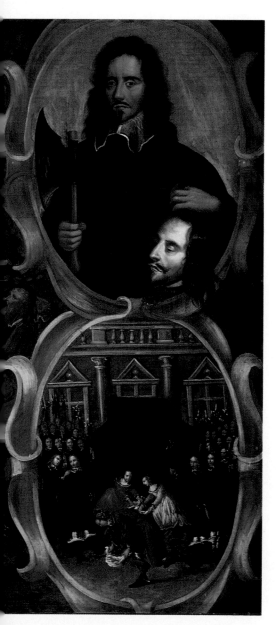

Rupert's pleas, they advanced no farther than the university city of Oxford, fifty miles northwest of the capital, which became their headquarters for the rest of the war.

At Oxford, colleges were turned into courts, council chambers, billets, arsenals, and stables. The quadrangles became sheep pens, open-air theaters, and dueling grounds. The whole atmosphere of the ancient seat of learning changed as it filled with fashionable women and poorly paid fighting men who lived mostly on plunder and sought to the best of their abilities to present themselves as the opposite of their pious enemies.

With the opening of armed conflict, the war of words intensified. Puritan pamphlets accused the Royalists of atrocities. One suggested that Prince Rupert was a witch and that his dog, Boye, was his familiar. Others tried to destroy morale by printing false lists of Royalist casualties, in response to one of which the following item appeared in the Royalist newspaper, *Mercurius Aulicus:*

> *Sir Jacob Astley, lately slain at Gloucester, wishes to know was he slain with a musket or a cannon bullet.*

While Roundhead generals mounted sieges and maneuvered aimlessly, the Cavaliers planned a three-pronged attack on the city of London, with one army coming from the north, one from Oxford, and one from the southwest. At the same time, however,

THE RELIGIOUS RADICALS

In the chaotic years of the Civil War, a diverse group of Nonconformist sects made their appearance in England, to the alarm of the moderate Puritans who made up a majority of Parliament's supporters. Among the groups satirized in the pamphlet illustration at right are the Arians, who rejected the doctrine of the Trinity; Soul Sleepers, who denied the afterlife; the Family of Love, who kept no sabbath; Seekers, who sought a personal relationship with God; and also the advocates of easier divorce, whose number included the poet John Milton. For good measure, the pamphlet's author included two old enemies, associated in Parliamentarian minds with the Royalist cause: Catholic Jesuits; and Arminians, who supported the High Church Anglicanism of Charles's archbishop of Canterbury, William Laud.

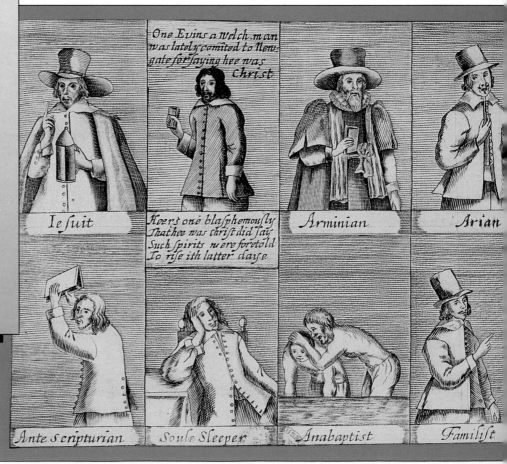

The Great Seal of England, which was affixed to official documents to guarantee their authenticity, shows the Speaker *(center)* presiding over a session of Parliament in 1651. Three years earlier, the house had been purged of moderate members opposed to the execution of the king. The Rump Parliament that remained set up the special court that condemned Charles I to death. It subsequently did away with the House of Lords and abolished the monarchy, proclaiming in its place a republican regime known as the Commonwealth.

Adamite　　*Libertin*

Seeker　　*Diuorcer*

the Parliamentarian leaders were making plans of their own. On September 25, 1643, little more than six weeks before his death from cancer, John Pym triumphantly concluded a crucial alliance with the king's Scottish opponents. The two parties accepted the Solemn League and Covenant: In return for a promise to bring the churches of England, Scotland, and Ireland "to the nearest conjunction and uniformity in religion," and a payment of £30,000 a month, the Scots agreed to send an army to England.

Events in eastern England were equally auspicious for the Parliamentary cause. The big, clever, melancholy member of Parliament for Cambridge, Oliver Cromwell, had been in the thick of the fighting at Edgehill and had seen how the Roundhead horsemen, whom he described as "old decayed serving men and tapsters," had fled in the face of Rupert's Cavaliers. Cromwell had returned determined to build the best regiments of cavalry in England from the ranks of the Nonconformist local yeomanry, men he described as being "of greater understanding than common soldiers." Furthermore, "I had rather," he wrote, "have a plain russet-coated captain that knows what he fights for and loves what he knows than what you call 'a gentleman' and is nothing else."

He dressed his recruits in red coats, and provided them with the best armor and weapons available. Believing passionately that everyone had the right to find his own way of God, he tolerated their differing and unorthodox Puritan faiths. But he also used their religious zeal as the basis of stern moral and military discipline. And he taught them the Swedish tactics that the Royalists had already learned.

At the end of June 1644, Cromwell and his new troopers joined forces with a combined army of Scots and Roundheads that had been forced to abandon a siege of York by a relief column under Prince Rupert. On July 2, the Puritan allies met Rupert and his army at Marston Moor, about seven miles west of the city. There were 27,000 Roundheads and Scots, and only 18,000 Cavaliers; but Rupert had received a letter from the king ordering him to fight, and he obeyed the order.

All day the armies faced each other, and in the evening, when Rupert had stood his men down and gone to the rear to have supper, Cromwell led his troopers in a charge against the cavalry on the Royalist right. After initial success, they fell back when Rupert joined in with his reserves, but the Cavaliers were then overwhelmed by the Scots cavalry that appeared on their flank. For the first time, Rupert's horsemen retreated; and as the Scots set out after them, Cromwell's disciplined soldiers turned back to rescue the hard-pressed Roundhead infantry.

By nightfall, a Parliamentary victory had been ensured. The Royalist cavalry's reputation for invincibility had been destroyed, and 4,000 of the king's soldiers lay dead on the battlefield. In the thick of the fighting, Cromwell himself had been wounded. Rupert, impressed by Cromwell's stubborn strength and courage, had referred to him as "Old Ironsides." It was an epithet that was soon to be applied to all Cromwell's cavalry.

Northern England was now at the mercy of the Parliamentarians. But the success was offset by disaster in the southwest, where the earl of Essex had been forced to surrender all his infantry at Lostwithiel after advancing too deep into Royalist Cornwall. It was time for the russet-coated captains to take over from the gentlemen.

At Cromwell's urging, the House of Commons agreed to reconstitute the Parliamentary army. Over the winter, the old, personally raised regiments were disbanded and the men were incorporated into new, highly disciplined units. Local conscription was imposed to increase their numbers. Overall command was given to Sir Thomas Fairfax, and command of the cavalry to Oliver Cromwell.

On June 14, 1645, the last great battle of the war took place at Naseby in Leicestershire. On one side, there were 7,000 Royalists commanded by the king himself. On the other, there were 11,000 soldiers of Parliament's New Model Army.

Once again, Rupert and his Cavaliers charged the horsemen on the Roundhead left and, though outnumbered, chased them from the field. But Cromwell was on the right. In their own charge, his new troopers broke the cavalry on the king's left; and since he had superior numbers, he was able to hold the rear ranks back from the pursuit and wheel them to attack the flank and rear of the Royalist infantry, most of whom surrendered. By the time that Rupert's men finally returned to the battlefield, the day was lost.

The Parliamentary victory at Naseby was not as bloody as at Marston Moor. Only 1,000 Cavaliers were killed, but more than 4,000 were captured, along with their cannon, 8,000 muskets, and all their ammunition. In addition, the righteous troopers of the New Model Army slaughtered 100 of the women they discovered in the king's camp and branded several hundred more women as prostitutes by slitting their noses or scarring their faces.

After Naseby, the New Model Army set about mopping up the remaining opposition and taking Royalist towns with bombardments and storming parties. Rupert, who had been sent to hold the vital west-coast port of Bristol, became convinced that the king's only hope was to come to terms with Parliament. By early September, he had barely 1,000 men left, and plague was spreading among the citizens. He agreed to surrender the city to Fairfax, who allowed the Cavaliers to keep their colors and march away as free men.

It was not long before King Charles as well was forced to accept that his cause was lost. In April of 1646, the last Royalist army in the field was defeated at Stow-on-the-Wold in Gloucestershire. Rather than give himself up to his Parliamentarian enemies, Charles chose to surrender to the Scots. Prince Rupert made a desperate attempt to dissuade him, but the king ignored him. On April 27, 1646, Charles left his nephew at Oxford and set out in disguise for the Scots camp at Newark. Eight weeks later, Oxford surrendered to Lord Fairfax, and once again, the commander of the New Model Army was chivalrous, allowing Rupert and his brother Maurice to leave England with their servants.

At Newark, the astonished Scots took King Charles as their prisoner. But Charles behaved as though he were a guest and negotiated haughtily with Parliament. In August, Parliament offered to restore him to his throne in return for the imposition of Presbyterianism in England, the punishment of his chief supporters, and the surrender of control of the army. When Charles refused, the Scots, who had approved the terms, handed him over in return for a down payment of half the £400,000 that Parliament still owed them. As the Scots marched northward to the border, the king, who had mocked them for selling him so cheap, was led away to become the prisoner of the Parliamentarians at Holmby House in Northamptonshire. The first phase of the fighting was over.

After the defeat at Stow-on-the-Wold, the vanquished Royalist commander, old Sir Jacob Astley, sat down on a drum among his captors and told them: "You have done your work, boys, and may go play, unless you will fall out among yourselves." The

A Dutch painting of 1660 commemorates a ball held at The Hague to celebrate the departure for England of Charles Stuart, son and heir of the executed Charles I, to be crowned as Charles II. After the death of Oliver Cromwell in 1658, army leaders and other influential figures came to see the restoration of the monarchy as the only way to avoid large-scale civil disorder. In the painting, the king is shown dancing with his sister Mary, princess of Orange. Two other future kings of England are also featured. Behind Charles, in a cloak, stands his brother James, duke of York, who was to succeed him as James II; and beyond the dancers, with the ladies of the Dutch court, stands Mary's nine-year-old son, Prince William of Orange, who later married James's daughter and, as King William III, ruled jointly with her in her father's place.

words proved prophetic, for the Parliamentarian forces soon found themselves bitterly divided. The members of the Long Parliament regarded themselves as arbiters of the new society that was to emerge with the ending of the war. But in creating the New Model Army, they had established a fresh power in the land, and one whose views were markedly different from their own. The officers of the New Model Army were more radical in their religion and their politics; many of them were zealous followers of a variety of independent Nonconformist sects, as were some of the ordinary soldiers.

In September 1646, without pausing to consider the consequences, the pro-Presbyterian majority in Parliament introduced bills ruling that proponents of certain sects—including the Unitarians, who denied the doctrine of the Trinity—could be put to death; less heretical Nonconformists, such as Baptists, who merely advocated adult baptism, could be imprisoned for life. And in December, they ruled that no layman should be allowed to preach. The army leaders protested vehemently, but Parliament continued blindly along the road to self-destruction. Eight months later, as a prelude to the sectarian persecutions promised by its ordinances, Parliament ordered the soldiers of the New Model Army to disband or else volunteer for service against the Catholic rebels in Ireland. The troops, already close to mutiny because their pay was badly in arrears, refused to do either and defiantly withdrew to their headquarters at Newmarket, east of Cambridge. As the local member of Parliament, Oliver Cromwell rode over to negotiate a compromise, but once he realized that the men were adamant, he remained among them and took their side.

A few days later, on his own initiative, a young officer called George Joyce led 500 troopers to Holmby House, arrested the king and brought him back to Newmarket as a prisoner of the army. When the king asked to see his commission, Joyce simply

THE CHRONICLER OF LONDON LIFE

The brilliant son of a London tailor, Samuel Pepys rose to become an important public figure. He was a member of Parliament and president of the Royal Society, which promoted the sciences. As Secretary of the Admiralty, he restored England's sea power, doubling the strength of the navy and enabling it to compete on equal terms with the fleets of France and the Netherlands. Yet he came to be remembered most for his intimate diary, which provides a vivid, detailed, and revealing portrait of social life in London during the 1660s.

Writing in shorthand for privacy, Pepys candidly admitted his own weaknesses and gave enthusiastic accounts of his dinners, his visits to theaters and concerts, and his many sexual adventures. But he also found room to discuss affairs of state, commenting on corruption among public servants and describing the two dramatic disasters visited on London during the decade: the Great Plague and the Great Fire.

The pestilence—bubonic plague, which caused soft black swellings on its victims—killed almost 80,000 people in 1665. The fire devastated the city in the following year, raging unchecked until Charles II gave orders for all buildings in its path to be blown up. In all, some 13,000 houses and 87 churches were consumed. But the disaster provided a unique opportunity for one of Pepys's many friends, the architect Christopher Wren, who supervised the rebuilding of the city and enriched it with 53 churches and a splendid new cathedral.

Dressed in an Indian robe hired specially for the occasion, the diarist Samuel Pepys sits for a portrait holding the manuscript of his favorite song, "Beauty Retire," with words by the poet Sir William Davenant and music by Pepys. The painting dates from 1666, when Pepys was thirty-three. On seeing it, he confided to his diary, "I am very well satisfied."

98

Lay long, being bitter, cold, frosty day, the frost being now grown old, and the Thames covered with ice.
—January 1, 1666

With its flow impeded by the thick arches of old bridges, the Thames froze in harsh winters, and citizens held Frost Fairs on the ice, as shown in this late-seventeenth-century painting. But the "bitter cold" of the 1665-1666 winter also helped to kill off the Great Plague, which had been spread by fleas on rats during an unusually long, hot summer.

*It being darkish we saw the fire
as only one entire arch of fire
from this to the other side of the
bridge, and in a bow up the hill,
for an arch of above a mile long.
It made me weep to see it. The
churches, houses, and all on fire
and flaming at once, and a horrid
noise the flames made, and the
cracking of houses at their ruin.*
—September 2, 1666

The Great Fire of London,
depicted here at its height
by a Dutch artist who was
almost certainly an eye-
witness, began in a baker's
shop near the Thames Riv-
er and raged for three
days through almost 400
acres of timber-framed
houses, leaving 200,000
people homeless.

*The people die so, that now
it seems they are fain to carry
the dead to be buried by day-
light, the nights not sufficing to
do it in. And my Lord Mayor
commands people to be within at
9 at night, all (as they say) that
the sick may have liberty to go
abroad for ayre.*
—August 12, 1665

Hand bells such as this
one were rung as a warn-
ing of their approach by
the drivers of the "dead-
carts" that carried the
contagious corpses of
plague victims. The bodies
were buried in quicklime
in huge "plague pits" by
ceaseless shifts of often
drunken gravediggers.

pointed to the men behind him. "Indeed," said His Majesty, "It is one I can read without spelling."

Cromwell and some of the other officers made an offer to restore the king to his throne in return for religious toleration and parliamentary control of the appointment of officers of state. It was the best offer that any of his opponents had ever proposed to him, but Charles refused it, now believing that he would be able to play his enemies off against one another.

For a time, it looked as though he might be right. The army bolstered its position by marching on London in order to protect its own interests, but its own members were divided in their aspirations. In the autumn, an elected army council met at Putney to determine the next move. Some spokesmen still hoped to reach a constitutional agreement with the king. Others, particularly from the rank and file, wanted to abolish the monarchy and the House of Lords and to establish a democracy with votes for all men. And while they debated, the king slipped away to the Isle of Wight and started secret negotiations with the Scots.

Suddenly the weary country found itself at war again. By promising to accept Presbyterianism for three years and to allow parliamentary control of the army for ten, the king managed to forge a strange alliance between forces that had been fighting one another little more than a year earlier. As the Scots army crossed the border in the north, Royalists rose in rebellion in Wales and in the south and west of England, and English Presbyterians who had previously fought against the king rallied in response to his promises. Half the navy mutinied in his favor.

The only force that stood against them all was the New Model Army, but it proved more than a match for them. Fairfax routed the Royalists in the south and west. Cromwell suppressed the Welsh and then marched north to defeat the Scots in a running battle at Preston, Wigan, and Warrington. When the soldiers returned to London, they were eager for vengeance against the king, who had in their view deceitfully played at negotiating with the army while secretly planning to renew the war. Their leaders also came increasingly to support this point of view.

Angry voices now urged that the king be killed. Yet such a drastic move could not be considered without the support of Parliament; and the great majority of its members, by now more frightened of the radical elements in the army than of the poor remnants of royal power, would not contemplate such a deed. The impasse was finally resolved by force. On December 6, 1648, Colonel Thomas Pride, at the head of a company of musketeers, secluded or arrested ninety-six members of the House of Commons. Pride's Purge, as the coup became known, left a rump of about sixty Nonconformist Parliamentarians who were prepared to support the army line.

The Rump Parliament did exactly what the army desired it to do. It set up a specially appointed high court of justice that brought the king to London and tried him for treason in Westminster Hall. King Charles was found guilty and sentenced to death. The less-politicized elements of the nation outside the army, who still tended to see the king as God's anointed sent to rule his people, reacted with stunned disbelief. Indeed, there were few people in England outside the ranks of the army who did not regard the sentence as a crime. But there was no one who could prevent its being carried out.

On January 30, 1649, the king stepped through a window onto a scaffold set up outside the beautiful Banqueting House, which Inigo Jones had designed for his father at the royal palace of Whitehall. For all his faults, Charles had never been anything but brave. Since it was a cold day, he wore two shirts so that there would be no shivers that the crowd could mistake for fear. He knelt in prayer, laid his head on the block, and stretched out a hand as a signal that he was ready. The ax fell, cutting through the king's neck with a single blow, and the huge crowd groaned as his head was held up to them.

The widespread revulsion at the execution of the king gave momentum to the last phase of the fighting. The Irish Catholic Royalists, who were still undefeated, transferred their allegiance to the king's nineteen-year-old heir, Prince Charles. And the Scots agreed to provide young Charles with an army in return for the promise of a Presbyterian England. But the New Model Army was now at the height of its power, and in the last campaigns, Cromwell led it.

After returning from Ireland, where he broke the resistance with ruthless and unforgettable brutality, he marched north to defeat the Scots at the Battle of Dunbar. When Prince Charles invaded England at the head of a second Scots army, collecting Royalist reinforcements as he advanced, Cromwell annihilated them at the Battle of Worcester. For six weeks after the battle, the young prince evaded Cromwell's troopers, hiding in an oak tree, disguising himself as a woodcutter, and passing through their ranks dressed as a lady's maid, until he found a boat at Brighton on the south coast and sailed away to France and safety at last.

The Battle of Worcester on August 24, 1651, secured the rule of the new government within the boundaries of Great Britain, and by the middle of the following year, it was secure beyond the seas as well. A squadron of Royalist ships, commanded by Prince Rupert, had been driven into the Mediterranean; and the Royalist colonies of Barbados, Virginia, and Maryland had submitted. In the years that followed, the commercial interests in Parliament led England into a fierce naval war with the Dutch, whose merchant ships were carrying much of the trade between England and the colonies in Asia, Africa, and America. They passed the Navigation Acts, which ruled that all such trade must be carried in ships built and manned by Englishmen; and in enforcing these acts, English warships asserted their control over the Channel and proved a match for what was then the most powerful and professional navy in the world. As a result, England's reputation rose in Europe to a level unknown since the days of the Tudors.

At home, it was a very different story. The triumph of the New Model Army was not the triumph of democracy. After the execution of the king, the House of Lords was abolished and England was declared a commonwealth. But antagonism grew between the Rump Parliament and the army, which disliked the many lawyers among Parliament's members, criticized the Dutch war, and wanted radical religious and constitutional reforms. On April 20, 1653, Cromwell forcibly dissolved Parliament and locked the doors of its debating chamber. Soon afterward, a new parliament purged of all those opposed to Cromwell declared him lord protector, and it was not long before he was ruling England as little less than a military dictator. It was not a position that Cromwell had wanted; and when his supporters offered to make him king, he refused. Yet, as he said himself, "No man climbs so high as he who does not know where he is going."

By the time Cromwell died in 1658, the English had had their fill of Puritan austerity. The old animosities rose again, and on a new tide of royalism, the throne was offered to Prince Charles—on no conditions other than a general amnesty,

This glazed earthenware bust of King William III was made at Delft in the Netherlands, where William had served as stadholder—military commander—for sixteen years before his accession to the English throne. Invited to England by Protestants discontented with the rule of the Catholic James II, William took power after a bloodless coup that ended in James's flight to France. He was to rule jointly with his wife, Mary—daughter of the deposed monarch—until her death in 1694, and then on his own for another eight years. For William, the price of the throne was acceptance of the Bill of Rights, a document that limited royal power and upheld the role of Parliament in the government of the land.

religious toleration, and payment of the army's arrears. On May 29, 1660, King Charles II entered London to a delirious welcome from its citizens. Prince Rupert soon returned as well; he spent the rest of his life in England, becoming a vice admiral and the first governor of the Hudson's Bay Company in North America.

Under the rule of Charles II, the cultural life of the kingdom found new energy to fill the void that had been left by the Puritans. The theater was revived. The architects who had traveled with the king in Europe began to build fine new classical houses. And guided by the advice of his first minister, Lord Clarendon, the king maintained a statesmanlike, if not always cordial, relationship with Parliament.

But the restoration of Charles II was not to be the end of the conflict between king and Parliament. Although Charles had many children, he left no legitimate heir, and he was succeeded by his brother James, who had become a Roman Catholic. James II promoted fellow Catholics to high office in the state and the army; when his subjects protested, he simply emulated his father and invoked the royal prerogative. Within a couple of years, members of Parliament were again plotting to overthrow their king. In secret negotiations, they offered the throne jointly to James's daughter Mary and her Dutch husband, Prince William of Orange.

On November 5, 1688, at the start of what became known as the Glorious Revolution, William landed in England, and James, knowing that he was without support, fled across the Channel to France. Six months later, William and Mary were jointly crowned. But the English Parliament set terms for its support. The price of their accession was the Bill of Rights, which barred Catholics from the throne, abolished the royal power to suspend laws and levy money by "pretence of prerogative," made standing armies illegal in time of peace, and insisted that there should be frequent parliaments and free elections.

The restoration of Charles II had simply reestablished the balance of power between the monarchy and Parliament. With the Bill of Rights, the Glorious Revolution tipped the scales in favor of Parliament. The struggle and the excesses were over. A constitutional monarchy had been created. At last, the basic liberties that English men and women had crossed the Atlantic to establish in a new world had been planted just as firmly in the blood-stained soil of the kingdom that they left behind.

hroughout Europe, the seventeenth century saw government concentrated in the hands of rulers with almost despotic power. This centralizing tendency found theoretical expression in the doctrine of absolutism—the belief that sovereignty was vested exclusively in a nation-state's ruler, who was under no obligation to share his authority with any person or body.

Although he was subject to no agency of the state, the new style of monarch appeared in the political thought of the time as a defender of individual rights and liberties. Theorists argued that the unconditional power of a king, exercised from a central seat of government, was an advance upon the warring influences of regional nobles and magistrates. Centralized rule brought greater efficiency and control, and when these in turn led to economic as well as military successes, they provided apparent justification for the system.

So it was in seventeenth-century France, where absolutism reached its most developed form. The nation's young king, Louis XIV, became for all Europe the apotheosis of the absolute monarch. He came to the throne in 1643 at the age of four, but it was not until the death of his powerful adviser Mazarin in 1661 that he established the personal control over every aspect of government that became central to his view of kingship. During his long reign—Louis died in 1715—he embodied an entire era of political development. He believed that "the profession of king is great, noble, a fount of

delight. It is through and for work that one reigns." His advice to a new king was, "God who made you king will give you the necessary guidance."

In 1662, Louis adopted the sun (above) as his personal symbol, citing "the unique quality of the radiance . . . the light it imparts to other stars . . . the good it does in every place." By then he had already made the decision to build a palace that would be a worthy setting for his conception of royal majesty. The court he created at Versailles was to be France's seat of government for more than a century; in its halls and gardens, a tableau of kingly power was played out day by day, as though on a stage.

AT THE COURT OF THE SUN KING

Louis XIV's palace at Versailles, twelve miles southwest of Paris, had its origins in a hunting lodge that the king's father began building in 1624. Successive stages of enlargement and remodeling over sixty years transformed the complex from a country retreat for the pleasure-loving young king and his circle into the administrative center of the realm and a symbolic monument to Europe's supreme monarch.

The scale of the building was huge—in the 1680s, it was reported that 36,000 bricklayers were at work daily—and the cost, though never precisely divulged, was astronomical. By the mid-1670s, the king was spending long periods at Versailles, accompanied by courtiers and some government ministers, and in 1682, the court with all its staff and functions was transferred from Paris.

Grandeur, rather than comfort, was the guiding principle. The palace, explicitly conceived as a formal setting for the art of kingship, abounded with allegorical statuary and symbolic references, but there were many complaints about the bad air, the cramped living quarters, and the vast grounds that were muddy in winter and scorching in summer.

Beneath the extravagant show lay political expediency. The removal of the court from Paris underlined the king's superiority to external influences. The courtiers who vied for a place at his side and beggared themselves to keep up with court life were constantly under Louis's eye, and they had neither the time nor the money to challenge his position.

Versailles also served as an international showcase that other monarchs came to marvel at and went home to imitate. Its glass, tapestries, marble, and lace, all produced locally, firmly established France as the arbiter of European taste.

Clad in coronation robes,
Louis XIV gazes from a
Hyacinthe Rigaud portrait.
The king's grace was noted
even by unsympathetic
observers; he was an accomplished dancer whose
"least gesture, his walk,
his bearing," was, in the
Duc de Saint-Simon's
words, "seemly, noble . . .
and withal very natural."

A long column of outriders
stream into Versailles's
circular forecourt as the
king and queen arrive at
the palace in separate
coaches. Painted by Pierre
Patel, the scene shows the
buildings in 1668 when
the original hunting
lodge—the central block
between the projecting
wings—was still clearly
discernible among the
grandiose additions.

Louise de La Vallière

Mme. de Maintenon

Mme. de Montespan

The first of Louis's three official mistresses was an officer's daughter, Louise de La Vallière, who shared the king's equestrian skill. She was succeeded by the intelligent and ambitious Mme. de Montespan, who kept the court lively and witty. The forty-eight-year-old Mme. de Maintenon became his morganatic wife after Marie-Thérèse died in 1683.

An allegorical painting by Jean Nocret represents Louis as the Greek god Apollo, surrounded by members of his family as fellow divinities. Portrayed as the earth mother Cybele, the king's mother, Anne of Austria, is shown seated at center even though she had died in 1666, three years before the painting was completed. To her right, the king's brother Monsieur and his wife are shown as Pluto and Flora. Queen Marie-Thérèse, sitting at the king's left hand, represents Juno, queen of the gods,

The world Louis created at Versailles was peopled with courtiers, civil servants, government officials, chamberlains, cooks, huntsmen, maids, governesses—all the inhabitants of a small city. After 1682, there were said to be 10,000 residents of the palace, with perhaps 50,000 other attendants and servants accommodated in the vicinity.

But the main players to whom all eyes turned were the king and his circle. The court, ruled by Louis's favor and patronage, was full of intrigue; even the king's own family jockeyed for position. Louis's brother, known as "Monsieur," was one of the most important members of the inner circle. Monsieur's wife, "Madame," and Louis's cousin, "Mademoiselle," also ranked high in the order of precedence. Louis's queen was his cousin Marie-Thérèse, by whom he had six children, only one of whom—the Dauphin—lived to adulthood. In addition, other women favored by Louis were accorded honor as the king's official mistresses. Two of his three principal favorites (*opposite*) bore him other children who were ennobled to become important members of the court and were eventually legitimized.

In spite of the exclusivity and privilege of the court, it was easy for the public to witness the spectacle provided by the king's daily life. It was a fashionable outing for Parisians to drive to Versailles to see the royal party dine on interminable courses that had been carried from the kitchens about half a mile away.

In the early days of Versailles, the newly enlarged palace was the scene of fetes of fantastic extravagance; but after the court had migrated to the palace and Louis had entered middle age, the round of pleasure and diversion that courtiers fought so hard to enter took on a clockwork regularity. Saint-Simon remarked that given a timepiece and an almanac, it would be possible to work out exactly what Louis was doing at any moment of the day.

The life of the court and all its attendants revolved around the king and his timetable. Louis was a man of great vigor who devoted eight or nine hours a day to matters of state, regularly rode and hunted, ate with phenomenal appetite—and exacted similar efforts from all his courtiers. His sister-in-law Elizabeth-Charlotte sent a friend a description of a typical day at court: "We hunted all morning, got back about 3 o'clock in the afternoon, changed, went up to gamble until 7 o'clock, then to the play, which never ended before 10:30, then on to supper and afterward to the ball until 3 o'clock in the morning . . . So you see how much time I had for writing."

The cardplayers in this 1695 engraving include Louis's daughter—the duchess of Bourbon—and his mistress Mme. de Montespan with her husband (seated on the left). At evening receptions, held every Monday, Wednesday, and Friday in the suite called the Grand Appartement, high-stakes gambling was de rigueur.

Playing an early form of billiards, Louis XIV, resplendent in a plumed hat, lines up a shot. The players include his brother Monsieur *(far left)* and other court grandees.

In a painting by Claude Guy Hallé, Louis welcomes the doge of Genoa in Versailles's Hall of Mirrors on a state visit made in 1685.

in old age, Louis remained the focus of courtiers' attention, as this painting by Pierre Denis Martin indicates. Behind him rise all the grand effects of the Versailles landscape, including the fountains of the Basin of Apollo—the pivotal point of the perspectives laid out by the architect André Le Nôtre.

A late-seventeenth-century painting shows a jostling crowd of richly dressed courtiers—men, women, and children—surrounding the young Louis as he rides past the Grotto of Thetis, a folly in the grounds of Versailles. Louis's love of hunting and the open air lasted all his life—even in his later days when growing piety led him to replace the grotto with a chapel.

THE RISE OF THE DUTCH REPUBLIC

On the face of it, there was nothing remarkable in the sight of four heavily laden cargo ships moving through the Zuider Zee and into the teeming port of Amsterdam. The city, in that year of 1599, drew its wealth and sustenance, as it had for generations, from seaborne trade. The tall brick warehouses lining the network of canals were crammed with all the goods of Europe: grain and fish, woolens and wine. The harbor was always full of traffic—a dense, floating forest of masts and rigging.

But on that July day when these vessels came home, Amsterdam celebrated with a fervor more commonly reserved for victory in war. Church bells pealed a message of triumph and thanksgiving that echoed even in the marshes beyond the town. Welcomed with pomp and ceremony, the ships' commanders and their commercial backers were regaled with a lavish banquet. Meanwhile, the junior crew members prepared to spend their wages in the town's notorious taverns and brothels.

As the city fathers rehearsed their laudatory speeches, the lightermen at the docks began to unload the precious cargo, releasing its pungency into the already-aromatic harbor air. The sacks emerging from the ships' bellies bulged with cloves and nutmegs from the East Indies, the fabled islands of spices on the far side of the world. The small, dark pellets might as well have been rubies: Counting-house clerks calculated that the expedition's backers would reap a 400 percent profit on their investment in the returning vessels, and four sister ships still awaited. "As long as Holland has been Holland," marveled one chronicler, "such richly laden ships have never been seen."

But the safe return of the Far Lands Company fleet was much more than a fat harvest for a few investors. For a community that lived by trade, this first successful foray to the distant East Indies was a turning point: a promise of untold riches, and a mark of heaven's favor. Such a sign of hope could not have come at a better time to a country engaged in a prolonged and bitter struggle for survival.

The Dutch were still becoming a nation. The merchants and mariners of Amsterdam, the peat cutters, cheesemakers, and farmers of the hinterland, the North Sea fishers, and the bargemen on the Rhine lived within a loose confederation of towns and provinces that had been joined for someone else's political convenience. Calvinists and dissenting Protestants rubbed shoulders with Catholics and people of little or no religious affiliation in a society of some 1.5 million souls. If they were united now, it was because they were fighting for their freedom against a common foe.

Early in the sixteenth century, the shifting fortunes and strategic marriages of Europe's ruling dynasties had brought the Netherlands—seventeen low-lying, French- or Dutch-speaking provinces on the shores of the North Sea—under Spanish domination. By the latter part of the century, the provinces had built up a stock of rankling resentments: Religious persecution and economic exploitation under the rule of inept or tyrannical governors had led to a series of bloody revolts. Unilaterally,

In a mid-seventeenth-century portrait by Pieter de Hooch, a soberly clad Dutch family exudes calm prosperity from the security of its well-swept courtyard in the city of Delft. Middle-class merchants were the backbone of the Dutch republic, which after winning independence from the Hapsburg rulers of Spain in the early years of the seventeenth century, rapidly became the world's most dynamic trading nation.

113

the Dutch-speaking people of the northern Netherlands declared their independence, committing themselves to a war that would not end until 1648.

Meanwhile, the Dutch contended with an enemy more intractable than Spain: topography. The country lay at sea level—or below it—and its inhabitants battled constantly to restrain the menacing waters of the North Sea.

A land too waterlogged to feed its population; a people without a common history, professing different—and hostile—forms of Christianity; a war of independence lasting for generations: together, they did not herald a good beginning. But, within a few decades, both the sea and the Spanish would be beaten, and the Dutch would rise with astonishing speed to become Europe's most important commercial power. Their wealth would excite the envy of the world; their domination of European and overseas trade would anger their neighbors. And they would achieve this without a prince to rule them. In an age of autocratic, empire-building monarchies, it was an anomoly: an autonomous republic, with more sovereignty lodged in its constituent towns and provinces than in any centralized organs of state.

In 1548, Charles V, ruler of Austria, Spain, Burgundy, and a multitude of smaller territories scattered across Europe, had made the seventeen provinces into a single administrative unit within his Hapsburg empire. Under Charles, the provinces had considerable autonomy. The towns, such as Amsterdam and the larger port city of

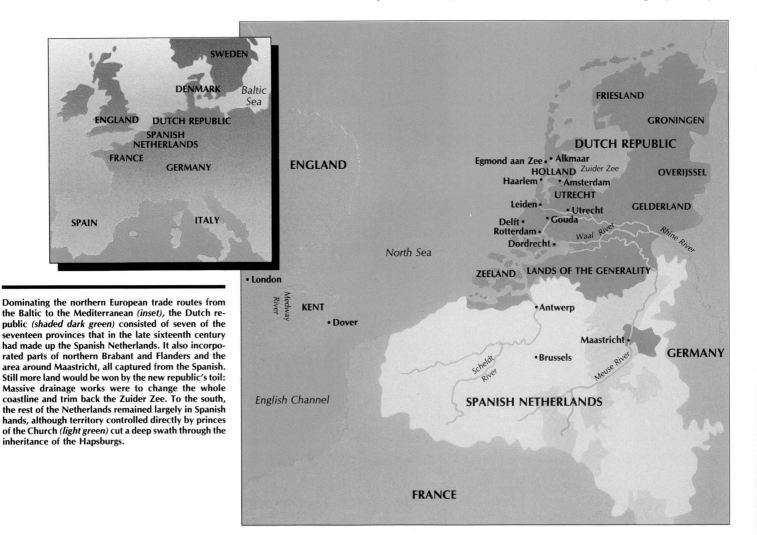

Dominating the northern European trade routes from the Baltic to the Mediterranean *(inset)*, the Dutch republic *(shaded dark green)* consisted of seven of the seventeen provinces that in the late sixteenth century had made up the Spanish Netherlands. It also incorporated parts of northern Brabant and Flanders and the area around Maastricht, all captured from the Spanish. Still more land would be won by the new republic's toil: Massive drainage works were to change the whole coastline and trim back the Zuider Zee. To the south, the rest of the Netherlands remained largely in Spanish hands, although territory controlled directly by princes of the Church *(light green)* cut a deep swath through the inheritance of the Hapsburgs.

Antwerp in the south, were controlled by wealthy mercantile families jealous of their municipal rights and privileges. In some rural districts, the local nobility dominated public life. But each of the seventeen provinces had its own chamber of representatives—the States; these bodies, in turn, sent deputies to a central forum, the States-General in Brussels, which the Hapsburgs had made their northern capital.

In 1556, Charles abdicated from power, and in the ensuing division of his domain, the Netherlands fell to his son Philip II, the king of Spain. Philip tried to impose his will upon his distant provinces without worrying unduly if his actions violated their traditional liberties. He sought to control their domestic policies, intervened in the appointment of their bishops, and reorganized the Catholic Inquisition set up by Charles V to persecute the Calvinist Protestants, whose heretical beliefs were gaining ground throughout the north. Still worse, he imposed new and burdensome taxes in an effort to replenish an exchequer drained by foreign wars.

Roused in equal part by matters of God and mammon, the Netherlands rebelled, and the battle for Dutch independence began. At their head, the rebels boasted a leader of outstanding ability. William the Silent, prince of Orange, was a Protestant nobleman with large estates in Germany, as well as the principality of Orange in southern France, and extensive estates in various parts of the Low Countries. Against all odds, he forged an alliance among divergent, often mutually hostile groups, winning the support of rural nobles, urban patricians, middle-class merchants, and the populace at large. His support was strongest in the north, where Calvinism had made the greatest gains. In 1579, under his leadership, the seven northern provinces solemnly bound themselves together in the Union of Utrecht. Two years later, these united provinces unilaterally declared their independence from Spain.

A stalemate ensued. Philip's shaky finances were depleted by the war effort. With his ill-paid and ill-fed army in a state of near-constant mutiny, he never succeeded in stamping out the rebel forces—although his agents eventually managed to assassinate Prince William in 1584. Meanwhile, the Orangeists made a little headway against Spain, but they lacked the financial and military aid from Europe's other Protestant countries needed to consolidate their gains.

Soon after William's death, however, Elizabeth of England, fearful that Spain might regain control across the Channel, decided that the time had come for active intervention on the rebels' behalf. The Dutch now had at least one powerful ally.

In 1588, the Spanish Armada, sweeping up the Channel to invade England, was destroyed by the joint efforts of the English, the Dutch, and the weather. Neither Spain's exchequer, nor its self-esteem, recovered from the blow. Philip directed his attentions elsewhere, to battles over the succession to the French throne. By 1598, he was dead, and the Spanish were driven out of their last strongholds in the northern Netherlands. Devastating plagues and famines in Spain made it impossible for Philip's heir to sustain anything more than a defensive war from his remaining fastnesses in the southern provinces. Even so, it was not until 1609 that Spain proved willing to sign a truce. Twelve years later, hostilities were renewed. Spain finally gave formal recognition to the independence of the seven northern provinces in 1648 by the Treaty of Westphalia. (The southern provinces, geographically approximate to modern Belgium, were to remain in Hapsburg hands as the Spanish—later the Austrian—Netherlands until 1794.)

Though not blessed by Spanish recognition, the United Provinces functioned as an independent political entity almost from the time of the Union of Utrecht in 1579.

WINNING FARMLAND FROM THE SEA

God created the world," went the saying, "but the Dutchman created Holland." Since the fifteenth century, the needs of a growing population had been met by a drainage system that won land from the sea for farming. The reclaimed acres, called polders, provided grazing and cropland, as the 1590 painting below shows.

By the seventeenth century, the Dutch had become the world's greatest hydraulic engineers, using windmills *(inset)* to reclaim up to 4,500 acres annually. For drainage, an expanse of shallow water was enclosed by a dike, and a ring canal was built around it. Then the mills pumped the water up to the canal, from which it ran off into the sea. A stepped array of mills, each passing its output to the next, could drain a sheet of water fifteen feet deep.

But the sea could always return. Despite careful maintenance, the web of dikes sometimes failed, and the engineers' steady progress was punctuated by occasional disastrous floods.

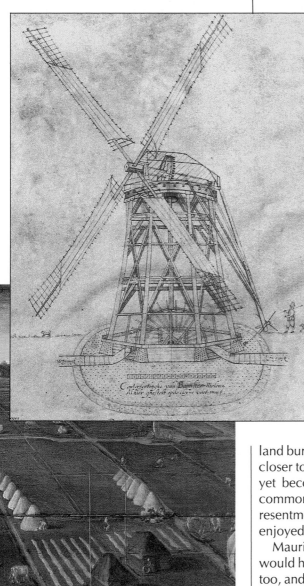

The fledgling state was a republic, with no single apex of power. By the terms of the union, each province governed its internal affairs through the provincial States, while continuing to send delegates—as they had done under Spain—to a central States-General to debate matters concerning the union's collective interests. Within this assembly, the patricians and burghers of Holland—the richest and most populous province—generally spoke with the strongest voice.

The provinces appointed a military leader, the stadholder, inevitably a member of the princely house of Orange or its allied family of Nassau. The post had been established during the early years of revolt, when William of Orange held the office. The stadholder's noble birth ensured him the military training and knightly prestige required for the job, but his lineage conferred no superior status. Sovereignty remained firmly in the hands of the provincial States.

Cooperation between the civil power and the stadholderate was vital, if not always easily achieved. After the death of William of Orange, his son Maurice of Nassau was named stadholder for Holland and Zeeland. His civil counterpart was Johan van Oldenbarnevelt, chief advocate of Holland in the States-General and, by extension, the leading minister of the republic. Their initial collaboration, in the last years of active combat against Spain and the early days of independence, was fruitful: Maurice's military skills kept the Spanish at bay, while Oldenbarnevelt, a consummate politician, forged the policies that placed the union on a firm foundation and negotiated with friendly foreign governments.

But tensions between the two leaders were never far from the surface. Oldenbarnevelt represented the oligarchy of wealthy Holland burghers, who saw no need for any higher sovereign power; Prince Maurice was closer to the Dutch nobility, some of whom may have hoped that the new state might yet become a monarchy under an Orange ruler. Yet he was also a hero to the common people, whose own royalist inclinations—if any—were rooted in their resentment of the patricians who ran the towns, controlled the magistrates, and enjoyed the lion's share of the wealth.

Maurice had not been in favor of the 1609 truce with Spain; his own preference would have been to fight until the enemy was hounded out of the southern provinces, too, and the whole of the Netherlands was free. In this, he had the support of the most zealously orthodox Calvinist clergymen, who now saw the conflict as a holy war against a papist foe. But Oldenbarnevelt, reflecting the pragmatic inclinations of his own constituency, supported the truce. It was time, he thought, to resume the business of amassing wealth through trade.

It was religion that proved Oldenbarnevelt's undoing. With the struggle for survival against Rome won, internal schisms threatened the young Reformed church. Two separate tendencies were at war within Dutch Calvinism, divided over, among other issues, the question of whether an individual's sins could keep him or her out of heaven. According to strict Calvinist doctrine, the precise number and names of God's elect had been set down for all time at the world's beginning, so personal morality could make no difference.

Oldenbarnevelt's faction, the Arminians, represented a more liberal school, which placed a higher value on individual thought and action. They favored a policy of greater religious tolerance, arguing against those zealots who would have liked to see papists, Jews, and members of dissident Protestant sects purged from the land. Their credo was: "In essentials unity, in doubtful matters liberty, in all things charity," a doctrine despised by extreme Calvinists, certain of their own monopoly on truth.

Matters came to a head in 1618. One winter's morning, five life-size snowmen representing Oldenbarnevelt and four leading fellow liberals appeared on a street in The Hague. Gangs of urchins began pelting them with stones and snowballs, chanting biblically, "An Arminian is a plague on the land; his house is a nest of salamanders! Arminians to the gallows!" Soon after, riots erupted in many towns. Oldenbarnevelt, on behalf of the States of Holland, passed an order allowing communities within the province to muster special militias to restore order. The States-General, dominated by anti-Arminians and under the sway of Maurice, ordered all the troops thus raised to be disbanded. Oldenbarnevelt himself was accused of flouting the expressed will of the States-General, taken prisoner, and following a rigged trial, beheaded as a traitor. Other prominent Arminians, including some of Holland's leading scholars and teachers, were purged, jailed, or exiled.

But Oldenbarnevelt's execution proved to be only a temporary setback for the advocates of religious tolerance. Without a strong, centralized state capable of enforcing censorship, there was neither the collective will nor the political machinery to curb the circulation of dissident ideas. Each municipality had its own, more or less liberal, regulations on freedom of the press; what the printers in one town feared to touch, their colleagues in the next province would often happily publish.

The liberty that the Dutch enjoyed from legislated religious orthodoxy was a rare luxury in Europe at that time. In other countries, to belong to a church that was not the state church was to suffer some loss of civil rights, if not outright persecution. Thanks to its religious tolerance, the Dutch republic possessed a climate of intellectual freedom unequaled anywhere in Europe. Attracted by its open atmosphere, the French philosopher René Descartes spent thirty years in Holland, producing his great work, *The Discourse on Method,* and other major texts. Others came in search of a haven. The political thinker John Locke, forced out of England for his "dangerous" ideas, passed his time of exile in Holland; and the philosopher Baruch Spinoza, excommunicated by his Jewish brethren for denying that the Bible was God's word, praised Amsterdam for its tolerance: "In this flourishing state, this city without a peer, men of every race and sect live in the greatest harmony."

The energies the Dutch saved from strife and bigotry they expended on the pursuit of wealth. The most prosperous areas of the young republic were the three westward-facing coastal provinces, where the inhabitants lived by fishing and maritime trade. Holland, by far the richest and most populous, embraced most of the great towns: Amsterdam, Rotterdam, Delft, Gouda, Leiden, and Haarlem all lay within a compass of thirty miles. Friesland, to its north, handled a substantial slice of the flourishing Baltic trade and a still higher proportion of the Norwegian timber business. To the south was Zeeland, a flat expanse of marshes and islands lying in the waters where the well-trafficked trade routes from Europe's heart—the Rhine, Meuse, and Scheldt rivers—flowed into the North Sea.

For the Hollanders and Zeelanders, the sea was, in equal measure, enemy and friend. For centuries, they had built dikes and other defenses to hold back its waters.

The Dutch had of necessity become experts in the technologies of drainage, canal building, and land reclamation; between 1590 and 1640, their efforts won them almost 200,000 new acres of agricultural land.

Even when the rich alluvial soil of this recovered ground brought forth crops, the Dutch were not self-sufficient in food. They had long ago learned that what their land could not provide must be brought in by sea. Large quantities of grain were imported from the Baltic countries, and every year, from June to December, the boats set out from Holland and Zeeland on an enterprise known as the great fishery, to sweep up the shoals of herring moving down from the Baltic and into the North Sea.

The Dutch fleet operated with prodigious efficiency. Their specially designed vessels, the herring buses, were commodious enough to house the crew throughout the six months of the season, and large enough to carry out the salting and packing of the fish on board. Instead of wasting precious time by returning to harbor, the buses relied on a fleet of smaller service boats shuttling between the ports and the fishing grounds, bringing out fresh provisions and taking away the barreled catches. At home, the industry was backed up by a vast network of other trades: shipwrights, chandlers, rope and sail makers, coopers, packers, warehousers, and brokers.

The business brought in foreign earnings too, for the oil-rich herring, salted to preserve it, was a prized source of protein all over Europe—not least in the Catholic countries with their many fast days on which meat-eating was banned. The fish became almost a form of currency. The barrels of herring sent to France and Germany bought luxury goods, and those sent to the Baltic lands came back as grain.

The buses formed only part of a fleet that was the envy of seamen elsewhere in Europe. The shipwrights of the Netherlands also devised the finest cargo vessels of the age: the capacious *fluyten*, which were cheap to build—in the shipyards, efficient mass-production techniques and the use of cranes as well as wind-powered sawmills kept labor costs down—and inexpensive to run. Equipped with simple rigging and fitted with winches and tackles for loading cargo, they needed fewer crewmen than other craft: Ten sailors on a fluyt did the work of thirty on an English vessel of the same size. Low wage costs and cheap provisioning meant that Dutch shipowners were able to undercut competitors' freight charges by as much as 50 percent. It made better financial sense for foreign merchants to buy or charter Dutch ships than to use their own.

The fountainhead of Dutch mercantilism was Amsterdam. The city had always been in the forefront of the Baltic trade, but its spectacular growth at the start of the seventeenth century came, in effect, from the spoils of war. Its major competitor, the southern port of Antwerp, suffered badly during the revolt, losing much of its trade to its northern rival. At the same time, Amsterdam benefited from the hordes of southern refugees who migrated into the northern towns. Some were Calvinists, drawn north on religious grounds; others saw a chance to improve their fortunes in a land that had freed itself from Spain. They came from all levels of society, bringing commercial acumen, capital, energy, intelligence, and a host of marketable talents.

Amsterdam, as befitted its new importance, became the processing center for the most valuable raw material of all: money. In 1609, the year of the truce with Spain, the city's financiers established an exchange bank to help Dutch merchants do business with one another. That year also saw the completion of the Bourse, whose handsome colonnades and stone-built cloisters sheltered the representatives of every financial interest group. In the shadow of one particular column, the Baltic grain merchants gathered; near another, investors in the young East India trade exchanged news of the latest voyages. It was a frenetic marketplace, raucous with the sounds of bidding, where deals were done, shares traded, and partners found for joint ventures.

The Dutch had long preferred collective financial effort to the derring-do of the lone entrepreneur. To pool resources and dilute the risks, investors formed consortia for every maritime project. The pioneering East Indian spice fleet of 1599 was the fruit of one such joint enterprise. Cloves and nutmegs were native to the Moluccas—a handful of tiny islands northeast of Java—and in the sixteenth century grew nowhere else. For centuries, these spices had reached Europe via a chain of merchants who each undertook part of the journey. Untold wealth awaited any trader who could eliminate all the middlemen. That was the aim of nine of Amsterdam's wealthiest merchant princes, who had come together for a series of secret meetings in an obscure wine shop to draw up plans for the Far Lands Company.

In March 1602, three years after the success of their first expedition, the Far Lands directors formed an even larger consortium, the United East India Company. Its express purpose was to eliminate wasteful competition between Dutch venturers and pool their resources to establish a monopoly of overseas trade in spices and in every other commodity. As well as edging out the Portuguese and English who were already active in the Orient, they planned to beat native Asian traders on their own ground.

The East India Company did not expect to achieve these goals simply by offering better commercial terms and more dazzling trade goods. With the blessing of the nation's political masters, its employees were empowered to wage war, conclude peace treaties, build forts, and recruit civil, military, and naval personnel, all bound by an oath of loyalty to the company itself. As the company's governor in the East Indies, Jan Pieterszoon Coen, reminded the authorities, "We cannot carry on trade without war, nor war without trade."

The first to feel the brunt of such policies were the Portuguese, who had been established in the East Indies for a century, but whose grip on these territories was weakening. Their energies were sapped by struggles at home, and their seamanship was inferior to that of their Dutch rivals. When the two nations' armed merchantmen clashed in maritime battles, the Netherlanders inevitably carried the day.

Although the Portuguese were dispatched with relative ease, England presented a greater problem. For a time, the English and Dutch East India companies tried to work together. But this policy, forged in the meeting rooms of London and Amsterdam, did not please Jan Pieterszoon Coen out in Batavia, his company's newly established trading base on the island of Java. With every outward show of cooperation, he proposed ambitious collaborative projects, well knowing that they required larger financial outlays than the English would be prepared to provide. When such ploys failed to drive the rival merchants away, he ordered a series of attacks on the English fleet, capturing several ships. For the English, the final provocation came in 1623, when one of Coen's subordinates arrested eight of their men on the island of Amboina, tortured them, and executed the whole party on trumped-up charges. The Anglo-Dutch partnership was over.

In addition to eradicating all European competitors, the company was also determined to prevent any large-scale native enterprise from undermining its monopoly. Total control of the East Indies was impossible; thousands of islands lay scattered across an area spanning some 2,800 miles from east to west, and another 1,200 from north to south. But Coen and his colleagues studied their charts and found strategic points where men and ships might be stationed to block access to whole island groups and archipelagos. At the least, unauthorized vessels that were apprehended had their cargoes confiscated. Often the fate of those who challenged the Dutch was more severe. When the inhabitants of the Banda Islands, for instance, defied the company's demands that they cease supplying rice to the Javanese, the Dutch launched a surprise attack in which approximately 15,000 Bandanese were massacred or sold into slavery.

Few areas of the world were left untouched by Dutch voyagers. The isolationist rulers of Japan were so impressed with the yellow-haired aliens that they gave them exclusive rights to maintain a trading post on their territory, a monopoly that would continue until 1853. At the Cape of Good Hope, a settlement grew up to service the East Indian ships with fresh provisions. Within a few years, the independent-minded colonists, already known as Boers, were pushing out into the hinterland in search of fresh pastures. And a North American colony, New Amsterdam, was established on Manhattan Island in 1611.

Some of the settlers prospered as farmers, cultivating the fertile shores of the river named after the English explorer Henry Hudson. Others made a comfortable living as smugglers, supplying cut-rate goods to the neighboring English colonies, whose inhabitants gladly ignored their mother country's ban on trade with any merchants but its own.

In 1616, the Dutch won a foothold in South America, in western Guyana. The Dutch West India Company was subsequently set up to challenge the dominance of Spain and Portugal in the Caribbean. Identifying a gap in the market, the company purchased slaves in West Africa, and sold them, in defiance of Spain's attempts at monopoly, to its labor-hungry American colonists. As well as supporting this venture, the company gave funds to privateers who raided Spanish settlements and hijacked their cargo ships. The

This model of a Dutch *fluyt*—anglicized as "flyboat"—was constructed for the future owner of a full-size vessel. Broad-beamed and robustly seaworthy, such ships were Europe's finest vessels for carrying bulky goods. Holland's advanced shipyards used wind-powered sawmills and standardized parts to build the craft cheaply as well as soundly; ingeniously designed winch-operated rigging kept crew levels low. Unlike rival merchantmen, weighed down by defensive armament, the flyboats carried no cannon: If protection was needed, they sailed in convoys escorted by warships. The extra cargo space thus provided allowed owners to undercut rivals' freight charges, giving the Dutch ascendancy over the European bulk transport trade.

greatest boost to the company's morale, and to its coffers, was Admiral Piet Heyn's capture, in 1628, of the Spanish treasure fleet laden with silver from the Mexican mines. The booty was valued at 11 million guilders, enough to pay two-thirds of the yearly costs of the Dutch army, by then once more enmeshed in war with Spain.

While Piet Heyn and his captains harried Spanish ships, many of their compatriots were content to do business with the enemy. Throughout the eighty years of official or undeclared hostilities on sea and land, Dutch merchants continued to trade, discreetly or overtly, with the Spanish. Not everyone approved. But when the stadholder remonstrated with one such entrepreneur, the merchant retorted that he would happily sail his ships into hell and risk singeing their timbers if he saw a profit in it.

By the middle of the century, the young republic's commercial supremacy was firmly established. Dutch merchants were at work from Siberia to the Cape of Good Hope. Closer to home, thirteen times as many Dutch ships as English ones passed through the Baltic Sound, carrying three-quarters of the Baltic countries' grain and timber, as well as half the metal exported from Swedish mines. No consumer in western Europe could be untouched by the activities of the Dutch. In a wealthy household in London or Paris, a visitor might be received in a room covered with Flemish tapestries, offered West Indian sugar in a Chinese porcelain bowl, invited to light a pipe of North American tobacco, and tempted with a goblet of Peruvian silver filled with German wine—all provided by Dutch traders and sailors.

According to some observers, among them the Englishman William Temple, these delights were for export only:

> They are the great masters of the Indian spices and of the Persian silks, but wear plain wool, and feed upon their own fish and roots . . . they furnish infinite luxury, which they never practice, and traffic in pleasures, which they never taste.

Temple's assertion was only partly accurate. The Calvinist burghers of Holland and Zeeland had a reputation for thrift and plain living, but they stopped far short of asceticism. They did, however, reserve the enjoyment of their enhanced incomes for the privacy of their own homes. Even families of moderate means had cabinets to display their crockery, and deep chests or ornately carved cupboards to hold the household linen, the quantity and quality of which was a yardstick of prosperity.

The laundering of all this clothing and napery formed part of a national obsession with domestic cleanliness. Dutch housewives believed that the dirt of the world should never be allowed to cross the threshold or sully the sacred hearth. In a poem by Pieter van Godewijk, a Dordrecht schoolmaster, a magistrate's daughter declares: "My brush is my sword, my broom my weapon."

The interiors of their carefully tended houses—tranquil chambers illuminated by a shaft of sunlight from a tall window; halls of polished tiles lighted by the gleam of brass and copper; neat backyards, paved in brick, leading to narrow, walled gardens—were objects of pride, and as such

A 1665 painting shows the Dutch East India Company's trading station on the Hooghly River in Bengal, its well-defended warehouses laid out with geometric precision. The depot was a key link in the network of bases that made up Holland's eastern trading empire. Through it, ships streamed to and from the Moluccas, Batavia—present-day Jakarta—and as far east as China and Japan, returning with lucrative cargoes of spices and fine textiles. By the end of the century, the Dutch controlled substantial territories in Ceylon and southern India as well as much of Indonesia.

were minutely recorded in the paintings that prosperous Dutch burghers purchased to adorn their walls. Not that the love of pictures was restricted to the well-to-do. An English traveler arriving in 1640 marveled that even "blacksmiths, cobblers, etc. will have some picture or other by their forge and in their stall. Such is the general notion, inclination, and delight that these country natives have to painting."

The art of painting flourished, nurtured by an enthusiastic public in love with color, realistic detail, and mirror images of their own lives. Every town of any size had its community of professional artists, women as well as men, who were regarded as ordinary tradespeople, much like carpenters or tilers. They strove energetically to meet the demand for paintings of every kind, from landscapes and naval battles through still lifes and biblical narratives to views of the lowlifes in taverns, bordellos, and gambling dens. The last were often the cheapest, produced for the low end of the market, but even the most elegant and ambitious works were relatively inexpensive.

While individuals and institutions alike built up picture collections, many paintings were exported. Dutch merchants in East Indian trading posts ordered pictures to embellish their overseas residences. Native princes bought them for their palaces. As the reputation of Dutch artists spread, people of taste in England, France, and Scotland got their works through agents or gathered them on their travels. Perspicacious Dutch collectors realized that something the rest of the world wanted so badly was likely to be a good investment; although great artists died in poverty, the price of their pictures gradually rose.

One reason was the lack of alternative investment opportunities in a crowded country. English diarist John Evelyn, touring the republic, noted: "The reason of this store of pictures and their cheapness proceeds from want of land to employ their stock, so that it is an ordinary thing to find a common farmer lay out two or three thousand pounds in this commodity."

Evelyn's assessment perhaps underestimated the aesthetic sense of the Dutch burghers, most of whom also found time to enjoy the life of the mind. The pleasures of intellectual disputation became a sociable pursuit in local literary societies known as chambers of rhetoric. These associations, which held poetry competitions and organized amateur dramatics and formal debates, flourished in towns and villages throughout the republic. Each one devised its own rituals and regalia, usually choosing a plant or flower for its name. Leiden boasted three—the Palm Tree, the White Columbine, and the Orange Lily; Alkmaar was home to the Green Laurel; Amsterdamers attended the White Lavender and

As depicted in this 1649 map, the swelling city of Amsterdam had grown into a metropolis by the mid-seventeenth century, with a population of 150,000. It was already spreading beyond its moated fortifications, where windmills posted on the breezy ramparts ground the citizens' grain; a new fortress line *(outlined on the left)* was being planned to cope with further expansion. With more than 1,000 oceangoing ships claiming it as their home port, Amsterdam boasted the world's busiest harbor, from which a network of canals carried goods to every corner of the city. With their locks and dams, these waterways also helped protect Amsterdam from flooding: The city stood an average of ten feet below sea level.

the Eglantine. Chambers generally met on Sundays, after church services, and members encouraged the muse with rounds of beer or wine. The house rules varied, but most societies required their meetings to be conducted entirely in verse—even orders for drinks had to be composed in rhyme.

Burghers of a less literary bent found comradeship in recreational clubs and trade associations. Musical societies offered concerts and communal singing; local militias became more social than strategic in their importance. And every convocation of like-minded extroverts provided an excuse for gargantuan feasts at regular intervals. One society of Amsterdam merchants, the Guild of Saint Martin, organized a banquet that lasted for two full days.

In the midst of this good living, the poor were not forgotten. Charity was a public duty and conducted—in the manner of many commercial enterprises—as a cooperative venture. Boards of male and female aristocrats supervised the almshouses, orphanages, and other institutions, which were supported by municipal funds and private bequests. Local magistrates or volunteer groups, including the chambers of rhetoric, sponsored vast public lotteries with a range of dazzling prizes to raise money for worthy causes. Items such as gold chains, silver tableware, and lace petticoats were raffled off to help build a new home for aged paupers in Haarlem, or raise funds for destitute widows in the flood-battered fishing village of Egmond aan Zee. Ticket sales could rise into the hundreds of thousands, and potential players with little money bartered goods instead: Sacks of peat, wheels of cheese, wine, textiles, and pictures were all grist to the lotteries' mill.

Whatever the hopes of its more enlightened inhabitants, the republic still fell far short of utopia. Large sectors of the population enjoyed no share of the newfound prosperity. In Friesland and the remote rural province of Overijssel, a small coterie of noble families forming about one percent of the population held nearly one-half of the region's wealth. In the more affluent mercantile provinces of Holland and Zeeland, homeless beggars still wandered the streets, and workers and artisans struggled to feed their families. Throughout the republic, bad harvests and periodic bouts of inflation could bring some districts to the brink of famine, and an economy heavily dependent on foreign trade was vulnerable to any trouble in the world outside.

Nor was the state free from political turbulence. By mid-century, relations between the urban patricians of Holland and the House of Orange had deteriorated. In 1647, William II of Orange, grandson of William the Silent, quarreled with the States of Holland over their refusal to allow him to launch another military action against Spain. They were ready for an end to the war that drained their finances and hindered their trade, and they wished to see the stadholder's expensive army—with its preponderance of foreign mercenaries—reduced to a modest domestic defense force.

The balance of power between States and stadholder, between provincial States and States-General, remained delicate. When William took office, the tensions came to a head. He had acquired considerable support within the other six provinces; Holland alone stood against him. In 1650, the States of Holland defied William by dismissing some of the troops stationed within the province and paid for out of its funds. Furious at this interference with his rights as supreme military commander, William, with the uneasy consent of the States-General, arrested six Holland deputies for treason and sent 10,000 troops to mount a surprise attack on Amsterdam.

But the soldiers got lost in a night fog in the marshlands near the city. They were spotted by a courier carrying post from Hamburg, who raised the alarm in Amsterdam that some foreign army was on the way. At dawn, when the Orange forces arrived at the city walls, they found the gates barred against them. Both sides were equally surprised. The officers were puzzled that their midnight maneuvers had been noticed, the Amsterdamers astonished that the invaders were Dutch.

Within a few days, the two parties reached a fragile compromise. The Amsterdam authorities agreed to dismiss the most militant anti-Orange faction from the city government; in return, William saw to it that the six imprisoned deputies were released. The States-General resolved that decisions on collective concerns thenceforth be unanimously agreed on by all seven provinces. It then sought to negotiate troop reductions with William, insisting that mercenaries should be the first to go.

For a few weeks, there was a standoff. William continued to make warlike noises against Spain, and there were rumors that he was plotting with the French to stage some sort of coup. The whole republic seemed to be holding its breath, waiting for something to happen, when fate intervened. The twenty-three-year-old William caught a virulent strain of smallpox and within weeks was dead. His widow, daughter of the late king of England, Charles I, gave birth a few months afterward to a son.

The States-General had made no provision for a successor. The result was a twenty-two-year interregnum, known by some as the "stadholderless period" and by others as the time of the "true freedom." During this interval, Holland's political leader, the grand pensionary, became the most powerful figure in the republic. Supreme military command was vested in the States-General itself, whose members appointed a field marshal or other chief officer for the duration of hostilities.

Inevitably, the need for mobilization did arise. In 1651, the English Parliament made a direct attack on Dutch commerce by passing a Navigation Act that had the effect of banning the Dutch from carrying goods from any country other than their own to England or England's colonies. The Dutch sent representatives to bargain with the English, but while the two parties met at the negotiating table, their naval commanders, the republic's Admiral Tromp and England's Admiral Blake, were also receiving instructions for war.

Blake was charged with harrying the republic's vital Baltic trade. He was also instructed to seize the Dutch East Indiamen returning from the Orient and encouraged to disrupt the herring fishery along the English and Scottish coasts and confiscate all captured buses and their catches. Tromp's orders were to defeat the English while defending all this vulnerable traffic.

Tromp chafed at the assignment. "I should wish to be so fortunate," he complained to the States-General, "as to have only one of the two duties, to seek out the enemy or to give convoy, for to do both is attended by great difficulties." His civilian superiors wanted him to give priority to the protection of their trade, shipping, and property. He wanted to take the offensive. Why settle for survival, he asked, when the nation could enjoy total victory?

The Dutch had more ships and better sailors, and the English coast was vulnerable to bombardment and blockade. The English—equipped with better warships and greater firepower—set up a blockade of their own, although their men grew mutinous inside the cramped vessels patrolling the republic's shores. Tromp himself died in the attempt to break the blockade, and the first Anglo-Dutch war ended with little real satisfaction for either side, although the English were, nominally, the victors.

By the 1660s, the two sides were at war again. The English made no secret of their

AN ORDERED DOMESTIC WORLD

Protected from the winds of Holland's polder landscape by wooden walls and high, well-trimmed hedges, a Dutch merchant's country villa near Haarlem boasts a carefully organized garden chock full of fruit trees and ornamental shrubs. As this contemporary painting shows, a private canal provided drainage and access by boat to a nearby river.

As was befitting of a mercantile republic, seventeenth-century Holland bestowed the great wealth its trade had won not on lavish palaces for kings and aristocrats but on middle-class traders' homes. The guilders spent were not always immediately obvious: Town houses were generally narrow, especially in Amsterdam, where everyone wanted a home with a canal frontage, and where by law no house could be more than 25 feet wide. To compensate, however, wealthier merchants constructed their dwellings up to 165 feet deep, decorated them with moneyed taste, and packed them with the fine furnishings shown overleaf.

Dirt was banished both indoors and out: Housefronts, steps, and even the streets themselves were scrubbed to a state of cleanliness that amazed foreign visitors, who were accustomed to the general squalor and filth of most towns of the day. The streets were so clean, marveled one Englishman, that people "even seem to take pleasure in walking them."

A painting by an unknown artist shows a typical morning scene: A maid dresses her mistress before tidying the room. Behind the four-poster bed—probably the most expensive item of furniture in the house—lies the bathroom, its door open to reveal the close-stool—a wood frame enclosing a chamber pot.

In a detail from Vermeer's *Girl with a Wineglass,* a Turkish rug serves as a tablecloth, while a lute rests on a fine silk cushion on a leather-backed chair. Oriental carpets were often too delicate, and too highly valued, to be consigned to the floor.

Oriental rugs, imported from the Ottoman Empire and Persia, were goods that only the wealthy could afford.

Brass chandeliers were exported to much of Europe from the Netherlands. They were hung low to allow for easy lighting.

Mirrors became larger and more decorative in the seventeenth century as a result of the introduction of plate glass.

Another Vermeer detail illustrates the seventeenth-century fashion for displaying family coats of arms in stained glass. Problems with sheet-glass manufacture meant that windows had to be assembled from many small panes, but Dutch artisans often managed to turn the drawback into an advantage by the quality of their workmanship.

In Emanuel de Witte's *Interior with a Woman at a Spinet*, the mistress of a prosperous Dutch household finds time for music practice while her husband remains comfortably in bed. Framed by twin doorways, a maidservant performs the daily ritual of most Dutch housewives: sweeping up.

The spinet was a novelty at the time; many people found the opportunity it offered for making music at home almost magical.

purpose. "What we want," said the duke of Albemarle, who commanded the English fleet, "is more of the trade the Dutch now have." But this time the republic's morale was better, and its naval strategies more clearly mapped. Clashes were not restricted to domestic waters; the two sides fought in the East and West Indies, up and down the coasts of the Americas, and off West Africa.

In a bold stroke, Admiral de Ruyter led a Dutch attack force up the Medway River, whose estuary cuts deep into the English county of Kent. Breaking the chain barrier that had been drawn across the waterway, his men-of-war pounced on the fleet that lay at anchor there. Some they burned; others were taken as prizes, among them the English flagship, the *Royal Charles*. With this booty in tow, and the English gaping in outrage, the invaders sailed safely home. In July 1667, the two nations met to make peace, this time on the republic's terms.

With the fighting scarcely over at sea, the United Provinces were shaken at home by dramas that threatened their status as a republic. Throughout the 1650s and 1660s, political continuity and stability had been provided by the grand pensionary of Holland, Johan de Witt. Equipped with formidable persuasive powers and political acumen, de Witt put the republic's financial house in order, strengthened and reorganized the navy sufficiently to bring victory in the second English war, and directed foreign and domestic policymaking with a skill and style not seen since the days of Oldenbarnevelt. He also made enemies, especially among the Orangeists, who hoped for the day when young William III would take his father's place as stadholder.

Within the States-General, de Witt and his supporters expressed the view that the republic was surviving very well without a stadholder, and that the nation's debt to William the Silent and his Orange heirs had now been paid in full: They no longer deserved that exalted post as a matter of right. Nevertheless, when the States-General took charge of the prince's education, de Witt agreed to instruct him in the arts of statecraft. As the grandson of one English king and the nephew of another, the youth was acutely conscious of his own royal blood. But he developed considerable respect for his republican tutor and later claimed that de Witt had taught him more about the world than all his other instructors.

Neighboring states watched the debate over the stadholderate with interest, for the Dutch were now important players on the chessboard of European power politics. England's Charles II, lately restored to a throne that had been taken away from his father, hoped that his own country's war with the Dutch would undermine their republican government and open the way for his Orange nephew to rule as a prince.

The French king, Louis XIV, was anxious to prevent the Orange's followers from taking power, fearing that any thaw in relations between the Dutch and the English would inevitably pose a threat to France. Meanwhile, he was engaged in his own war against Spain and in May 1667 marched his armies into the Spanish Netherlands. The Dutch and the English, sensing that France was now more dangerous to each of them than either was to the other, hastily concluded a peace treaty and formed a triple alliance, with Sweden, to force an end to the Franco-Spanish war.

To break up this triumvirate, Louis began to pay court to Charles II. He suggested that it would be to England's financial, as well as political, advantage to join him in a campaign against the Dutch. In 1670, the two monarchs signed the Treaty of Dover, resolving to remove de Witt, destroy the Dutch republic, and replace it with a puppet monarchy, ruled by William under the joint control of Charles and Louis.

Despite strong personal ties between the English king and the young prince of Orange, William knew better than to trust his uncle; he was not willing to purchase a crown by sacrificing Dutch sovereignty. He was also a devout Protestant, and the heir to a princely house that had long been the standard-bearer for the Protestant cause; his English uncle was revealing himself as far too papist in his preferences for William's liking, and Louis was, above all else, a staunchly Catholic king.

Two years after the Treaty of Dover, the crisis came to a head. With their enemies breathing down their necks, the Dutch could no longer do without a military leader. William was duly named captain-general and joined forces with his old tutor to build up the army. The mobilization was quickly accomplished; for twenty years, de Witt had kept the nation's finances on a healthy footing, so there were sufficient funds, or good sources of credit, to organize the necessary troops, weapons, and supplies.

In April, France declared war. Two months later, its army marched along the fringes of the Spanish Netherlands, through the German Rhineland, and entered the United Provinces from the east. The troops forced their way halfway across the country and were west of Utrecht when the Dutch opened the dikes and flooded the low-lying polder lands to keep the invaders from advancing farther.

Instead of uniting in the face of a common enemy, the Dutch now began fighting among themselves. Riots broke out in towns throughout the republic; witnesses observed that the mobs appeared to include numbers of respectable citizens as well as the rougher elements usually associated with public disorder. Possibly outside agitators were behind some of the outbursts; rumor certainly had it so.

De Witt, passing along an Amsterdam street, was attacked by four unknown, but apparently well-dressed, young men. They left him half-dead, bleeding from wounds that took many weeks to heal. While he lay recovering from his injuries, the States-General hastily sent emissaries to Louis XIV, encamped in Utrecht province, offering sizable financial and territorial concessions in return for peace. Louis, enjoying the advantage, bided his time and refused to negotiate.

The Orangeists insisted that the republic could no longer fend off its enemies without a strong leader at the helm, and they demanded that William be appointed to a restored and more powerful stadholderate. Shortly after he took up his post, a scandal erupted that showed William up in an unattractive light.

Johan de Witt's brother Cornelius, a magistrate and senior member of the government of the province of Holland, was accused of conspiring to assassinate the prince. The charges were false, brought by a barber-surgeon of dubious reputation who had once been tried by Cornelius on a charge of rape. Even under torture, Cornelius would not admit to a crime of which he was innocent. But his brother's powerful Orangeist enemies saw their opportunity and persuaded or coerced the judges to ensure an unfair trial. During these proceedings, the grand pensionary, recovered from his wounds, resigned from public office.

Despite the best efforts of Cornelius de Witt's opponents, the court was unable to find him guilty of conspiracy. Nevertheless, the judges stripped him of all his public offices and declared him banished for life from the province of Holland.

The day the trial ended, a message reached Johan de Witt to the effect that his brother wished him to escort him home from the prison in which he was being held. When Johan de Witt reached the jail, he found it surrounded by an angry crowd, with troops of cavalry struggling to keep order. Shortly after he had entered the building the soldiers disappeared, called to the outskirts of the city to quell a supposed peasant riot that in fact turned out to be a hoax. Meanwhile the de Witt brothers found themselves besieged inside the prison. An appeal to William to send troops to restore order proved fruitless; the stadholder declared that, between French invaders and public strife elsewhere, he had no soldiers to spare.

Late in the afternoon, the mob broke into the prison, dragged out the de Witts, slaughtered them with pikes and muskets, and tied the bodies upside down from the public gallows. Witnesses reported that the attackers included prominent Orangeist citizens and members of the civil guard. When these local worthies left the scene, the populace fell upon the corpses and tore them to pieces. It was later whispered that parts of the bodies were auctioned off to the highest bidders, cooked, and eaten in an orgy of vengeance.

In the towns of Holland, the crowds went wild. "King Mob," remarked one contemporary pamphleteer, "plays boss." Many among the poorer sectors of the population had loathed the de Witts as representatives of the clique of urban patricians who in their view ran the nation for their own advantage. The rioters now demanded a purge of republican magistrates and local officials.

William, though no more a populist than de Witt had been, exploited this fever of Orangeist enthusiasm. He restored calm, refilled public offices with his own loyal supporters, and left them to manage domestic affairs while he pursued his own highest priority: the war against France.

The stadholder launched a bold attack against Louis. In the dead of winter, a time when hostilities were usually suspended, he led an army up through the Rhineland to launch a surprise assault against the main French arsenal at Bonn. Caught off balance, the French began to lose ground. The Dutch struggle gradually expanded into a general European war. The English eventually dropped out, and the French, though slower to give up the

Tulipmania

In the 1630s, tulips seemed the ideal commodity to Holland's adventurous investors: The flowers, a recent import from Turkey, were fashionable in European courts, horticulturists were vying to create new varieties, and the bulbs fetched high prices. The result was a speculative frenzy in which tulips, and tulip futures, were traded on credit for spiraling prices. At the height of the boom, flower beds were guarded by armed men and a house in Haarlem was swapped for just three bulbs.

In a rising market, it seemed no one could lose. But when prices reached a level at which no buyers could be found, the bubble burst and thousands found themselves ruinously in debt—fair game for satirical artists like Crispin van de Pass the Younger, who portrayed the goddess Flora's triumphal car as a ship of fools (right).

fight, finally signed a peace treaty with William in 1678, returning all captured Dutch territory and agreeing to drop the restrictive tariffs they had imposed to hinder the republic's foreign trade.

During the war, the prince had strengthened his ties with the English crown by marrying his cousin Mary, daughter of the duke of York and second in line to the throne after her father. The wedding made Mary a far more popular figure in Britain than her father the duke, whose Roman Catholic faith alarmed his future subjects. When the duke succeeded to the throne as King James II in 1685, William found himself under pressure from English Protestants to cross the Channel and intervene. In 1688, backed by a Dutch army and carried by a Dutch fleet, he responded to the English invitation. James II fled the kingdom, and William and Mary were proclaimed joint monarchs in his place. The Orangeists were elated: Their prince had now taken his rightful place among the crowned heads of Europe, even if on a foreign throne.

Within the republic, he would remain as stadholder, officially the servant of the States-General but capable of wielding considerable power. Yet with fresh demands upon his energies elsewhere, the States-General and its leaders were by and large left free to manage their own affairs.

It would be more than a century before the stadholderate was transformed into a monarchy, but in the eyes of its own inhabitants, the golden age of the Dutch republic seemed to be drawing to a close. The economy, though reasonably stable, had ceased to grow. Crippling taxation was sending skilled artisans and entrepreneurs out in search of more congenial fiscal environments; European nations were becoming more self-sufficient and less dependent on Dutch traders; and such was the republic's newfound importance that it could not avoid being sucked into Europe's political upheavals, which grew ever more commercially disruptive. The eighteenth century would see the Dutch involved in prolonged wars over the succession to the Spanish and Austrian thrones, invaded once more by the French, and at loggerheads once again with England.

If the poor suffered under the high tax burden, the patricians, at least, still had money to spend. Yet the old days, when merchants plowed profits back into new ventures and lived comfortably but with a certain simplicity, were over. Those who could afford to purchase land built themselves suburban or rural estates and lived off their investments, far away from the warehouses full of Baltic timber or salt herring that had made their first fortunes.

Observers lamented that the Dutch were giving up the virtues that had brought them success. Some blamed the French for sapping Dutch vitality by encouraging a lamentable vogue for extravagant fashions. Certainly, the befrilled and periwigged burghers of the United Provinces no longer looked like their republican grandparents, clad in no-nonsense Puritan black. The Dutch, as they themselves realized, were becoming much like other Western nations.

But if the Dutch were being transformed into conventional Europeans, then they could reflect with some satisfaction that they, too, had played their part in changing Europe. They had supplied the world not only with such material goods as butter, cheese, and herrings but with a rich cargo of enlightened values and ideas: They demonstrated that it was possible to be tolerant as well as pious, charitable as well as rich, visionary as well as hardheaded. They also showed that a self-governing, secular, republican state might not only survive but flourish beyond all expectations.

NEWCOMERS TO THE NEW WORLD

There was nothing spectacular about the low strip of land on the horizon, scarcely distinguishable from the surface of the sea. For the devout passengers on board the little ship, however, this first glimpse of the New World represented an answer to prayer and a vision of the future. Sixty-seven days of sickness and fear, of close confinement in a malodorous, heaving prison, made the prospect of any solid land irresistible. On November 11, 1620, the *Mayflower* cast anchor where God had directed her, sheltered from Atlantic storms by the sandy northern hook of Cape Cod. For 102 English men, women, and children, the long ordeal was over. In the words of William Bradford, their chronicler and future leader, "they were not a little joyful."

On dry land, according to Bradford, the new colonists relished the luxury of exercising their aching limbs at last. The men explored the forests along the shore for food, water, and signs of habitation; the women washed the party's clothes in a brackish pool near the beach, while the children—amazed by the space suddenly available to them—scrambled over the grassy dunes and raced along the flat sands.

More thoughtful members of the party realized that the immediate future promised nothing but hardship. Winter was nearly upon them, "and they that know the winters of that country, know them to be sharp and violent," observed Bradford. They had no shelter except the cramped and fetid ship and no provisions except the dwindling supplies that they had brought with them. "What could they see but a hideous and desolate wilderness?" asked Bradford, confronting their situation with stoic objectivity. But not in their worst imaginings could Bradford and his companions have envisaged the horrors of the ensuing winter. Over the next few months, disease and malnutrition took the lives of nearly half of the colonists.

Throughout these misfortunes, battling for a foothold on the unwelcoming continent, they began to build the village of New Plymouth. That this frail settlement even survived is a tribute to the faith, courage, and common sense of the Pilgrims, as they became known. "It pleased the Lord to give the plantation peace," Bradford humbly wrote home after five years of struggle. Just ten years later, the Pilgrims could see the smoke rising from the kitchen fires of communities that had sprung up around Plymouth. New England's wilderness was in retreat.

The New World was hardly new to Europe by 1620. For more than a century, ballads, histories, and plays had acquainted poor and rich alike with the vast land lying to the west of the Atlantic Ocean. In the course of the sixteenth century, the Spanish had firmly entrenched themselves in the old Aztec lands of Mexico and had colonized much of the continent to the south, while conceding Brazil to the Portuguese. North America, however, had been relatively neglected.

It was not for lack of effort by Iberian explorers. Their expeditions had ranged far

An engraving by the Flemish artist Theodore de Bry shows the English explorer Captain Bartholomew Gosnold making a landfall in 1602 on the island of Martha's Vineyard off the New England coast. Working in Europe from written accounts, de Bry got many details wrong; Gosnold had a single ship, and the native inhabitants greeting him are portrayed fancifully. Nonetheless, Gosnold did trade successfully for skins with the Indians and returned with such glowing reports of the area that further exploration was ensured. Four years later, Gosnold commanded one of the boats that brought settlers to Jamestown, Virginia, 500 miles to the south—the first permanent English outpost in America.

In the first decades of the seventeenth century, most of the maritime nations of Europe, including Sweden, the Netherlands, France, and Britain, laid claim to parts of eastern North America. But by the end of the century, the French and British were the dominant powers; the Spanish, who had made many pioneering journeys over-land and were established in New Mexico, were con-fined on the east coast to the Florida peninsula. The pattern of English and French settlement—shaded green and yellow respectively on the map—reflects the dif-ferent priorities of the colonists. The English were pri-marily farmers drawn to the fertile lands of New Eng-land, Virginia, and Pennsylvania. The French were less interested in land than in the fur trade, which took them far inland along the country's great waterways.

and wide across the continent. In the 1520s, the Portuguese, who had already explored Newfoundland and Labrador, attempted a settlement on Cape Breton Island in Nova Scotia—the first by Europeans in North America since Viking days. The Spanish visited the Saint Lawrence River in 1525 and briefly established colonies in the Carolinas. By sea, they traveled up the Pacific coast, perhaps as far as the southern boundary of modern-day Oregon. By land, an expedition from Mexico reached Arizona, encountered the Grand Canyon, and found the Great Plains to the east of the Rocky Mountains. Another expedition marched from Florida in 1539 into the territory that is now Arkansas and Oklahoma. But the distances involved were enor-mous, the costs were huge, and the rewards seemed slight; there was no sign that North America boasted the vast resources of silver that lured Europeans to the lands farther south. In addition, the native peoples were hostile. Consequently, Spanish interest in the lands to the north declined. San Juan and Santa Fe, two struggling

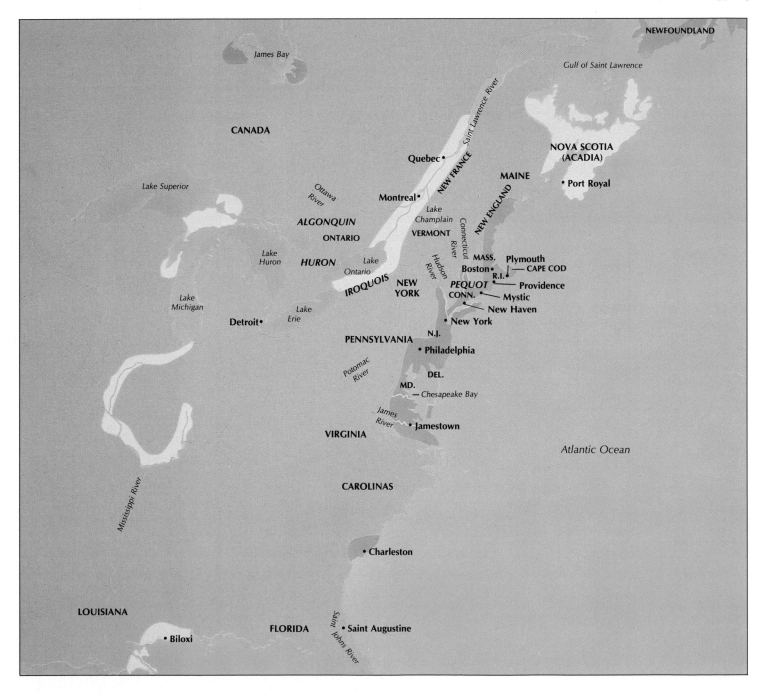

settlements in what is now New Mexico, remained Spain's solitary seventeenth-century outposts in the southwest. Saint Augustine, established on the Florida coast in 1565, represented Spanish influence in the east of the continent.

Explorers from other nations also had little immediate luck. To the nations of northern Europe, the New World at first appeared as primarily an inhospitable obstacle between Europe and Asia. John Cabot, the Italian mariner who led English expeditions across the North Atlantic in the late fifteenth century, remained convinced that Japan lay just beyond Newfoundland. He even carried with him a letter—never to be delivered—from King Henry VII to the Great Khan of China. What Cabot did discover were vast breeding grounds of cod in the shallow seas between Newfoundland and Nova Scotia—fish could be scooped from the water with a basket, he claimed. But cod lacked the glamour of gold and spices, and Cabot never lived to appreciate the importance of this finding.

Sailing farther into the same waters forty years later, the French explorer Jacques Cartier was charged by King Francis I "to discover certain islands and lands where it is said a great quantity of gold and other precious things are to be found." In this commission Cartier failed. The gold he triumphantly brought back to France turned out to be pyrite, the diamonds worthless quartz. But he sailed deep into the Gulf of Saint Lawrence, discovering furs and forests in what he described as "as goodly and pleasant a country as possibly can be wished for."

As this first century of exploration wore on, it became clear that furs and forests were principally what North America had to offer. Trees covered the entire Atlantic coastal plain, creating a near-continuous carpet of foliage sixty-five or more feet above the ground from the Gulf of Saint Lawrence to the Gulf of Mexico. Hickory, oak, tulipwood, basswood, cherry, and other great hardwoods were abundant in the southern temperate forests. White pine and hemlock mixed with the beech, maple, and birch of northern regions. This did not represent instant wealth, but to the business-minded European it suggested a vast repository of masts, spars, and planks. Here also was one of the world's great breeding grounds for animals whose pelts had commercial value: bear, deer, otter, marten, and—especially—beaver (page 146).

To the disappointment of French and English explorers, however, there was no sign that the native peoples—the very name given to them by Europeans, Indians, perpetuated the Asian error—had developed civilizations of the kind that Spain had so profitably exploited in the south. In all of North America there may have been about 10 million indigenous inhabitants when European exploration began. Those along the east coast lived in loosely associated tribes belonging mainly to the Algonquian or the Iroquois language groups. Although they cultivated crops, using sophisticated techniques, their copper ornaments held no allure for acquisitive Europeans.

With no easy pickings to lure them, England and France were slow to establish settlements. When they did try later in the century, the first experiments were failures. An attempt by French Protestants—Huguenots—to settle near the Saint Johns River in Florida ended in their brutal massacre by an expeditionary force sent from Spain. On Roanoke Island off the coast of present-day North Carolina, where Sir Walter Raleigh established a colony that he named Virginia in honor of England's Virgin Queen, Elizabeth I, more than 100 English men and women simply disappeared. The fate of the colony is still an enigma of American history.

The vanishing of the Roanoke colonists did not discourage other would-be settlers, although it was not until after the start of the seventeenth century that the first such

Most revealing of all White's drawings were his portraits. The series at right shows a man decorated with body paint for hunting or feasting; a shaman; and an elder dressed for winter in a deerskin mantle. The tattoos adorning the women below, one of whom is holding a sturdy child, probably indicate their status as wives of chiefs or counselors.

One of White's drawings shows a man and woman sharing a meal of hominy—corn kernels swollen by soaking and boiling. Corn was the staple crop, planted in three sowings. After the late-September harvest, most Indians left the villages to fish, hunt, and trap, or to gather fruit, berries, and nuts.

Theire sitting at meate.

FIRST GLIMPSES OF INDIAN LIFE

Thousands of years before European explorers discovered North America, Palaeolithic immigrants from Asia had colonized the land. By the time the first white settlers arrived, the peoples they called Indians numbered as many as 10 million, divided into dozens of different language groups and hundreds of tribal entities.

Unlike the Aztec or Inca, the North American Indians did not establish urban cultures. Whether farmers or hunters, they lived within their available resources, adapting their livelihoods to the contours of nature and expressing a deep reverence for the land and its wildlife.

Among the first Indians encountered by European settlers were an Algonquian-speaking group who lived by fishing, hunting, and slash-and-burn farming in what is now North Carolina and the most southerly part of Virginia. A unique glimpse of these people at the time of contact is provided by the works of John White, official artist on a series of colonial ventures promoted by the English courtier Sir Walter Raleigh between 1584 and 1590.

White's rendering of the Indian village of Pomeioc shows houses of bent and tied poles covered with matting or bark. Such settlements, scattered along coast and rivers, contained as many as 200 inhabitants each. Some were undefended; others, including Pomeioc, were protected by a palisade.

venture took root. In 1620, when Bradford apprehensively contemplated the isolation of New England, he was not alone in North America. About 500 miles south of Plymouth, around Jamestown and along the rich river valleys of Virginia, other English colonists had already cut back the forests and begun cultivating tobacco, the cash crop that was to make the fortune of the South. Far to the north, in a wilderness sterner than New England, French fur traders and priests were bargaining for beaver pelts and human souls in what is now Nova Scotia and the Gulf of Saint Lawrence.

"There were never Englishmen left in a foreign country in such misery as we were in the new discovered Virginia," wrote George Percy, a settler who survived Jamestown's tragic first summer of 1607. There was, in fact, even worse misery to come. During its early years, starvation, disease, and warfare constantly threatened to destroy what was to be England's first permanent settlement in the New World.

The establishment of a colony in Virginia made sense to English statesmen and merchants at the dawn of the seventeenth century. This huge territory stretched from present-day North Carolina to northern Maine. It was an area claimed by both Spain and France, but England argued that there was no possession without occupation. A settlement on the fertile shores of Chesapeake Bay in southern Virginia would defy Spain, while still keeping a safe distance from aggressive Spanish colonies.

To the London entrepreneurs who backed the venture, Jamestown made good sense too. Many still believed that the American continent was merely a strip of land dividing the Atlantic from the riches of Asia. A colony in Virginia would be a useful trading station. Besides, there was the prospect of gold and silver in the great Indian kingdoms that optimists hoped to find in the North American forests. More realistically, English merchants had by now begun to appreciate the value of the fish, furs, and timber that were North America's most accessible raw materials. Buoyed by the expectations of an attractive return, they formed a joint-stock company, an association of shareholders who funded the colony for a share of the profits. Many shareholders in the Virginia Company would rue the day they had invested in Jamestown.

It was not difficult finding volunteers for the Jamestown expedition. Young Englishmen had read with excitement the colorful accounts of sixteenth-century voyages compiled by Richard Hakluyt or Thomas Harriot's *A Briefe and True Report of the New Found Land of Virginia,* describing the New World's wonders. The New World seemed to offer both adventure and the chance of a good living.

The long and stormy passage, which lasted more than four months, may have drained some of the young adventurers' high spirits. Few, however, could resist the beauties of Virginia in April. Here were broad rivers meandering to the sea through woodland and meadows. "I was almost ravished at the sight thereof," wrote Percy, who also marveled at strawberries four times the size of England's, as well as the shellfish that lay on the beach "as thick as stones."

There followed a succession of tragic mistakes. The first was to establish their settlement—named after King James I—

Samuel de Champlain, explorer and champion of French settlement in Canada, is shown in armor at the center of a battle between rival Indian tribes in 1609. The previous year Champlain, with the help of friendly Indians, had founded Quebec as a post for the Indian-French fur trade. Eager to expand the commerce into hostile Indian territory, he and three armed companions joined a Huron war party in a raid against their enemies, the Iroquois. Panic-stricken by the unaccustomed gunfire, which killed three of their number, the Iroquois fled. The incident greatly increased French prestige among the Huron and their allies, but made enemies of the Iroquois, who later supported the British in their struggle against the colonists of New France.

on a marshy, mosquito-infested peninsula in the James River. The brackish water was scarcely drinkable, and the highest ground was only ten feet above the level of the river. Then there was endless bickering and fatal idleness. Few of the young gentlemen of Jamestown had anticipated blistering their hands with agricultural labor, and even fewer had any useful skills. The result was that insufficient land was cultivated the first spring for an adequate harvest. By midsummer, the stores of salt beef, cheese, and hardtack were gone. Even in this season of plenty the settlers began to starve.

Throughout summer and fall, the Jamestown settlers died. Malaria and intermittent war with the Indians—mainly the Paspaheghs, on whose hunting grounds they had settled—accounted for a few deaths, but "for the most part, they died of famine," wrote George Percy. "Their bodies trailed out of their cabins like dogs to be buried." Of the 104 settlers living in June, all but 38 had died by the next January. Those who survived were saved by their wits, their strength, and handouts from the Indians.

More tragedies ensued as additional shiploads of unskilled and unprepared English gentlemen—along with a few women—disembarked at Jamestown. In vain did John Smith, the colony's leader, entreat the parent company to send carpenters, gardeners, fishers, smiths, and "diggers up of trees." In August 1609, some 400 ill and hungry new arrivals precipitated a crisis known as the Starving Time. It is even asserted that one man killed, salted, and ate his wife. By spring, only 60 were alive.

In the end, it was a simple weed that preserved England's colony in Virginia; *Nicotiana tabacum*. Although King James himself had condemned the habit as "harmful to the brains and dangerous to the lungs," smoking tobacco had become a popular pastime in Europe by the early seventeenth century. The variety of tobacco native to Virginia and smoked by the Indians was "poor and weak and of a bitter taste," according to one contemporary. In 1612, however, an enterprising settler named John Rolfe introduced the esteemed and expensive West Indian plant. Within two years, his experiments at growing and curing this variety proved so successful that the fortunes of the colony were transformed. Suddenly, everyone was cultivating tobacco on every available patch of land, even in the streets of Jamestown itself.

The discovery of a successful cash crop imposed a new way of life upon Virginia. Because tobacco was grown most economically on large estates, prosperous Englishmen were tempted now to try their hands at this lucrative profession. Their plantations soon extended well beyond the immediate vicinity of Jamestown, reaching inland along the shores of the James River. From private riverside quays, English captains collected valuable shipments of cured Virginia tobacco.

Most of the work in the fields and tobacco warehouses was done by indentured servants, immigrant English people contracted to work for three to seven years for the master who "purchased" them. When the contract expired, an indentured servant was theoretically rewarded with seeds, tools, and often land; in reality, few were so lucky. Recruited mainly from the homeless and unemployed of the Old World, some of these young Englishmen had virtually been kidnapped by agents—or "spirits," as they were called—who made a handsome profit from this trade in human souls. Women too were press-ganged, or "spirited away," to provide mates for the men.

Both sexes found themselves subjected to conditions that were tantamount to slavery. Their movements were restricted; those who ran away were subjected to corporal or even capital punishment. They could be sold like slaves and flogged senseless for even minor misdemeanors. Some of the men escaped to become pirates; others ran off to live among the Indians, assuming Indian ways. A few—perhaps two

Portrayed here in Elizabethan dress, Matoaka—better known by her pet name, Pocahontas, or "little wanton"—was the daughter of Powhatan, leader of a powerful Indian confederation in Virginia. In 1608, when she was about thirteen years old, she interceded for the life of Captain John Smith, who had come to ask her father's help for the starving Jamestown colony. Abducted by the English in 1612, she converted to Christianity, took the baptismal name Rebecca, and married John Rolfe, who is credited with turning the fortunes of the colony by planting its first crop of tobacco. With her husband, Pocahontas went to England in 1616; the following year, she contracted smallpox and died. Five years later, her father's successor, alarmed by the expansion of the Jamestown colony, led a massacre of 347 settlers. From then on, the colonists' goal was the extermination of the Indians.

Matoaks als Rebecka daughter to the mighty Prince Powhatan Emperour of Attanougskomouck als virginia converted and baptized in the Christian faith, and wife to the worth.ᵗᵉ Mr. Joh Rolff.

FORECASTLE
Food was cooked over a
brick firebox in the galley.
Behind it were the tiny
cabins where the ordinary
seamen slept on straw
beds, doubling up on four-
hour shifts in which one
man rested while his mate
kept watch on deck.

MAIN HOLD
Sacks of flour, seeds, and
dried beans vied for space
with casks of salt beef and
pork, water, and beer
in the vessel's main stor-
age area. Here too were
tools and weapons the settlers would require in the
New World. It was the
seamen's task to bring up
goods from the hold as
they were needed, using a
block and tackle.

'TWEEN DECK
The 102 passengers were
accommodated here in
cramped quarters with
headroom of five and one-
half feet. Here too they
stored their belongings.
Light came from candles
and oil lamps; hatches and
gunports would also have
been open in fine weather.
There was no privacy; passengers could not change
clothing on the trip.

MASTER'S CABIN
Christopher Jones, the *Mayflower*'s sailing master, had his own room, in which to sleep and to chart the ship's course.

THE GREAT CABIN
This roomy area was reserved for the ship's five officers, who dined here with the captain off a linen-covered table with iron cutlery and pewter plates. Here too were sleeping quarters for the surgeon and the mates.

BREAD HOLD

When the *Mayflower* left England on September 6, 1620, carrying Puritan settlers to the New World, it was the third time the ship had set sail for America. The Pilgrims on board had intended to travel in two boats, but twice leaks in the smaller vessel, the *Speedwell,* forced both ships to return. Demoralized, some twenty Pilgrims abandoned the enterprise, leaving 102 men, women, and children to brave the perils of the Atlantic crossing.

The *Mayflower* was a three-masted merchant vessel approximately 100 feet long, carrying a crew of twenty-five. Since about 1609, the *Mayflower* had been engaged in the wine trade between France and England, and as a result, she was known as a "sweet ship," the bilges being free from the residues of noisome cargoes.

Nevertheless, shipboard life for the Pilgrims was extremely uncomfortable and unsanitary. With only about ten square feet of space per person belowdecks, some of the passengers chose to sleep on deck in the ship's boat. There were no toilet facilities aboard; for cooking, the crew had access to a galley on deck, but the Pilgrims had to make do with braziers.

As a result of her late departure, the *Mayflower* soon ran into fierce storms that opened the deck seams and soaked the passengers' sleeping quarters. During one gale, a main beam cracked. And in another incident, a young Pilgrim was swept overboard but managed to grab a rope and was hauled back to safety.

CRAMPED QUARTERS FOR THE PILGRIMS

out of every ten—were more fortunate; at the end of their term of service, they might manage, through hard work, to become successful craftsmen or farmers.

There were others against whom the odds were to be even more heavily stacked. In 1619, a tragic social revolution began with the arrival in Jamestown of twenty slaves on a Dutch privateer. By then, African slavery was already well established in South America and the sugar plantations of the West Indies. At first, however, blacks in Virginia were employed under the same terms as white indentured servants. Only later in the century were the Africans denied all rights. By the early 1700s, black slaves made up about 20 percent of the population of Maryland.

In addition, there was vigorous Indian slaving in the south. In the Carolinas, the settlers provided local tribes with weapons and drink, and encouraged intertribal wars. Prisoners taken in the fighting, which reached as far south as Spanish Florida by the turn of the century, were enslaved for service in the Carolinas—there were 1,400 such Indians in Charleston in 1708—or were shipped to the West Indies, New York, or New England. For slavery was by no means restricted to the south. It was a Boston schoolmistress at the end of the century who complained that Connecticut farmers were too indulgent to their slaves, "permitting them to sit at table and eat with them . . . and into the dish goes the black hoof as freely as the white hand."

Virginia's economy required a fresh political order as well as a reliable work force. Initially ruled by a local council appointed in London, the colony found itself under

martial law supervised by an absolute governor after Jamestown's disastrous first two seasons. In 1619, a new era began with the convening of Virginia's—and America's—first elected assembly. The House of Burgesses, as it was known, made laws concerning nearly all aspects of life, from farming to churchgoing. Even when James I dissolved the Virginia Company in 1624 and established royal control, he permitted the Burgesses to continue as a lower legislative assembly. This early example of self-government was important to the colonies' future political independence.

The demise of the Virginia Company followed hard on the heels of a nearly fatal disaster that had befallen the colony: the Indian uprising of 1622. The Jamestown colonists had unwittingly settled among a powerful confederacy of about thirty Indian tribes under a chief known as Powhatan. At first relations were edgy; skirmishes alternated with periods of cooperation. Peace seemed assured, however, when John Rolfe, the man who revolutionized Virginia's agriculture, married Powhatan's witty and beautiful daughter, Pocahontas. At the age of about thirteen, this remarkable woman reputedly saved the life of the colonist's leader, John Smith—then her father's prisoner—by throwing herself between him and his intended executioner. As Mistress Rolfe she traveled to London, awing the English court with her queenly bearing.

The untimely death of Pocahontas in 1617, followed by her father's demise a year later, released pent-up resentments among the Indians, on whose lands the colonists were increasingly encroaching. The Indians laid careful plans for a surprise attack. Until the last minute, the assailants mixed amicably with the settlers. But then, on Good Friday, 1622, in the words of Smith's *General History of Virginia,* "they came unarmed into our houses with deer, turkeys, fish, fruit, and other provisions to sell us; yea, in some places sat down at breakfast with our people, whom immediately with their own tools they slew most barbarously." Nearly one-third of the colony's population—347 English men, women, and children—died that morning.

Had the Indians pressed home their advantage immediately, they might have driven the immigrants off the continent. Instead they withdrew to their villages, satisfied that they had subdued the white man's appetite for expansion. This gave the settlers a chance to rearm and launch a ferocious campaign of reprisal, systematically destroying Indian villages and crops. For nearly a decade the wars continued. It was better, claimed Virginia's governor, Sir Francis Wyatt, "to have no heathen among us, who are at best but thorns in our sides, than to be at peace and league with them." His policies were vigorously pursued. By mid-century, the Indians had withdrawn to the edge of the retreating forests, and the coastal farmers of Virginia had virtually lost contact with the people who until so recently had been in possession of their lands.

Unlike the English of Virginia, North America's French pioneers quickly proved themselves skillful at dealing with the Indians. According to its charter of 1627, New France extended from Florida to the Arctic. But early on, most of its citizens lived within the boundaries of modern-day eastern Canada: the Maritime Provinces, the Gulf of Saint Lawrence, and the forests of Ontario. The first French settlement was at Port Royal in Acadia, now Nova Scotia. Although this outpost changed hands five times between the French and English during the century, it had little more than symbolic value. More central to the development of New France was Quebec on the Saint Lawrence River, founded in 1608 by the remarkable Samuel de Champlain.

In Champlain, New France found a tireless and many-faceted champion. Soldier, sailor, author, explorer, fur trader, and governor, "he bore the whole burden of

Plymouth, the settlement established by the *Mayflower* pilgrims on the Massachusetts coast in December, 1620, had become within seven years of their landfall a self-sufficient community of more than 200 souls. Its wooden houses lined a road leading to a two-story building that served both as a fort and as a meeting house. The community's trim prosperity had not been easily attained. In the first winter, half the immigrants died of disease or exposure. The colonists would not have survived without help from local Indians, who taught the newcomers how to plant and fertilize corn. But the settlers remained on their guard against attack, and after 1622, when they received news of an Indian massacre in Virginia, they enclosed the plantation with a palisade 2,625 feet long.

INDIAN
ENCAMPMENT

An eighteenth-century engraving shows a beaver pool dammed with trees felled by the animals. The sketch also reveals the ways in which the Indians hunted beavers—with traps, guns, bows and arrows, trained dogs, and, in winter, with nets spread over holes cut in the ice around the beavers' "kennels," or lodges.

A FORTUNE IN FUR

Of all the animals sought by hunters in the forests of the New World, none offered richer rewards than the beaver, shown second from top—between an otter and two species of seal—in the seventeenth-century drawing below. The creatures' smooth, dense pelts, which had long attracted Indian hunters, found an enthusiastic market in Europe, relieving the Continent of overreliance on the unpredictable Russian fur trade. Beaver hats soon became the height of gentlemanly fashion, while fur muffs and tippets were popular items of female attire. Seeking to exploit the demand, French and British traders ventured ever deeper into the interior in search of new sources of fur, and it was this quest more than any other activity that opened up the North American wilderness.

A brook

A savage killing a beaver with a fusee

A savage killing a beaver with his bow

a beaver cutting a tree

Beavers dragging a tree in ye water

a Beaver kennel

A BEAVER POOL

Beavers taken with nets

holes in the Ice

A savage grapples a beaver

a dog worrying a beaver

another dog worrys a beaver

beavers going to work

beavers dragging a tree as they swim

a beaver cau in a trap

The bank rais'd by the beavers

water falling over the bank

f.54   Nika ou loutre

amic ou castor

I

Loup marin

3. tigre marin

administration on his own shoulders," according to a contemporary historian. Champlain himself explained his achievements as arising from "the desire I have always entertained of making new discoveries in New France for the welfare, advantage, and the glory of the French name, as well as of bringing these poor people to the knowledge of God." The "poor people" were, of course, the Indians. No one was more influential in setting the course of French-Indian relations than Champlain.

Although he was committed to establishing a successful colony in New France, Champlain was also convinced that by exploring farther along the waterways of Canada he could, as he put it, "open the road to China." To aid him in this endeavor, he enlisted the help of Indian nations along the Saint Lawrence and Ottawa rivers, promising in return to assist them in their war against the dreaded Iroquois, based in what is now upstate New York. In 1609, accompanied by only one other Frenchman, Champlain set out by canoe with a war party of sixty Huron and Algonquin warriors. On the banks of the long lake (now called Lake Champlain) that forms the northern borders of New York State and Vermont, they came upon a party of 200 Iroquois. With a single shot of his harquebus, Champlain killed two Iroquois chiefs. Terrified by this unfamiliar weapon, the Iroquois fled in wild panic. This easy victory gained Champlain the undying gratitude of his Indian allies. But he had made a dangerous enemy in the Iroquois, whose frequent raids and subsequent alliance with the New England English proved a constant menace to New France.

Champlain never discovered a route to the East Indies, but many of his compatriots found riches enough in the forests of New France. Friendly Indians sailed down the tributaries of the Saint Lawrence, their canoes laden with furs that they had accumulated during the long winter trapping season; these were exchanged for axes, scalping knives, guns, blankets, and shoes. The annual spring fair at Montreal, founded in 1642 by priests and fur traders, was an important business occasion—and a riotous celebration until the bishop of New France forbade giving alcohol to the Indians, except, he wisely allowed, "in long, fatiguing, and extraordinary voyages."

Not all Frenchmen were content to wait for the furs to come to them. A breed of lawless young trappers, known as *coureurs de bois,* took to the wilds, becoming as adept at tracking on snowshoes and shooting rapids in birchbark canoes as the Indians among whom they lived. Their familiarity with Indian languages and society made them invaluable sources of information in times of war.

Perhaps the most remarkable immigrants to New France were the Jesuits. These tough, intellectual clerics first arrived at Quebec in 1626 and immediately set to work converting the Indians—not in the relative comfort of a white settlement, but in the villages of the Indians. Some were horrified by their strange companions: cannibalism, torture, incest, polygamy, and uncontrollable vermin were more than they had bargained for. "It is enough to say that they were altogether savage," wrote one early missionary, "from morning until night they have no other thought than to fill their stomachs." Many, however, developed a sympathetic relationship with their new parishioners. "There are Indians as there are Frenchmen," wrote an appreciative Ursuline nun, "but generally speaking they are more devout than the French."

A very different kind of society was taking shape on the coast between New France and Virginia. The men and women of New England, as the area north of the Hudson River became known, had not come to the New World to convert the savages or discover gold. Their aim was freedom of worship. These were the Puritans, English

Protestants who insisted on simplicity, or "purity," of worship, and felt that religion should be stripped of popish ritual and that bishops should be denied their lordly role in church administration. Their intellectual, moral, and political convictions were to exert a profound influence on the future of America. Some extreme Puritans, including the *Mayflower* pilgrims of 1620, sought complete independence from the Anglican church, and were consequently known as Separatists. Most of the later arrivals, however, were prepared to pledge loyalty to the English church and state.

Such was the case with a fresh wave of English settlers who arrived ten years after the *Mayflower*, bringing with them a royal charter to establish a colony named Massachusetts Bay. Although the newcomers did not call themselves separatists, the colony they established was politically and religiously the most headstrong in the New World. Despite the great hardships that attended its foundation—200 settlers died over the first winter—the progress made by Massachusetts was astonishing. In the first ten years of the colony's existence, 20,000 immigrants arrived. Many were highly educated or skilled; all were single-mindedly dedicated to establishing a pure society. Communities quickly sprang up along the bay or on the banks of the Charles River, including Boston, spiritual and financial heart of the colony.

Commercially these hard-working Englishmen did not make a misstep. The immigrants were far wealthier than the impoverished idealists on the *Mayflower*; in addition, they came in groups from clearly defined areas of England, East Anglia in particular, so the makings of a social structure were soon in place. Within five years of their arrival, the Puritans were exporting locally grown wheat to the West Indies. But it quickly became apparent that agriculture was not an easy way to prosper. A

Sketched in the 1650s, this view of New Amsterdam was completed after 1664, when the city was captured by the English, who renamed it New York. In the center lies the little wharf where passengers and goods landed; behind it stand a weighing beam and a crane. The large building in the background on the left is the fort, which contained a church as well as a barracks and a jail. New Amsterdam was founded in the 1620s as a Dutch center for the fur trade. The city prospered, exporting more than 7,000 beaver pelts to Holland in a single cargo in 1626—together with the news that the people of New Netherland had bought the island of Manhattan from the Indians for sixty guilders, about three months' wage for a craftsman. With the loss of the city, Dutch colonization in North America came to an end.

man took sixty days, it was said, to clear one New England acre of the great glacial boulders that studded his fields; and the following year, a fresh crop of rock, heaved up by the winter's frost, would have arisen from the earth.

The Puritans of Boston turned instead to the sea, where the codfish provided a reliable source of revenue. (It was later to become the symbol of the Commonwealth of Massachusetts.) The sea also became the high road to wealth for New England's shrewd merchants. By the latter part of the century, Boston had come to dominate North American trade, carrying New England fish and timber, Virginia tobacco, and West Indian sugar to Europe, then distributing English manufactured goods to the east-coast colonies on their return journeys. The success of the Massachusetts Bay Colony as a center of trade was to aggravate London merchants and influence English policy well before the end of the century.

Financial success was, however, not the main concern of Massachusetts Bay. The church was the center of colonial life. The Puritans' outspoken aim was to create a new Zion, a society in which laws, where possible, were derived from the Bible. "We shall be as a city upon a hill, the eyes of all the people are upon us," Massachusetts' first governor, John Winthrop, claimed in 1630.

In their efforts to establish a godly state, the Puritans enjoyed total freedom. Like Jamestown, Massachusetts Bay was funded by a stock company, but while the Virginia Company ruled from London, the Massachusetts Bay Company moved its governing council to New England, far from the eyes of the English church and state.

Religious freedom for the Puritan settlers meant freedom from the Church of England, by no means freedom of conscience for the individual living in the colony.

Although Puritan ministers did not hold political office, elders became increasingly influential interpreters of law. The result was theocracy, a government dominated by the church. Sunday was rigidly observed; in the Boston area, all work, play, and travel stopped at six o'clock on Saturday evening. Churches doubled as political meeting houses; those not attending risked a fine, and only church members—a select group of males considered suitable by the clergy to receive Communion—were permitted to vote. "If people shall be governors, who shall be governed?" asked one Puritan cleric in defense of such limited suffrage.

Laws became ever more severe. In an attempt to stamp out "the hideous clamor for liberty of conscience," political or religious dissent was promptly stifled. Some offenses were minor. A willful settler named Ursula Cole was sentenced to pay a fine or be whipped for saying she had "as lief hear a cat meow as Mr. Shephard preach." Those perceived as heretics, however, met with severe punishment. Few suffered more than the Quakers, members of a radical religious movement initiated in England in the mid-seventeenth century. By teaching that God could communicate directly to the common people, these eccentric outsiders threatened to undermine the authority of the Puritan leaders. Exile was the mildest punishment a Quaker could expect. If he came back to the colony he lost an ear; a second return cost the other ear. If he foolishly came back again, the authorities bored a hole in his tongue with a red-hot iron. This law was later simplified: A Quaker returning from exile was hanged. Several in fact died before popular resentment forced the repeal of this cruel ordinance.

The most remarkable opponent of the regime was Roger Williams. Although an orthodox Puritan in most doctrinal matters, this distinguished minister dared to contend before the elders of Massachusetts Bay that church and state should be separated and that the colony's land was held illegally because it had not been purchased from the Indians. Exiled in the dead of winter for these subversive opinions, he established Providence, which became the capital of Rhode Island. This tiny new colony, presided over by Williams, became a haven for the misfits of New England. Rogues' Island, its opponents mockingly called it; but Rhode Island remained the one place in North America that those of any belief—or none—could officially call home.

Other colonists left Massachusetts Bay for more worldly reasons, lured by the rich farmland of the Connecticut River valley. Connecticut became self-governing in 1639, later absorbing the independent colony of New Haven.

In spite of its self-righteous elders and official policy of intolerance, Massachusetts was not the gray, cheerless society that it was later painted. The Puritans wore bright colors, enjoyed sports, and were hardly teetotalers. There were taverns in Boston where a man could drink, smoke, and gossip. "Drink is in itself a good creature of God," wrote Increase Mather, a pillar of Boston's Second Church. The Puritans also had a devout respect for education. Harvard College, established in 1636 as a theological institution, soon became an internationally respected center of learning. Harvard Commencement Day was an annual holiday in Massachusetts, starting with sermons and ending with exuberant celebrations. Harvard was, according to Cotton Mather, Increase Mather's son, "the best thing that ever New England thought upon."

During the first years of colonization, the Puritans of New England had been more kindly disposed toward the Indians than toward Christians of differing views. Indeed, the Plymouth Pilgrims had cultivated excellent relations with the local Wampanoag tribe under its chief Massasoit. Toward the end of their first, starving winter, an English-speaking Pawtuxet Indian named Squanto had descended on Plymouth like a gift from God. He had taught the Pilgrims to fish, farm, and hunt, thereby saving many lives. The joyous first Thanksgiving of 1621—a three-day harvest celebration of food and friendship to which Massasoit brought ninety of his people—was a genuine and spontaneous expression of racial harmony.

Relations soon turned sour. In the 1630s, when feuding broke out in Connecticut between settlers and the Pequot tribe, there was no question of the immigrants' loyalty. Surrounding the Pequots at Mystic, the Puritans gave no quarter. "In a little more than one hour, five or six hundred of these barbarians were dismissed from a world that was burdened with them," wrote Cotton Mather. To confront the menace more effectively, Massachusetts Bay, Connecticut, Plymouth, and New Haven formed the New England Confederation in 1643, the first such alliance of colonies.

While New England and Virginia were developing their own characteristic societies 500 miles apart, other communities sprang up along the shores of the bays and rivers in between. One of the most promising experiments was undertaken by Cecilius

Calvert, Lord Baltimore, whose family had been granted by Charles I about 10 million acres of land north of the Potomac River. For this, Lord Baltimore was to pay the king two Indian arrows per year plus one-fifth of any gold and silver discovered.

The new colony was ideally situated. The climate was not too hot or too cold for the English, game abounded, and the forests were free of undergrowth. "Even the peas in those parts grow ten inches long in ten days," marveled one contemporary. And the Indians greeted the newcomers enthusiastically, offering every assistance.

The idyll was short-lived. A Roman Catholic, Calvert intended the new colony, which he called Maryland, to serve as a haven for his persecuted coreligionists. From the beginning, he insisted on religious toleration between Catholics and Protestants. Early on, however, conflicts arose between the proprietors of Maryland's great plantations—mainly Catholics—and their Puritan tenants, who soon constituted a majority of the population. Economically, the colony prospered, but Lord Baltimore's dream of religious harmony collapsed into political bickering and occasional civil disorder. Even the Act Concerning Religion of 1649, conceived by Lord Baltimore as a law to ensure toleration, was corrupted by bigotry. A paragraph insisted upon by strict Puritans declared that anyone denying the divinity of Christ or even making "reproachful speeches" concerning the Holy Trinity was to be punished with death.

Greater tolerance could be found in the colony of New Netherland, founded by the Dutch West India Company, which exercised a monopoly over Dutch trade in the New World. The Dutch built trading posts along the Atlantic coast and up the Hudson and Connecticut rivers, frequently clashing with Indians and English settlers in their efforts to acquire furs, timber, and other natural resources. In 1655, they annexed New Sweden—later to become the state of Delaware—Scandinavia's only colony in the New World. Yet New Netherland had problems of its own. It had immense difficulty in attracting settlers, not least since few emigrants could be tempted to leave

An engraving depicting the forced departure of prostitutes to New France is captioned: "The sad embarkation of Parisian ladies of joy in December 1687, and their farewell to the apothecaries and surgeons as well as to their lovers." The scene is obviously satirical, for some of the ladies have surnames that signify good birth—suggesting that they did not really go to America but perhaps had morals that classed them as fit for such. Nevertheless, the French government did transport prostitutes and criminals in an attempt to populate the great empty spaces of the New World. Many died during the passage or soon after arriving, and by the end of the seventeenth century, the population of New France was still no more than 10,000, compared with about 250,000 in the English colonies.

their rich and tolerant mother country to start afresh in a hostile land. It therefore had to draw in such peoples as it could, which meant that its population lacked the social cohesiveness of its English neighbors.

The main Dutch settlement was New Amsterdam, at the southern tip of Manhattan Island, which was named for the tribe from whom it had been purchased in 1626. The town was a secular, cosmopolitan place. Drunkenness was a perpetual problem and a law had to be enacted prohibiting the playing of golf in the streets. The city was run autocratically by its peglegged governor, Peter Stuyvesant, who administered the colony for seventeen years; but even he was unable to subdue this unruly community. "Shut your eyes," wrote the West India Company directors to Stuyvesant, "allow everyone his own belief as long as he behaves quietly and legally."

England remained the nation with the greatest stake in the development of North America, and by the middle of the seventeenth century, its rulers were waking up to the realization that unless they tightened the reins on their semi-independent colonies, they might lose control entirely. Once the trauma of the English Civil War had ended, first Oliver Cromwell, as lord protector of the commonwealth, and then the restored king, Charles II, took steps to clamp down on the economic and political freedoms that the New World had begun to take for granted.

During the years of confusion and war in England, colonial merchants had relied upon the ships of other countries, particularly the Netherlands, to transport their goods. To end this practice, England enacted two Navigation Acts aimed at debarring the Dutch and other foreign competitors from the colonial trade.

An early casualty of the acts was the Dutch colony of New Netherland. In 1664, four English warships dropped anchor off Manhattan Island and demanded the surrender of New Amsterdam. Peter Stuyvesant stood on the parapet of the fort, a gunner with a lighted match by his side, prepared to answer with cannon fire. Fortunately for the city, Stuyvesant's senior advisers talked him out of defending his colony; there was a small Dutch militia, but of the town's 1,500 or so inhabitants, only 250 were capable of bearing arms, and many flatly refused to do so. The English marched in unopposed and claimed New Amsterdam in the name of King Charles's brother James, duke of York. That day, Captain Richard Nicolls informed New England of the action, signing his letter "from New York." With the fall of New Amsterdam, the colony of New Netherland also changed its name and passed to the English.

The transition from New Amsterdam to New York was remarkably peaceful. It remained a worldly, tolerant, untidy town, quite willing to absorb the Scots, Huguenots, Catholics, Quakers, Anabaptists, and Jews, all of whom made it one of the New World's major centers of trade. The governor had absolute power; not until the end of the century did a representative assembly give the ordinary New Yorkers a say in running their city. But the governor was under instructions from England to tolerate people of all religions, "provided they give no disturbance to the public." So relaxed was the atmosphere of New York that Peter Stuyvesant himself remained in the colony, retiring to his farm in lower Manhattan, where he died in 1672.

In the English colonies themselves, the Navigation Acts were regarded with hostility and were widely and openly disregarded. Angered by such insubordination, England began to investigate the administration of her colonies, and in nearly all cases found it wanting. King Charles had need of money, and the colonies seemed to offer an attractive source of revenue that would not be dependent on the constant

THE LIMNERS' HONEST ART

Sturdy and plain of faith, the Puritans of New England had a correspondingly unvarnished attitude toward art. Their painters were themselves plain folk—usually craftsmen for whom portraiture was a sideline of their work as sign or coach painters. These mostly anonymous artists, called limners, worked in a medieval convention, making only a rudimentary attempt at three-dimensional representation and usually setting their subjects against a simple background. But as is apparent from the examples reproduced here, they recorded their compatriots with unsparing realism, for they believed that the smallest details of life were an expression of the will of God.

The earliest surviving portrait, dated 1664, is of a Mrs. Elizabeth Eggington *(below)*. Wealth and social standing are discreetly conveyed in the painting of John Freake, a Boston merchant and attorney *(top right)*. Freake's anonymous portraitist also painted Freake's relative, Elizabeth *(bottom right)*, shown tenderly holding her baby. There is no tenderness, however, in the self-portrait of Captain Thomas Smith *(below, left)*, whose stern outlook is summed up in the first two lines of the paper in his hand: "Why should I the world be minding therein a World of Evils Finding."

The Fairest Dealer

Of all the English colonies in North America, Pennsylvania had the most enlightened policy toward the Indians, and as a consequence, saw the least warfare. The colony was founded in 1682 by William Penn, son of a wealthy admiral, who was granted the territory in lieu of a debt owed by the Crown to his father. A convert to Quakerism, imprisoned in England several times for preaching the virtues of religious tolerance and pacifism, Penn considered his colony a "holy experiment" and established it with high idealism, treating the Indians fairly, acknowledging their title to the land, and trying to protect them in their dealings with settlers and traders.

Power was concentrated in the governor and his council, but liberty of conscience was guaranteed, and in an age when the death penalty was meted out to petty thieves, Penn made only murder and treason capital crimes. He was also a shrewd promoter, writing glowing reports of the colony that helped attract 9,000 settlers within three years of its founding.

supervision of the English Parliament. The result was increased interference in colonial affairs, with agents from London attempting to ensure that colonial governors enforced the law. In Virginia, a one-crop colony where the governor was a royal appointee, it was easy enough to insist upon obedience. Massachusetts, however, remained rebelliously independent for much of the century.

So consistent was Massachusetts Bay's flouting of the Navigation Acts, and so worrying the tales of discrimination and persecution told of the colony, that King Charles sent a special agent named Edward Randolph to investigate its affairs in 1676. Randolph, an orthodox royalist, quickly developed a loathing for the stubborn, pious Puritans of New England and wrote a damning report, asserting that Massachusetts was not only openly trading with other states, but had established its own customs office, which was pocketing all the revenue from foreign trade.

England's solution was to revoke the charter of the delinquent colony. In 1686, Charles's successor, the Catholic James II, incorporated it into the newly created Dominion of New England. This huge new colony, which stretched from Maine to the Hudson River, was intended to strengthen the colonies in the face of the threat from the French to the north, with whom the settlers were increasingly in conflict.

The man sent to govern the dominion was a political appointee named Sir Edmund Andros, whose policies seemed calculated to antagonize the elders of Massachusetts Bay. Legislation was no longer initiated by a representative assembly; taxation was imposed arbitrarily. Worse still, Boston churches were used for Anglican services. Andros even permitted the erection of a maypole on Boston Common and encouraged the celebration of Christmas, regarded as a pagan festivity by the Puritans.

It seemed as if God himself had raised his hand against this profane administration when, in 1688, William of Orange—a devout Protestant—overthrew James II to become king of England. The jubilant Puritans imprisoned Andros and shipped him home to London. The Dominion of New England was dissolved.

The new administration devised a fresh charter for Massachusetts Bay. Plymouth and Maine were included as part of the colony. This document was carefully drafted to prevent repeating previous abuses. Suffrage would be determined by ownership of property, not by church membership. But sixty years of theocracy were not to die with a charter. One last spasm of religious violence rocked the colony to its core.

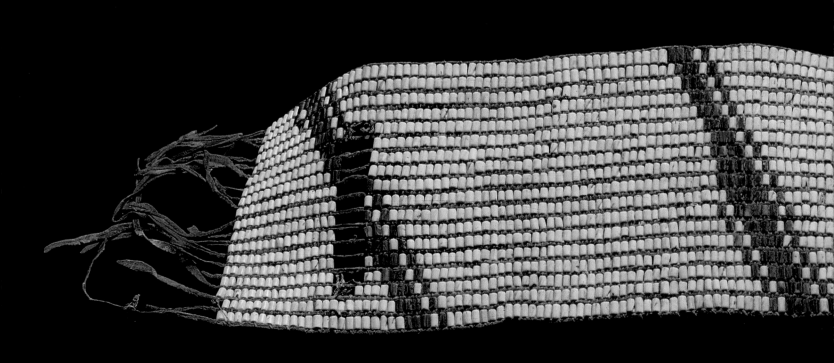

The Delaware Indians commemorated their 1682 treaty with William Penn—shown below in a portrait sketched by Francis Place in about 1698—in wampum belts made from seashells acquired by trade with coastal tribes. In the example below, a hatted white man and an Indian clasp hands in friendship, while territorial information is given in the diagonal stripes on each side.

In 1691, the daughter and a niece of the minister of Salem village, a settlement north of Boston on Massachusetts Bay, suffered recurring hysterical seizures. The two teenagers claimed to have been visited by spectral forms of local women, who urged them to sign a pact with the devil; their torments, it seemed, resulted from the devil's anger at their refusal to collaborate. Before long, several other women, all of them young and unmarried, confessed to similar visitations. The women they named were accused of witchcraft and arrested.

By the time the new governor of the colony, Sir William Phips, established a court of inquiry into the matter, more than 100 people—mostly women between the ages of forty and sixty—had been imprisoned. After a summer of trials, during which evidence often could not be heard above the howling of the possessed, nineteen were found guilty and hanged. One man who refused to answer charges was crushed to death with stones; two dogs were also executed. By this time, the whole district was in the grip of a collective hysteria, and few people were safe from accusation. Only when rumors began to circulate that the governor's own wife was in league with the devil did the authorities step in to bring the trials to an abrupt end. The frenzy soon ebbed, but the Salem witch trials had offered a frightening glimpse of the fear and suspicion simmering under the surface of New England life.

The last substantial area of the North American coast not colonized by Europeans lay between Virginia and Spanish Florida. In 1670, with Spain no longer strong enough to resist, King Charles II awarded this region to eight of his court favorites. The new colony, known as Carolina in honor of the King, comprised a northern and southern territory. It was run along undemocratic lines, the proprietors appointing a governor and half the members of his governing council. French Huguenots were among the early settlers; English immigrants came largely from the other colonies. Charles Town (now Charleston) soon became a properous center for the export of rice, the staple crop of southern Carolina's marshy coastal plantations.

The new colony was not entirely peaceful. Threats from Spain had been anticipated. What came as a surprise to Carolina's settlers, however, was the discovery that they were contesting the deer-hunting lands on their western frontier not so much with Indians as with the French.

"We have turned our eyes to New France," announced Louis XIV in 1663, "where to our regret, we see few inhabitants established . . . and these are in daily danger from the Iroquois." The Sun King, who had only recently acceded to the throne, had every reason for concern. Between 1641 and 1653, the Iroquois had waged two ruinous campaigns against the French. Generally regarded as the fiercest and best-organized Indian people north of Mexico, they had decimated the Huron, France's loyal allies in trade and war. "I would make this paper blush and my listeners would shudder," wrote one Jesuit, declining to describe the tortures inflicted upon his Christian charges by the Iroquois.

With New France on the brink of destruction, Louis and his chief minister, Jean-Baptiste Colbert, reorganized the huge colony. They abolished the Company of New France and the old order under which a small number of aristocratic landowners sublet their holdings to peasant farmers. A governor acting as head of state, a bishop, and an officer called an intendant, in charge of civil affairs, now took their place, but the ultimate authority lay with Louis and Colbert. They encouraged new colonists, especially artisans, and urged women to emigrate as wives for the soldiers. These policies proved effective. Between 1665 and 1690, the population of New France increased from 3,000 to 15,000. Security also improved after a successful winter campaign against the Iroquois. The Indians themselves vanished on their snowshoes into the forests, leaving the pursuing French to lay waste the territory.

Still searching for the great river that would carry them westward to the Pacific Ocean, the French found instead the greatest river of North America, flowing south to the Gulf of Mexico. Jacques Marquette, a Jesuit priest, and Louis Jolliet were the first to explore the Mississippi, followed by Robert de La Salle, who descended the river to its mouth. On the basis of this voyage, La Salle claimed the entire Mississippi valley for France, naming it Louisiana after the king. A series of forts, from Detroit to Biloxi, sought to establish French rights to this vast territory.

In spite of reforms and expansion, New France remained a beleaguered colony. The last two decades of the century were blighted by continual war with England, fought on several fronts. There had long been battles over possession of Newfoundland and Acadia. To these were added new conflicts in the far north over fur trading in the Hudson Bay region, as well as over the Carolina deer trade in the south. Meanwhile, the savage dispute over the hinterland of northern New York and New England continued to drain the resources of both nations.

By the waning decades of the century, a new order was taking shape in North America as the populous and aggressive English colonies expanded. All along the coast, tribal peoples had been pushed back from their traditional lands. In many regions, political weakness, together with European diseases to which they had no natural immunity, left them powerless to offer any organized resistance.

But this was not the case in New England. After the Pequot War in 1637, the Puritans showed a new interest in the Indians, largely as a result of the efforts of John Eliot. A fervent missionary, he translated the Bible into Algonquian—it became *Up-Biblum God*—and established two Indian churches, where more than 1,000 "praying Indians" could worship. There was even an Indian college at Harvard.

The great majority of Native Americans, however, were not interested in the white man's religion, and resented the loss of their hunting grounds to the settlers. The peace came to an end abruptly in 1675, when Massasoit's son Metacomet, known to the English as King Philip, led an alliance of tribes living in the region from Maine to Rhode Island in a remarkably well-coordinated campaign. "I am resolved not to see the day when I have no country," Metacomet said to an English friend.

In the summer of that year, Metacomet's warriors launched a series of lightning raids on English villages and homesteads. At first, these guerrilla attacks were successful, pushing the colonists back to within twenty miles of Boston by that winter. But English firepower and manpower—the settlers outnumbered the Indians by four to one—inevitably prevailed. By the following summer, the Indians were running out of food and ammunition and had begun to surrender. The fight may have gone out of Metacomet as well, for his wife and child were captured and sold as slaves to Bermuda. He soon died at the hands of an Indian in the service of the settlers. His head was carried to Plymouth and impaled there on the blockhouse wall.

King Philip's War, as it became known, severely tested the colony. One in sixteen of the male settlers died. Of ninety Puritan towns, fifty-two had been attacked and twelve totally destroyed. The colonial frontier was pushed back some forty miles.

The war was even more disastrous for the coastal Indians. Most withdrew westward. Those who chose to remain were either forced to accept Christianity and live in "praying villages" or else to work as tenant farmers, a sight that Metacomet, happily, never lived to see.

Meanwhile, Indian trouble had also broken out in Virginia, where settlers in the hilly frontier country known as the Piedmont persuaded themselves that they too were to be the victims of an all-out assault. Led by a fiery and charismatic aristocrat named Nathaniel Bacon, the upcountry Virginians marched on Jamestown. "I come for a commission against the heathen who daily, inhumanly murder us and spill our brethren's blood," announced Bacon to the assembled burgesses. Having duly obtained his commission by the threat of force, Bacon launched a ruthless campaign

By the time this view of Harvard was engraved in 1725, the college had been in existence for eighty-nine years, making it the oldest in North America. Named after a benefactor who endowed the institution, it was founded to provide a Puritan education and especially to prepare young men for the ministry. In order to gain admission for the three-year course, students had to be literate in Latin verse and prose, and had to demonstrate a familiarity with Greek nouns and verbs. When classes began in 1638, there was only one master in a single frame house. Old Harvard, the college building to the left of the quadrangle, was built in 1674, and Stoughton College opposite was opened in 1689. By the end of the century, Harvard's educational regimen had become too liberal for some New Englanders, who founded their own college, now Yale University.

against the Indians. Then, outlawed for his conduct, he turned his anger on the colony's governors. He marched again on Jamestown, burning it to the ground.

For a time, it seemed that Bacon might take over the colony, but before he could engage the governor's troops, he was struck down by "the bloody flux," probably dysentery, and died. The revolt he had inspired thereupon collapsed, to the relief of the rich coastal tobacco famers who had considered him, in the words of a royal commission set up to investigate the uprising, "of a most imperious and dangerous hidden pride of heart."

Bacon's Rebellion had little effect upon Virginia society, which remained divided between rich and poor. The only real beneficiary of the conflict was Charles II, who took advantage of the situation to replace the governor and tighten royal control. There were losers too: Apart from the rebel leaders, who were hanged for the uprising, the Indians of the Piedmont retreated into the wilderness, a broken power.

A happier story was told in the last colony to be established during the first century of settlement, and its founder's idealism illuminated the early history of America. William Penn was the son of an admiral with close connections to the court of Charles II. Early in his life, the young man enraged his father by becoming a Quaker at a time when many members of the sect were being persecuted for their beliefs. Young Penn himself served terms in both Newgate jail and the Tower of London. "My prison shall be my grave ere I budge a jot," he wrote, "for I owe obedience of my conscience to no mortal man."

It was presumably with a sense of relief that King Charles found a way of ridding England of this troublesome aristocrat. Money he had borrowed from Penn's father had accumulated to the tune of £16,000 by 1680. The king wrote off the debt by granting the younger Penn absolute proprietorship over a large tract of land north of Maryland, to which the king's brother James added the territory of Delaware.

The colony of Pennsylvania, established in 1682, was conceived by Penn on the highest of principles. "I went thither to lay the foundation of a free colony for all mankind," he wrote. Its chief settlement of Philadelphia—meaning City of Brotherly Love—was spaciously laid out in a formal grid of streets with large lots for each house, conforming to Penn's instructions "that it may be a green country town, which will never be burnt and always be wholesome." By the turn of the century, it numbered at least 5,000 inhabitants—as many as New York.

Although Pennsylvania's colonists—among them many Germans—chafed under Penn's paternalistic rule and the relatively limited representation in government that he granted them, the colony prospered. Above all, it came to serve as a model in its relations with the Indians, with whom Penn made several treaties promising tolerance and respect for property. "I am very sensible of unkindness and injustice that hath been too much exercised toward you by the people of these parts of the world," he wrote to the Indians, "but I am not such a man." He lived up to his word.

William Penn's "holy experiment" was the last piece to fall into place in the jigsaw of settlements that made up seventeenth-century North America. By the year 1700, some 250,000 settlers owing allegiance to England inhabited a string of colonies stretching from Canada to the Carolinas. Ranged against them in growing hostility were the 10,000 inhabitants of New France. The conflict between the two was to be resolved only in 1763, in favor of the English. But soon after that triumph, the king of England would face the wrath of his own rebellious colonists—an outcome few people could have foreseen in the pioneering days of the seventeenth century.

ELUCIDATING THE LAWS OF NATURE

The new philosophy calls all in doubt." So wrote the English poet John Donne in 1611, lamenting that a fresh world view that he had seen gaining acceptance in his lifetime left "all in pieces, all coherence gone." Old certainties had indeed been challenged over the course of the previous century, and by no one more disturbingly than the Polish ecclesiastic Nicolaus Copernicus, who had argued that the Sun, not the Earth, was the center of the universe.

In the decades following Donne's complaint, students were to push onward with the investigation of the natural world, showing ever-greater concern for direct observation and making use of experimentation in a more systematic way than their learned forebears had done. In their quest to discover the fundamental laws governing the behavior of objects and substances, they would develop a view of a world ruled by natural forces rather than by the direct supervision of God. Although their discoveries fundamentally changed the way in which people viewed the universe, these

seekers were generally far from revolutionary in their intentions. Most of them believed that if Nature resembled a machine, it was nonetheless one that had been created by God, and in the intricate regularity of its workings, they saw a reflection of divine perfection.

Alongside the scientific work itself, new methodologies evolved that emphasized objective investigation. The English philosopher Francis Bacon advocated induction, a method of logic whereby systematic, controlled observation and experimentation establishes specific facts, which are then used as a foundation for determining general principles. In contrast, the French philosopher René Descartes championed the deductive method of reason—the development of a logical, step-by-step argument from basic premises. The two approaches were to dominate Western scientific thought in the centuries to come.

A NEW VIEW OF THE HEAVENS

Ottavio Leoni's crayon portrait of Galileo dates from 1624, when the scientist was in Rome arguing for papal acceptance of the Copernican theory. Eight years later, he published a book comparing the Copernican with the traditional view of the universe. Pope Urban VIII's initial approval of this project turned to animosity when the work seemed to mock his opinions, and Galileo was condemned to house arrest.

Astronomy, the study of the heavens, places the Earth in a cosmic context. The radical advances made by sixteenth- and seventeenth-century astronomers forced a change in the way people regarded the world and themselves—and were greeted by many with suspicion and hostility.

Previously, Christians had accepted the view handed down by ancient astronomers that the Earth lay at rest at the center of the universe. The heavenly bodies moved around it in orbits that were either circles or combinations of circles. This view was first challenged in modern times by Copernicus in *On the Revolutions of the Heavenly Spheres* (1543), which set down in print the theory he had held

for at least thirty years that "the center of the Earth is not the center of the universe. . . . All orbits encircle the Sun."

The astronomer Johannes Kepler (1571-1630) confirmed and refined Copernicus's Sun-centered theory. He derived more accurate laws for planetary motion, and his Rudolphine Tables—named after his patron, the Emperor Rudolf II—predicted with unprecedented accuracy the positions of the planets. Galileo Galilei (1564-1642)—a scientist of great versatility who also established central principles of motion and mechanics—was the first to demonstrate the astronomical use of the telescope in his book *The Starry Messenger*, published in 1610.

One of about 100 telescopes made by Galileo, this had the basic design of a tube *(diagram, below)* with a convex lens at one end directing light through a concave lens near the eye to create an enlarged image. With the telescope Galileo could see craters on the Moon.

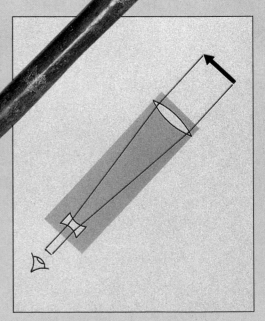

An engraving by Jacob van Heyden shows Johannes Kepler when he was working as imperial mathematician in 1620. Kepler initially intended to enter the Roman Catholic church, but an aptitude for mathematics led him to a career in astronomy. Combining aesthetic sensibility with a deeply religious view of Creation, he believed that the universe had been made in accordance with a harmonious design.

The solar system, shown here as it was known in the seventeenth century (though not to scale), was described by Kepler's three laws of planetary motion as a self-contained system of planets moved by force from the Sun. His third law, set forth in his *Harmony of the World* of 1619, described the systematic way in which the size of orbits is related to their periods—the length of time the planets take to complete them.

According to Kepler's second law, if Mars travels from point A to point B in the same time that it takes to cover the much shorter distance from C to D, then the shaded sections of the diagram are of equal area. His first law stated that the planetary orbits were simple ellipses rather than combinations of circles. Both laws were first stated in Kepler's *New Astronomy* of 1609.

SATURN 29.5 years

JUPITER 11.75 years

MARS 687 days

EARTH 365.25 days

VENUS 224.75 days

MERCURY 88 days

SUN

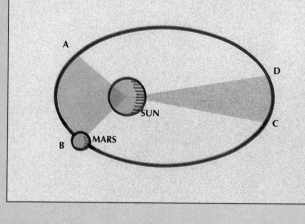

A

D

SUN

C

B MARS

BREAKTHROUGHS IN MEDICINE

For physicians of the early seventeenth century, the basic principles of medicine had been expounded in the distant past by two Greeks, Aristotle and the second-century-AD writer Galen. A Flemish anatomist, Andreas Vesalius (1514-1564), had refined some of Galen's anatomical descriptions, while his Swiss contemporary, Paracelsus, had introduced the idea that disease could be a localized rather than a general disturbance. But it was the English physician William Harvey (1578-1657) who stimulated a surge of fresh physiological ideas by disproving an important element in Galen's description of how the body worked. Veins, Galen had claimed, carried nutrition derived from food in the intestines to the liver and then to the rest of the body. The arteries formed a separate system that transmitted blood carrying "natural heat" from the heart and "vital spirit" inhaled from the air.

In his *On the Motion of the Heart* of 1628, Harvey—shown at right in a portrait painted the previous year—recorded the detailed experiments on the exposed hearts and blood vessels of live animals that had led him to a different view. The heartbeat, he claimed, corresponds with a constriction of the heart's walls to expel blood, forcing it "from the right (ventricle) into the lungs, and from the left (ventricle) into the aorta whence the pulse of the arteries." He reasoned that the large amounts of blood transferred from veins to arteries required a return flow at some point. The subsequent discovery of capillaries at the extremities of the body by the Italian physiologist Marcello Malpighi provided the missing connection between arteries and veins, thus confirming blood's circulatory passage.

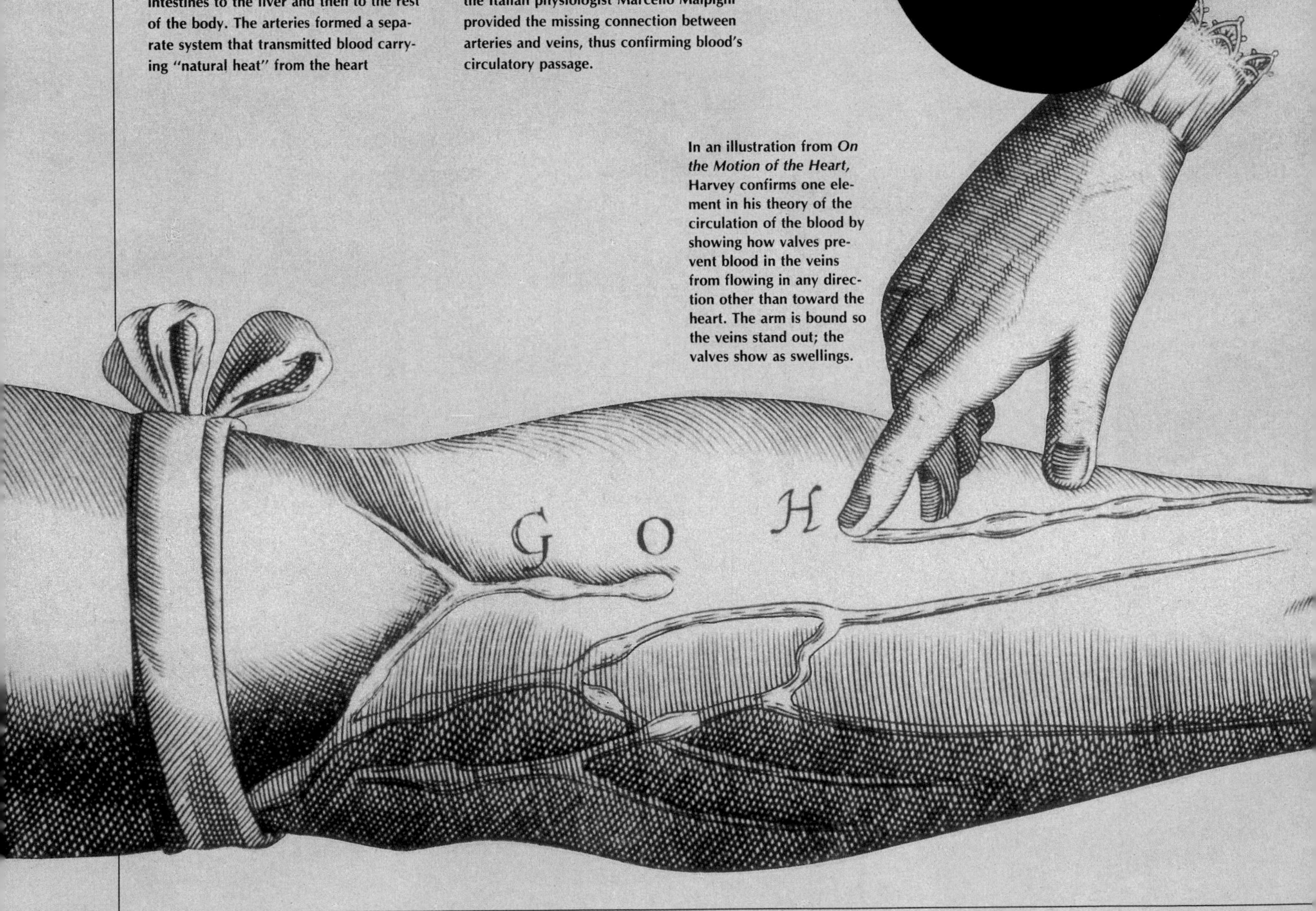

In an illustration from *On the Motion of the Heart*, Harvey confirms one element in his theory of the circulation of the blood by showing how valves prevent blood in the veins from flowing in any direction other than toward the heart. The arm is bound so the veins stand out; the valves show as swellings.

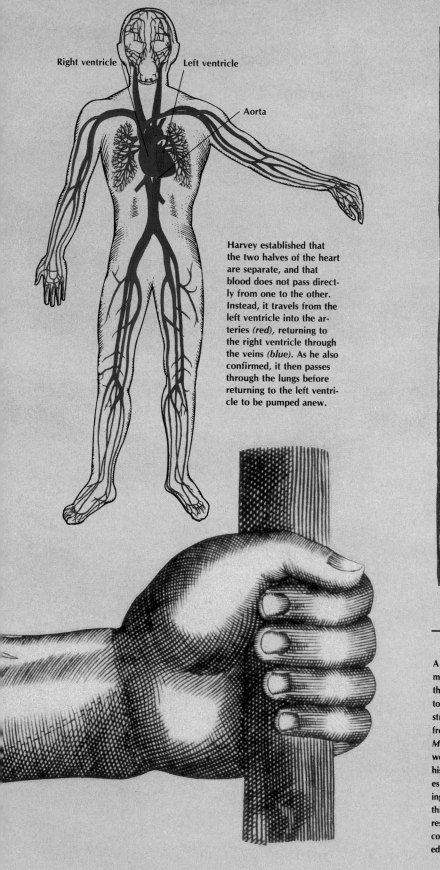

Right ventricle

Left ventricle

Aorta

Harvey established that the two halves of the heart are separate, and that blood does not pass directly from one to the other. Instead, it travels from the left ventricle into the arteries (red), returning to the right ventricle through the veins (blue). As he also confirmed, it then passes through the lungs before returning to the left ventricle to be pumped anew.

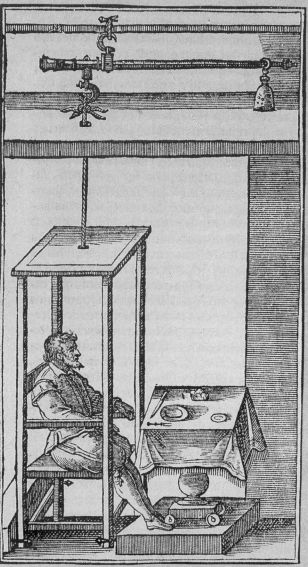

A Patient Pioneer

A pioneer of accurate measurement in medicine, the Italian physician Sanctorius (1561-1636) demonstrates, in this illustration from his book *On Medical Measurement* of 1614, a weighing device used in his study of weight changes in the body following ingestion and excretion. In thirty years of systematic research, during the course of which he invented instruments to measure humidity and body temperature, he conceived the view that the body loses weight through the skin by a process he termed "insensible perspiration." Believing, mistakenly, that measuring this exudation could be diagnostically useful, Sanctorius hoped to explore the traditional idea of health as a balance between what the body consumes and what it rejects.

L

M

I

R

R

R

R

R

R

𝓕𝒾𝓰: 3.

E D

F C

H G

K

B

A

T

V

S

Q

P

O

A 1686 mezzotint portrays Leeuwenhoek, by that time a scientist of international renown, with one of his microscopes. Lacking a university education, he more than compensated with a sharp mathematical mind, great manual dexterity, and keen eyesight. Such was his reputation that he received kings as admiring guests.

Leeuwenhoek included this picture of an ichneumon fly in a letter—one of many such—to London's Royal Society, giving an account of the hatching of these insects out of the bodies of dead aphids. The clarity of the illustration (commissioned from an artist, since Leeuwenhoek was a poor draftsman) complements the detail of his verbal description.

EXPLORING A MINIATURE WORLD

Whereas the astronomer used the telescope, the tool of the biologist was the microscope, also invented during the first decade of the seventeenth century and similarly designed to make visible what was previously invisible.

The microscope's scientific value was only fully realized in the middle of the century, when Malpighi used it to discover capillaries. Then in 1665 Robert Hooke, a founding member of London's Royal Society, published his superbly illustrated *Micrographia*—the first major work

to display the potential of the instrument—which revealed the cellular structure of plants.

But it was a Dutch civil servant named Antoni van Leeuwenhoek (1632-1723) who made the most remarkable advances in this field. At the age of forty, he decided to develop the magnifying glasses used by drapers to inspect cloth, and in so doing, he created an instrument powerful enough to discern red blood cells and bacteria. Indeed, Leeuwenhoek invented not only an instrument but a high-

quality lens-grinding technique, the secret of which he never divulged. True to the rigorous scientific standards then being established in intellectual circles, he presented his observations precisely and in full before attempting any interpretation. Leeuwenhoek's methods revealed the existence of a host of micro-organisms and allowed him to produce informed theories on the subject of sexual reproduction (he identified sperm) and the transport systems for air and fluids within plants and animals.

Lens

Magnifying Lens Power

Designed by Robert Hooke (1635-1702), this microscope had a three-lens arrangement *(diagram, right)* as opposed to Leeuwenhoek's single-lens system. Finished luxuriously in gold-embossed leather, the microscope would no doubt have been kept in a library among handsomely bound books. Hooke excelled as an instrument-maker, inventing an efficient air pump, improving clocks and microscopes, and developing meteorological equipment.

A typical Leeuwenhoek microscope, this instrument, two and one-third inches long, consists of a minute, hand-ground lens clamped between two plates. The specimen to be examined was fixed on the pin; its position in relation to the lens could be adjusted by screw threads.

Robert Boyle (1627-1691) embodied the spirit of seventeenth-century scientific inquiry. A pioneer in chemical classification using acid-alkali color indicators, in the physics of gases, and in theories of basic matter, Boyle found in the orderliness of the universe further evidence for the existence of God.

One of the greatest challenges for seventeenth-century scholars was the investigation of gases. That air had substance had been shown in the fifth century BC by the Greek philosopher Empedocles: An empty vessel upturned and immersed in water did not fill with the liquid because trapped air resisted the inflow. But further experimentation proved difficult, for air was elusive, invisible, and almost intangible. Consequently, the Aristotelian view that nature abhors a vacuum and that the effects of a suction pump were produced by a mysterious force remained unchallenged.

Galileo reopened the question by pumping air into a sealed vessel and weighing it on a balance (the more air pumped in, the heavier the vessel), and Evangelista Torricelli in Rome and Otto von Guericke *(opposite)* in south Germany demonstrated conclusively the existence of air pressure. The first person to formulate a law accurately describing the behavior of air, however, was Ireland's Robert Boyle, a founder of London's Royal Society. To show that even gases could be measured, Boyle demonstrated how air, trapped at the end of a sealed tube, would halve its volume in response to doubled pressure. He thus arrived at Boyle's law, which states that, for gases, pressure and volume are inversely related.

Boyle's 1662 book *New Experiments* describes how a kitten was suffocated and a lighted candle was extinguished in the vacuum jar *(far left)* when the air was pumped out of it, thus proving air's importance for life and combustion. He also used a jar containing a bell *(left)* to investigate air's behavior as a conductor of sound.

EVANGELISTA TORRICELLI

A brilliant pupil of Galileo, Evangelista Torricelli (1608-1647) demonstrated that if glass tubes full of mercury were upturned and immersed in bowls or tubs, the mercury was supported at the same height, whatever the shape or size of the tube. This effect was due, he said, to pressure exerted by the "sea of elementary air" in which we are submerged.

A diplomat and mayor of the German town of Magdeburg, Otto von Guericke (1602-1686) had sought since his student days to demonstrate the existence of vacuums, thereby proving Aristotle wrong. In one experiment, two teams of horses tried unsuccessfully to pull apart two copper hemispheres emptied of air, thereby illustrating the force of air pressure.

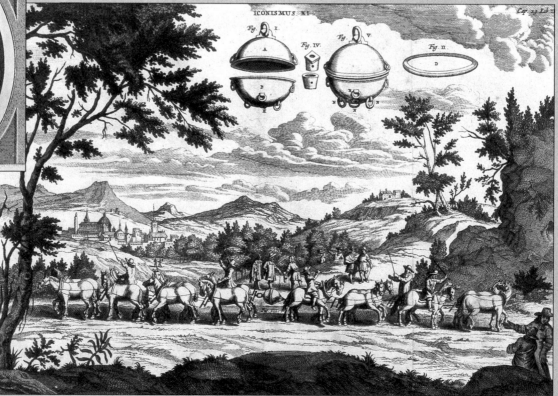

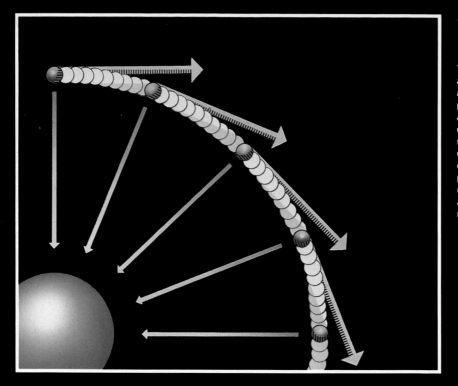

The Moon is diverted from a straight path *(thick arrows)* by the gravitational pull of the Earth *(thin arrows)*, resulting in an equilibrium that holds the satellite in orbit. A similar explanation for the motion of planets around the Sun provided Newton with a cosmic exemplar of the applications of his mathematical law of gravitation.

Light fans out into the spectrum of colors when passed through a prism. Newton's work on light and color, presented in his *Opticks* of 1704, demolished the theory that colors arise as modifications of white light. White, said Newton, is a combination of colors, each refracted to a different degree on passing through a dense medium such as glass.

THE FATHER OF MODERN SCIENCE

Isaac Newton (1642-1727) drew together many of the scientific advances of the century into a coherent, universal picture. Unexceptional at school, he blossomed intellectually at Cambridge University, where he was introduced to the work of Descartes and discovered his own gift for mathematics and science.

While still a student, Newton invented the mathematical technique of calculus to analyze movement and change quantitatively. This was followed by work on optics and the reflecting telescope, which in turn gave way to Newton's abiding interest: motion and "force," the cause of change in motion. He dedicated much of his masterpiece, the *Mathematical Principles of Natural Philosophy* of 1687, to exploring the action of forces on bodies. This work contains his three laws of motion, which state that a body continues in a state of rest or of uniform motion in a straight line unless acted on by a force; that a body's acceleration is proportional to, and in the same direction as, the force applied to it; and that to every action there is an equal and opposite reaction.

Newton also proposed the existence of a universal force of gravity, an attraction exerted by every body in the universe on every other body, and varying with the masses of the bodies and the distances between them. Thus, the force drawing an apple to the earth was the same as the one determining the orbits of the planets around the Sun—a unifying principle for the universe.

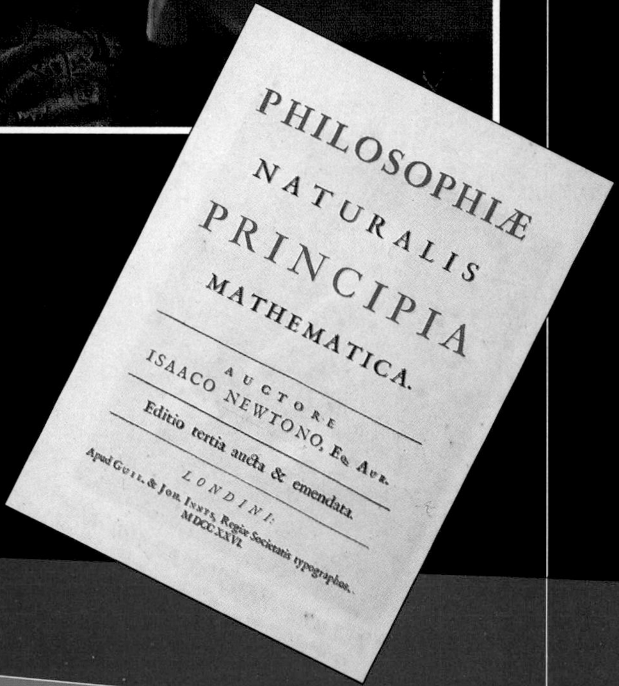

"I now demonstrate the frame of the system of the World," Newton—sitting by a celestial globe in the 1726 portrait above—declared with justifiable immodesty in his *Mathematical Principles (right)*. This three-part treatise deals with dynamics—the study of the forces producing motion—and links the planetary laws of Kepler with the terrestrial physics of Galileo.

PHILOSOPHIÆ
NATURALIS
PRINCIPIA
MATHEMATICA.

AUCTORE
ISAACO NEWTONO, Eq. Aur.

Editio tertia aucta & emendata.

LONDINI:
Apud Guil. & Joh. Innys, Regiæ Societatis typographos.
MDCCXXVI.

1600-1610	1610-1620	1620-1630	1630-1640	1640-1650

The accession of the Tianqi emperor accelerates the decline of China's Ming dynasty (1620).

In Japan, Hidetada dies, and Iemitsu becomes shogun (1623).

Ieyasu's troops besiege and take Osaka castle. Its lord, Hideyori, commits suicide (1615).

Tokugawa Ieyasu dies (1616).

Ieyasu's successor, Hidetada, embarks on a large-scale persecution of Japan's Christians (1618).

The Manchu ruler Nurhachi launches an invasion of China (1618).

At the Battle of Sekigahara, the army of Tokugawa Ieyasu defeats the forces of rival warlord Ishida Mitsunari, effectively reuniting Japan (1600).

Tokugawa Ieyasu is appointed shogun (military governor) of Japan—a position his family will hold for the next 264 years (1603).

The Manchu establish a new capital on former Chinese territory at Shenyang (1625).

The Manchu are defeated by the Chinese at the Battle of Ningyuan. Nurhachi is killed (1626).

A Manchu army reaches the gates of Beijing before withdrawing north of the Great Wall (1629).

Iemitsu introduces the first of a series of measures designed to limit Japan's contacts with the outside world (1633).

Iemitsu applies measures to keep Japan's feudal nobility in check (1635).

Iemitsu's forces crush rebels holding out in the castle of Shimabara (1638).

Li Zicheng, leader of a peasant rebellion, enters the Chinese capital, Beijing. The last Ming emperor commits suicide (1644).

The Ming general Wu Sangui invites the Manchu to help him drive out Li's rebels. The Manchu then proclaim their own Qing dynasty as the successor to the Ming and place their five-year-old ruler on the Chinese throne under the reign title of Shunzhi (1644).

THE FAR EAST

The Dutch East India Company is founded to foster trade with the Orient (1602).

On the death of Queen Elizabeth, James VI of Scotland accedes to the English throne as James I, establishing the Stuart dynasty (1603).

The Gunpowder Plot—an attempt to blow up England's king and Parliament—is foiled (1605).

After forty-one years of war, the Dutch arrange a truce with their former rulers, the Hapsburg kings of Spain (1609).

In the Plantation of Ulster, James I gives land forfeited by Catholic rebels in northern Ireland to Protestant settlers (1611).

A Protestant revolt in Bohemia against the authority of the Holy Roman emperor signals the outbreak of the Thirty Years' War (1618).

Holland's leading statesman, Johan van Oldenbarnevelt, is executed on charges of treason (1619).

The Dutch resume their war with Spain (1621).

The Dutch West India Company is founded (1621).

James I dies. His son Charles I becomes king of England, Scotland, and Ireland (1625).

Admiral Piet Heyn captures a Spanish treasure fleet (1628).

Charles I unwillingly gives his assent to the Petition of Right, outlawing taxes without parliamentary consent (1628).

Charles I dissolves Parliament, arresting nine of its leaders (1629).

A speculative boom in tulip prices in Holland ends in a dramatic crash (1637).

Alarmed by an attempt to impose the Anglican prayer book, supporters of Scotland's Presbyterian church swear by the Solemn League and Covenant to defend the reformed faith (1638).

Civil war breaks out in England between forces loyal to the king and to Parliament (1642).

Louis XIV succeeds to the French throne at the age of four (1643).

Charles I's Royalist forces are decisively defeated at the Battle of Naseby (1645).

The Treaty of Westphalia brings to an end the Thirty Years' War. As part of the peace settlement, Spain finally agrees to recognize Dutch independence (1648).

Charles I is executed (1649).

WESTERN EUROPE

The Mayflower brings the Pilgrims to Massachusetts (1620).

Indians massacre 347 Virginian settlers—nearly one-third of the colony's population (1622).

King James I of England dissolves the Virginia Company and establishes royal control of the colony (1624).

The Dutch purchase Manhattan Island from the Indians (1626).

Cardinal Richelieu grants a charter permitting the colonization of New France from Florida to the Arctic Circle (1627).

Dutch emigrants settle on the island of Manhattan (1611).

The introduction of the West Indian tobacco plant transforms the fortunes of the colony of Virginia (1612).

The governor of Virginia convenes a representative assembly called the House of Burgesses—the first in North America (1619).

A group of English settlers establishes the colony of Jamestown on the James River in Virginia—the first permanent English settlement in the New World (1607).

Samuel de Champlain founds Quebec (1608).

Lord Baltimore establishes the colony of Maryland (1632).

Harvard College is founded as a theological institution (1636).

New England settlers defeat neighboring Indian tribes in the Pequot War (1637).

Connecticut becomes a self-governing entity, separate from Massachusetts (1639).

French priests and fur traders found Montreal (1642).

The New England Confederation links the colonies of Connecticut, New Haven, Plymouth, and Massachusetts Bay, for purposes of defense (1643).

NORTH AMERICA

Persia's ruler Shah Abbās captures Tabrīz from the Ottomans (1603).

Abbās wins the Armenian city of Erevan from the Ottomans (1604).

Persian forces defeat an Ottoman army in the battle at Sufian (1605).

Making peace with Abbās, the Ottoman sultan Ahmed I agrees to renounce his predecessors' conquests in Persia (1612).

Suspecting a plot, Abbās arranges for the assassination of his eldest son (1615).

An Anglo-Persian force captures the Portuguese base of Hormuz in the Persian Gulf (1622).

In renewed conflict with the Ottomans, Abbās's troops relieve a Turkish siege of Baghdad (1626).

Abbās dies. He is succeeded by his grandson Safi (1629).

Renewing warfare, the Ottomans seize Hamadan. Kandahār is lost to the Uzbek rulers of Bukhara (1630).

The Ottomans reconquer Baghdad (1638).

Abbās II accedes to the throne at the age of nine (1642).

Abbās reconquers Kandahār, now in the hands of the Mogul rulers of India (1649).

PERSIA

TimeFrame AD 1600-1700

an's ruler Iemitsu dies, to be ceeded by his ten-year-old , Ietsuna. A plot by discon- ted ronin—masterless samu- warriors—to do away with Tokugawa government is covered and crushed (1651).

ssacks expanding eastward d the fortress of Albazin on Amur River, posing a threat China's northern frontier 55).

rebel leader Zheng Cheng- g, known to Westerners as xinga, narrowly fails to cap- China's largest city, Nanjing 59).

Coxinga captures Taiwan from the Dutch. Chinese authorities evacuate a long coastal strip in the face of the threat (1661).

An eight-year-old accedes to the Chinese throne as the Kangxi emperor (1662).

Kangxi arranges the murder of his regent, Oboi, and personally takes over the reins of command (1669).

A trio of rebel generals known as the Three Feudatories starts a seven-year uprising against Kangxi (1674).

Kangxi launches a campaign against the Russians in the Amur River region (1680).

Chinese forces capture Taiwan from Coxinga's successors (1683).

The Treaty of Nerchinsk—the first formal agreement between China and any European pow- er—ends the fighting between Russians and Chinese in the Amur Valley (1689).

Matsuo Bashō, Japan's master of haiku, dies (1694).

Kangxi crushes a Mongol upris- ing under the leadership of Gal- dan, who commits suicide (1697).

---

lliam II, stadholder (military der) of the Dutch Republic, , leaving a posthumously n son as his heir (1650).

an de Witt becomes pension- of Holland (1653).

ver Cromwell is declared d protector of England, Scot- d, and Ireland (1653).

First Anglo-Dutch War, in- red by commercial rivalry, s inconclusively (1654).

ver Cromwell dies (1658).

The exiled son of Charles I re- turns to England to take the throne as Charles II (1660).

Louis XIV reaches his majority and takes charge of the govern- ment of France (1661).

The Second Anglo-Dutch War breaks out (1665).

Plague afflicts England (1665).

The Great Fire of London devas- tates England's capital (1666).

The Treaty of Breda ends Anglo- Dutch hostilities on terms favor- able to the Dutch (1667).

Louis XIV of France invades the Dutch Republic (1672).

Following the murder of Johan de Witt by a mob, William III assumes control of the Dutch Republic, bringing to an end the so-called stadholderless period (1672).

By the Treaty of Nijmegen, France agrees to restore all cap- tured Dutch territory and drop restrictive trade measures (1678).

The French court moves from Paris to Versailles (1682).

James II, a Catholic, succeeds his brother, Charles II, as king of England (1685).

The English scientist Isaac New- ton publishes his Mathematical Principles (1687).

William III invades England at the invitation of Protestants dis- contented with James's Catholi- cism. James flees to France. William agrees to rule England jointly with his wife, Mary, daughter of the deposed mon- arch (1688).

William defeats an Irish uprising in favor of James II at the Battle of the Boyne (1690).

Queen Mary dies (1694).

England's King Charles II estab- lishes the colony of Carolina between Virginia and the Span- ish settlements in Florida (1670).

Jacques Marquette and Louis Joliet explore the Mississippi River as far as its confluence with the Arkansas River (1673).

King Philip's War pits an Indian confederation against the New England settlers. It ends with the defeat and death of the Indian ruler (1675-1676).

Robert de La Salle reaches the mouth of the Mississippi River, claiming the entire valley in the name of New France (1682).

The Dominion of New England is created to consolidate the ar- ea's colonies under royal control (1686).

On James II's deposition, the Dominion of New England is dissolved (1689).

Louis XIV and his chief minister, Colbert, reorganize New France under royal control (1663).

The English seize New Amster- dam, renaming it New York (1664).

Dutch annex New Sweden, only Scandinavian colony in New World (1655).

Witchcraft trials shake the com- munity of Salem in Massachu- setts Bay Colony (1692).

Cossack horsemen raid deep in- to Persia—the first of a series of incursions on the Caspian front (1664).

On the death of Abbās II, the throne passes to his son Süleyman, a dissolute and drunken ruler (1667).

Persian troops conquer Khiva. Its khan becomes a vassal of the shah (1688).

Süleyman is succeeded by the last Safavid shah, Husayn, a de- vout ruler whose attempts to impose Shiite orthodoxy stir up unrest (1697).

ACKNOWLEDGMENTS

The following have been reprinted with the permission of: Page 32: "On a withered branch . . .," quoted in *An Introduction to Haiku*, transl. by H. G. Henderson, New York: Anchor Books, 1958. Page 32: "On a journey, ill . . .," quoted in *The Bamboo Broom*, transl. by H. G. Henderson, Boston: Houghton, 1934. Page 35 and passim: "How can they presume . . .," quoted in *Emperor of China: Self-portrait of K'ang-hsi*, by Jonathan Spence, London: Jonathan Cape, 1974, reprinted by permission of Peters Fraser & Dunlop Group Ltd., 1975. Page 145 and passim: "he bore the whole burden . . ." quoted in *The French Regime*, ed. by Cameron Nish, Scarborough, Ontario: Prentice-Hall, 1965.

The editors also thank the following individuals and institutions for their help in the preparation of this volume: **England:** Blackburn—The Reverend F. J. Turner, Librarian, Stonyhurst College. Cambridge—Peter Kornicki, Lecturer in Japanese Studies, Faculty of Oriental Studies, University of Cambridge. Leigh-on-Sea—D. M. Ryan, Partizan Press. London—Michael Birch, Tea Ceremony Master, Urasenke Foundation; Yu Ying Brown, Oriental Collection, British Library; Sarah Coombe; Victor Harris, Department of Japanese Antiquities, British Museum; Sydney L. Moss Ltd.; Thom Richardson, The Royal Armoury, Tower of London; Rosemary Scott, Percival David Foundation of Chinese Art; Peter Thornton, Curator, Sir John Soane Museum; Brian A. Tremain, Photographic Service, British Museum; Jennifer Wearden, Textile Department, Victoria and Albert Museum. Oxford—Oliver Impey, Assistant Keeper, Head of Eastern Arts, Ashmolean Museum; Linda Proud. Whistable, Kent—Brian Lavery. **France:** Paris—François Avril, Conservateur, Département des Manuscrits, Bibliothèque Nationale; Béatrice Coti, Directrice du Service Iconographique, Éditions Citadelles; Antoinette Decaudin, Documentaliste, Département des Antiquités Oriéntales, Musée du Louvre; Marie Montembault, Documentaliste, Département des Antiquités Grecques et Romaines, Musée du Louvre. **Italy:** Florence—Mara Miniati and Franca Principe, Istituto e Museo di Storia della Scienza. **Japan:** Tokyo—Tokyo National Museum. **Scotland:** Edinburgh—Robert Hillenbrand, Professor of Islamic Art, University of Edinburgh. Fife—H. M. Scott, Lecturer in Modern History, University of Saint Andrews. **Sweden:** Stockholm—Göran Schmitt, Head of the Photographic Department, Livrustkammaren. **U.S.A.:** Plymouth, Massachusetts—James Baker and Randall J. Mason, Plimoth Plantation; New York—Methodact Ltd. **West Germany:** Göttingen—Helmut Rohlfing, Handschriftenabteilung, Niedersächsische Staats- und Universitätsbibliothek. West Berlin—Heidi Klein, Bildarchiv Preussischer Kulturbesitz.

PICTURE CREDITS

BIBLIOGRAPHY

EUROPE

Ashley, Maurice, *The English Civil War.* London: Thames and Hudson, 1974.

Bixby, William, *The Universe of Galileo and Newton.* New York: American Heritage, 1964.

Boxer, Charles, *The Dutch Seaborne Empire.* New York: Knopf, 1965.

Bracegirdle, Brian, ed., *Beads of Glass: Leeuwenhoek and the Early Microscope.* Leiden: Museum Boerhaave & Science Museum, November 1982-October 1983.

Burne, Alfred Higgins, and Peter Young, *The Great Civil War.* London: Eyre & Spottiswoode, 1959.

Dow, F. D., *Radicalism in the English Revolution, 1640-1660.* Oxford: Basil Blackwell, 1985.

Fauvel, John, et al., eds., *Let Newton Be!* Oxford: Oxford University Press, 1988.

Haley, Kenneth H. D., *The Dutch in the Seventeenth Century.* London: Thames and Hudson, 1972.

Hibbert, Christopher, *Charles I.* London: Weidenfeld and Nicolson, 1968.

Hill, Christopher, *The World Turned Upside Down.* London: Penguin, 1984.

Hyde, Edward, earl of Clarendon, *Selections from the History of the Rebellion and Civil Wars.* Ed. by G. Huehns. Oxford: Oxford University Press, 1979.

Israel, Jonathan, *The Dutch Republic and the Hispanic World.* Oxford: Oxford University Press, 1985.

Kenyon, J. P.:
The Civil Wars of England. London: Weidenfeld and Nicolson, 1988.
Stuart England. London: Pelican Books, 1978.

Kroll, Maria, transl. and ed., *Letters from Liselotte.* London: Golancz, 1970.

Langer, Herbert, *The Thirty Years' War.* Poole, Dorset: Blandford Press, 1980.

Lewis, W. H., *The Splendid Century.* London: Eyre & Spottiswoode, 1953.

Mitford, Nancy, *The Sun King.* London: Hamish Hamilton, 1966.

Norton, Lucy, ed. and transl., *Saint-Simon at Versailles.* London: Hamish Hamilton, 1980.

Ogg, David, *England in the Reigns of James II and William III.* Oxford: Oxford University Press, 1984.

Ollard, Richard, *This War without an Enemy.* New York: Atheneum, 1976.

Parker, Geoffrey:
The Dutch Revolt. Harmondsworth, Middlesex: Penguin Books, 1979.
The Military Revolution: 1500-1800. Cambridge: Cambridge University Press, 1988.
The 30 Years' War. London: Routledge & Kegan Paul, 1984.

Richardson, Joanna, *Louis XIV.* London: Weidenfeld and Nicolson, 1974.

Schama, Simon, *The Embarrassment of Riches.* London: Collins, 1987.

Smith, Alan G. R., *Science and Society in the Sixteenth and Seventeenth Centuries.* London: Thames and Hudson, 1972.

Stone, Lawrence, *The Causes of the English Revolution.* New York: Harper and Row, 1972.

Thornton, Peter, *Seventeenth-Century Interior Decoration in England, France and Holland.* New Haven: Yale University Press, 1978.

Trease, Geoffrey, *Samuel Pepys and His World.* London: Thames and Hudson, 1972.

Tyacke, Nicholas, *Anti-Calvinists: The Rise of English Arminianism.* Oxford: Clarendon Press, 1987.

Walton, Guy, *Louis XIV's Versailles.* London: Viking, 1986.

Wedgwood, C. V.:
The King's War. London: Collins, 1958.
The Trial of Charles I. London: Collins, 1964.

Wilson, Charles Henry:
The Dutch Republic. London: Weidenfeld and Nicolson, 1968.
Profit and Power. The Hague: Nijhoff, 1978.

Woolrych, Austin, *Soldiers and Statesmen.* Oxford: Clarendon Press, 1987.

Young, Peter, *Naseby, 1645.* London: Century Publishing, 1985.

Zumthor, Paul, *Daily Life in Rembrandt's Holland.* London: Weidenfeld and Nicolson, 1962.

THE FAR EAST

Backhouse, E., and J. O. P. Bland, *Annals and Memoirs of the Court of Peking.* London: William Heinemann, 1914.

Clunas, Craig, ed., *Chinese Export Art and Design.* London: Victoria and Albert Museum, 1988.

Cooper, M., *They Came to Japan.* Berkeley: University of California Press, 1965.

Dawson, Raymond:
Imperial China. London: Hutchinson, 1972.
Emperor, Scholar, Artisan, Monk. London: Sydney L. Moss, 1989.

Henderson, H. G., transl.:
An Introduction to Haiku. New York: Anchor Books, 1958.
The Bamboo Broom. Boston: Houghton, 1934.

Hsü, Immanuel C. Y., *The Rise of Modern China.* New York: Oxford University Press, 1975.

Keene, Donald, *The Battles of Coxinga.* London: Taylor's Foreign Press, 1951.

Kessler, Lawrence, *K'ang-hsi and the Consolidation of Ch'ing Rule.* Chicago: University of Chicago Press, 1976.

Kikyooka, Eiichi, *The Autobiography of Fukuzawa Yukichi.* Tokyo: Hokuseido Press, 1934.

Mote, Frederick W., and Denis Twitchett, *The Ming Dynasty, 1368-1644, Part I.* Vol. 7 of *The Cambridge History of China.* Cambridge: Cambridge University Press, 1988.

Sansom, G. B., *A History of Japan, 1615-1867.* London: The Cresset Press, 1964.

Seizo, Hayashiya, *Chanoyu: Japanese Tea Ceremony.* Tokyo: Japan Society, 1979.

Shimizu, Yoshiaki, ed., *Japan: The Shaping of Daimyo Culture.* Washington, D.C.: National Gallery of Art, 1988.

Spence, Jonathan D.:
Emperor of China. London: Jonathan Cape, 1974.
The Memory Palace of Matteo Ricci. New York: Viking, 1984.

Spence, Jonathan D., and John E. Wills Jr., eds., *From Ming to Ch'ing.* New Haven: Yale University Press, 1979.

Wakeman, Frederick:
The Fall of Imperial China. London: Collier Macmillan, 1975.
The Great Enterprise. Berkeley: University of California Press, 1985.

Watson, William, ed., *The Great Japan Exhibition.* London: Weidenfeld and Nicolson, 1981-1982.

NORTH AMERICA

Adams, Brooks, *The Emancipation of Massachusetts.* Boston: Houghton Mifflin, 1886.

Bradford, William, *Bradford's History of the Plymouth Settlement.* London: Alston Rivers, 1909.

Cumming, W. P., S. E. Hillier, D. B. Quinn, and G. Williams, eds., *The Exploration of North America.* London: Paul Elek, 1974.

Debo, Angie, *A History of the Indians in the United States.* Norman: University of Oklahoma Press, 1984.

Gill, Crispin, *Mayflower Remembered.* Newton Abbot, Devon: David & Charles, 1970.

Hall, Clayton, ed., *Narratives of Early Maryland.* New York: Barnes & Noble, 1910.

Hulton, Paul, *America 1585: The Com-

plete Drawings of John White. London: British Museum Publications, 1984.
Jameson, J. Franklin, ed., *Narratives of New Netherland.* New York: Barnes & Noble, 1909.
King, Jonathan, *The Mayflower Miracle.* Newton Abbot, Devon: David & Charles, 1987.
Miller, Perry, and T. H. Johnson, *The Puritans.* New York: Harper & Row, 1938.
Nish, Cameron, ed., *The French Regime.* Scarborough, Ontario: Prentice-Hall, 1965.
Savelle, Max, and Robert Middlekauff, *A History of Colonial America.* New York: Holt, Rinehart & Winston, 1964.

Soderland, Jean R., ed., *William Penn and the Founding of Pennsylvania, 1680-1684.* Philadelphia: University of Pennsylvania Press, 1983.
Tyler, Lyon Gardiner, ed., *Narratives of Early Virginia.* New York: Barnes & Noble, 1907.
Tyler, Ron, *Visions of America, Pioneer Artists in a New Land.* London: Thames and Hudson, 1983.
Williams, Roger, *The Complete Writings of Roger Williams.* New York: Russell & Russell, 1963.
Zee, Henri van der, and Barbara van der Zee, *A Sweet and Alien Land.* London: Macmillan, 1978.

PERSIA
Arberry, A. J., *Sufism.* London: George Allen & Unwin, 1968.

Bellan, Lucien-Louise, *Chah 'Abbas I.* Paris: Paul Geuthner, 1932.
Bier, Carol, ed., *Woven from the Soul, Spun from the Heart.* Washington, D.C.: The Textile Museum, 1987.
Blunt, Wilfrid:
Isfahan: Pearl of Persia. London: Paul Elek, 1966.
Pietro's Pilgrimage. London: James Barrie, 1953.
Browne, Edward Granville, *A History of Persian Literature in Modern Times.* Cambridge: Cambridge University Press, 1924.
Herbert, Thomas, *Travels in Persia, 1627-1629.* Ed. by W. Foster. London: Routledge, 1928.

Jackson, Peter, and Lawrence Lockhard, eds., *The Timurid and Safavid Periods.* Vol. 6 of *The Cambridge History of Iran.* Cambridge: Cambridge University Press, 1986.
Robinson, Francis, *Atlas of the Islamic World since 1500.* Oxford: Phaidon, 1982.
Rogers, J. M., *Islamic Art and Design, 1500-1700.* London: British Museum Publications, 1983.
Savory, Roger, *Iran under the Safavids.* Cambridge: Cambridge University Press, 1980.
Sherley, Anthony, *His Persian Adventure.* Ed. by E. Denison Ross. London: Routledge, 1933.
Welch, Anthony, *Shah 'Abbas & the Arts of Isfahan.* New York: The Asia Society, 1973.

INDEX

Numerals in italics indicate an illustration of the subject mentioned.